PREACHING AS WEEPING, CONFESSION, AND RESISTANCE

Also by Christine M. Smith

Weaving the Sermon: Preaching in a Feminist Perspective

PREACHING AS WEEPING, CONFESSION, AND RESISTANCE

Radical Responses *to* Radical Evil

CHRISTINE M. SMITH

Westminster/John Knox Press
Louisville, Kentucky

Book design by ediType

First edition

Published by Westminster/John Knox Press
Louisville, Kentucky

This book is printed on acid-free paper that meets the American National Standards Institute Z39.48 standard. ∞

PRINTED IN THE UNITED STATES OF AMERICA
9 8 7 6 5 4 3 2

Library of Congress Cataloging-in-Publication Data

Smith, Christine M. (Christine Marie), 1953–
    Preaching as weeping, confession, and resistance : radical responses to radical evil / Christine M. Smith. — 1st ed.
        p.   cm.
    Includes bibliographical references and index.
    ISBN 0-664-25216-8 (pb : acid-free)
    1. Preaching. 2. Church and social problems. I. Title.
BV4211.2.S623 1992
251—dc20   92-9739

When they come for the innocent
without crossing over your body,
cursed be your religion and your life.

—*From a Catholic Worker Poster*

CONTENTS

ACKNOWLEDGMENTS

Between the pages of every book there are countless feelings of grati-tude and thanksgiving. This is the place where I want to acknowledge publicly the people, events, and institutions that helped make this cre-ation possible.

I want to thank my colleague and friend Mark Kline Taylor for the insights of our team teaching, the challenges of our trips to Guatemala, and the richness of sharing life together. This book grew out of our common work.

I am grateful to Princeton Theological Seminary. The study leave it graciously supported gave me the time and opportunity to write most of this book. I want to acknowledge also the many students at Princeton who deeply touched my life and thus changed me as a teacher, scholar, and human being.

I remember with thanksgiving the Princeton Guatemala group, sum-mer 1989. The weeks we spent together in Guatemala, and the reflection time afterward, allowed me a time to struggle toward new theological understandings and deeper global commitments.

I am grateful for two colleagues and friends and our work together for the Women and the Word Conference, spring 1990 in Boston. Joan Martin's friendship has been utterly sustaining, and her confrontations have been challenging, demanding, and filled with some of the deepest meaning life offers. Sungmin Haesun Kim has touched my life deeply with her willingness to stay in the dialogue with me and with her work to build bridges of love and mutuality across our differences.

Life has been very tumultuous and hard during the months of writ-ing this book. Being constantly immersed in the magnitude of human suffering represented within these pages has been perhaps the most transforming experience of my adult life. I could not have sustained the personal and professional work required of me without many steadfast friends. The friendship and support of Kathleen Greider, Elizabeth Van-degrift, Jane Heckles, Ron Payne, Elaine Hinnant, Darlene Prestbo, Ann Deibert, Elizabeth Reed, Ida Thornton, Bev Shaw, Judy Mintier, Gray Thornton, Brian Roberts, Kadi Billman, Sandra Roberts, and Pam Sparr have given me life and joy during these days.

Holly Elliott, Laurel Glass, Kathy Black, Helen Betenbaugh, Ralph Uth, Pam Sparr, and Virginia Pharr read various parts of the manuscript and gave me treasured insights and critique. Janis Best worked with me toward the end caring for a multitude of details that make this a much better book.

I want to express deepest gratitude to my editor, Harold Twiss. He believed in the project from the beginning. His sensitivity to my process and work was outstanding. I always appreciated and respected his careful and insightful readings of the manuscript, and his suggestions improved the quality and content of this work.

The community at United Theological Seminary of the Twin Cities, where I presently teach, has welcomed my passions, my commitments, and my scholarly work. The encouragement of students, staff, and faculty empowered me to finish this project. The appreciation I receive in that community gives me courage to look forward to the book's release in the world.

The family of my origins provides the kind of love, security, and ultimate acceptance that I need to do my work in the world, to be most fully who I am, and to live a life of passion and conviction. There are never adequate words of thanks for mom (Betty), dad (Smitty), Pam, Charles, and Elizabeth.

Finally, I want to celebrate and acknowledge the role Barbara Weaver had in the shaping and evolution of this work. She prodded me to write this particular book with all its risks and demands. She has read or listened to every single page with attentiveness and sensitivity. Her social analysis, global awareness, and human compassion have transformed many aspects of my life. Her faithful work continually inspires and informs my own.

These communities, places, and individuals remind me poignantly that all books are expressions of collective work. Ultimately these are my words, and I take full responsibility for them, but I also am gratefully aware that many dimensions of this book simply represent all our voices and actions toward a world without violence and oppression.

Grateful acknowledgment is made for permission to reprint the following copyrighted material:

"The Blessing Song," from the recording titled *Circling Free*, by Marsie Silvestro. Copyright © 1983 Marsie Silvestro.

"The Diamonds on Liz's Bosom," from *Horses Make a Landscape More Beautiful*, copyright © 1984 by Alice Walker, reprinted by permission of Harcourt, Brace, Jovanovich, Inc.

"Investment of Worth," by Terri L. Jewell, in *When I Am an Old Woman I Shall Wear Purple* (Manhattan Beach, Calif.: Papier-Maché Press, 1987), p. 76.

"A Litany for Survival," by Audre Lorde, is reprinted from *The Black Unicorn: Poems by Audre Lorde*, by permission of W. W. Norton & Company, Inc. Copyright © 1978 by Audre Lorde.

"Okasan/Mother," from *Making Waves*, by Asian Women United of California. Copyright © 1989 by Asian Women United of California. Reprinted by permission of Beacon Press.

"Transit," by Adrienne Rich, is reprinted from *The Fact of a Doorframe: Poems Selected and New, 1950–1984*, by Adrienne Rich, by permission of W. W. Norton & Company, Inc. Copyright © 1984 by Adrienne Rich. Copyright © 1975, 1978 by W. W. Norton & Company, Inc. Copyright © 1981 by Adrienne Rich.

"What Does It Take?" by Cherrie Moraga in *Loving in the War Years* (Boston: South End Press, 1983), pp. 65–66. Reprinted by permission of Cherrie Moraga.

"Women Die Like Trees," in *Abiding Appalachia*, by Marilou Awiakta (Memphis: St. Luke's Press, 1978), p. 35.

✧ Introduction ✧

PREACHING AS
A THEOLOGICAL ACT

In the craft and act of preaching at least three worlds converge: the world of the text; the world of the preacher and community where proclamation occurs; and the world of the larger social context in which we live our lives of faith. Often in homiletics there is a primary emphasis on the world of the text. Homileticians and preachers alike are concerned with such things as how sacred texts function in the life of a community, how texts are interpreted, how texts have evolved in meaning and interpretation in the life of the church, and how the literary and distinctive qualities of texts function in the liturgical and religious life of a people.

In homiletics there is also a deep concern for the world of preacher and community. There are resources in the field that help us understand some of the many spiritual and psychological dimensions of individuals and communities as we anticipate a preaching ministry. Also, the role of the preacher as communicator and pastor has received considerable emphasis among homileticians. Some attention has been given to the social location of religious communities and to the impact of particular dimensions of a community's life on the preaching ministry that emerges there. Preachers and homileticians attend to these important worlds in the task and act of preaching.

In this book, however, I want to reflect on the third world of preaching, the larger social context in which we live our lives of faith. The focus of this work will be the particular issues, social systems, pervasive values, and theological understandings that dominate and structure the world in which we preach.

Preaching is a theological act. A vital preaching ministry includes the skills of the sophisticated communicator, the attentiveness of the biblical exegete, and the social analyses of the most discerning sociologist, but first and foremost it is the craft and act of a working theologian. It is a theological act because preachers are called to reflect upon, and struggle with, ultimate religious questions in life. The very act of preaching situates the preacher in the midst of the mysterious and perplexing nature of life and faith, trying to discern and proclaim the nature of God, the nature of human existence, the nature of the relationship between God and humanity, and the nature of human responsibility for creation.

Preaching is also an act of naming. The naming of reality functions in many ways, but whether naming calls persons to claim the fullness of their own created worth and the worth of all creation, or whether naming enables the demonic powers of hatred and injustice to be exposed and dethroned, one can hardly dispute the power of publicly proclaimed words. Preaching is an act of public theological naming. It is an act of disclosing and articulating the truths about our present human existence. It is an act of bringing new reality into being, an act of creation. It is also an act of redeeming and transforming reality, an act of shattering illusions and cracking open limited perspectives. It is nothing less than the interpretation of our present world and an invitation to build a profoundly different new world.

THEOLOGICAL EVOLUTION

In the summer of 1989 I spent six weeks traveling and studying in Guatemala. I returned from that immersion fundamentally changed. Even though the dramatic experience of being in Guatemala was, in itself, life transforming, I now understand it as a catalyst for the renaming and reshaping of my theology and faith.

During the past fifteen years a primary focus of my personal and professional life has been exploration and analysis of a web of "isms" that structures a foundation of oppression worldwide. As a woman, my first and primary experience of this web was through the painful and systematic oppression of sexism. My entry into an understanding of these oppressive structures and systems was through feminism. As my own critique has expanded, so have my exploration and transformation. As I have come to acknowledge and understand the breadth and depth of oppression in the human community, I have come to see the interlocking partners of oppression more clearly as handicappism, ageism, sexism, heterosexism, racism, and classism. There are other systems and ideologies that form part of this reality of oppression, but these are the ones that structure the fabric of the pages that follow. They will be considered in dialogue with each other, for when they are separated, analysis becomes fundamentally limited and superficial.

My world reality, my theology, my faith, and my preaching have shifted over these years in direct relationship to my deepening analysis and experience of these expressions of oppression. Because of my experience in Guatemala, I now must name this interlocking mass of oppression "radical evil." Yet even as I write these words, I am confronted by the depth of my own denial for so long. Why has it taken me this many years to give the name "radical evil" to this web of oppressive structures and systems? I have understood these systems and ideologies as expressions of injustice, as sources of immense suffering, even as demonic repercussions of human greed, fear, and hatred. It is only at this stage in my life, somewhat overwhelmed and enraged at the magnitude of the reality that confronts us, that I can no longer name this complex reality as anything but evil.

Once a theologian, a preacher, or a person of faith names the pervasive world reality that permeates the globe as radical evil, her or his entire theological thinking, writing, and interpretation of the world shift. I have not wanted to give up my deep, abiding belief that human beings are basically good. I have not wanted to face fully the ultimate questions of how to understand the nature of God and God's relationship to creation in the midst of such massive human suffering. I have not wanted to relinquish a somewhat naive eschatological hope that the human community is moving toward a day in which justice will prevail. I have not wanted to experience the deep abyss of human horror, and the haunting silence of indifference. Nor have I wanted to confront the depth and breadth of my own white, North American, middle-class privilege and complicity. At times I find these confrontations and transformations disorienting and terrifying. They call my world and my Christian faith into question. For me, the process of facing radical evil more directly has been, and continues to be, both a shattering and an exhilarating experience.

Naming this web of oppression as the expression of radical evil has everything to do with preaching. I find myself asking how any person can preach a word of hope, a word of faith, in a day such as this. And yet, a voice just as strongly imbedded in my spirit says, "How can we not preach a word of hope and faith in a day such as this?" As the breadth of evil becomes clearer to me I experience both despair about the focus of present preaching and renewed commitment to the possibility that preaching can be an expression of faith that enlightens and unleashes the compassion and convictions of religious communities. The task of preaching seems more difficult than it ever has to me, yet more urgent, critical, and needed. If we are to continue to be preachers ourselves, and if some of us are to continue to teach those who preach, how can we live out this calling with relevance and with passion?

WEEPING, CONFESSION, RESISTANCE

When I look at the task before us in homiletics, I am instructed and encouraged by three words: *weeping, confession,* and *resistance.* These words have begun to help me understand what preaching ought to feel like, look like, and be like, in a world where radical evil dominates our everyday reality. These words have helped me understand more fully the awesome responsibility of the preacher, for the preacher is accountable not only to the church, but to God, and to all of creation.

As my understanding of preaching deepens, I have found myself saying over and over again, "Preaching is weeping." Often when people weep, they are most in touch with the deepest passions, strongest yearnings, and greatest desires of their lives. These are some of the most difficult and richest moments in life. People weep when they are alive to those things they cherish and value the most and are touched by something they can hardly name or utter. This is not always so with weeping. Tears can also be sources of manipulation and condescension, or expressions of utter despair and chaos. However, I am speaking about that deep human experience that most of us have known, and will know again, of passionate weeping. In a world filled with human suffering, inequity, and oppression, surely preaching is a kind of weeping. In sermons and in acts of preaching, those who preach need to engage their deepest passions, their highest values, their surest convictions and make them present and alive in moments of proclamation. When preachers body forth passionate justice, it is life in the midst of death. When congregations respond by bodying forth dimensions of justice, it is hope in the midst of despair. That common work of preacher and community striving toward a fidelity to life might often feel like weeping.

But weeping is not enough. A world infected and diseased by radical evil also needs truth just as radical. Much of the Christian community has come to understand confession as speaking about the sinfulness of our lives and receiving God's forgiveness and grace. For many individuals and communities this liturgical act is neither clarifying nor empowering. Far too often confessional acts happen in our worship services as empty ritual moments at best, and guilt-inflicting individual and communal experiences at worst. How might confession change in the liturgical expressions of Christian communities if we understood it as profound truth telling? Confession is a time to speak truth about our lives and about the nature of our world. How powerful confession could be if we spoke the truth about life in the times for spoken prayers, and had the courage to tune our hearts and spirits to the joyous *and* harsh realities of the world in those moments of communal silence. This is the kind of confession our world needs.

Preaching might also be an act of confession, a moment in the life of the Christian community where truth is spoken. Hope is not engendered by illusions or lies; hope is engendered by truth. In the act of preaching we strive to speak the truth about life in the perpetual belief and abiding hope that such truth, as devastatingly ugly and as frighteningly beautiful as it is, is precisely what we bring to be offered, blessed, and transformed by God in the sacred act of preaching. If preachers believed that their sermons were acts of confession, they would be pulled back time and time again to the real world in which we live.

Far too often in preaching classrooms I find myself asking the preacher, "Is this the way life really is?" The preacher needs to resist the seductions of segmenting life, reducing life's complexities to false simplicity, or collapsing life's paradoxes to immobilizing moralisms. Preachers are often better at describing a world they hope for than articulating truth about the real world. It is in response to that real world, not an imaginary one, that the Christian community is called to live and speak and act. If preachers speak the truth about life and faith with clarity and courage, preaching could be an act of confession that heals, confronts, and enlivens.

Even confession is not enough. In the face of radical evil, preaching must be weeping, it must be confession, but it also must be resistance. Resistance is not just our reaction to the evil we experience and participate in, but it is our stand against it. It is not an act of standing still and defending ourselves against the evil that surrounds us, but it is a movement into it, and through it, with speech and presence and action. The church's resistance to evil needs to be strong and compelling. If preaching is to be a transforming act, then the power and integrity of our proclamations will surely be measured by their ability to mobilize communities to resist the reality that confronts us.

Resistance takes myriad forms for us as individuals, and is embodied in distinctly different ways by our different faith communities. To speak honestly about our individual lives and the conditions of the human family is a powerful act of resistance in a world committed to the denial of truth. In recent years the honest speech of incest survivors, victims of domestic violence, and those whose lives have been scarred by addiction and abuse has taught the church about the urgent need to break silence and speak truth. African-American womanist theologians are speaking powerfully about economic and cultural survival, and about black women's particular moral agency. Asian women theologians are speaking clearly about the ways Christianity has violated and repressed their indigenous cultural values and religious expressions. These are forms of resistance. For religious people, this speaking is an ethical imperative and one essential expression of resistance.

In our lives of faith and in our preaching, resistance demands even more than truthful speech. It is a theological affirmation to suggest that preaching be an act of resistance. The moment we commit ourselves to resisting evil we literally place our lives in a fundamentally new place. To resist evil is to position one's passion and being in the realm of life, and to position one's self in the realm of life is to accept the call to be a redemptive agent. For preaching to become resistance, we must be clear about what is ultimate in our lives of faith. To affirm preaching as resistance is to suggest that preaching is not only about the hearing and receiving of good news, but that it is an act that must enable and sustain persons to *be* good news in the larger world. To affirm preaching as resistance is to encourage the faithful community to be about God's redemptive activity in the world in concrete, particular ways. Throughout the world there are resistance movements to particular governments as well as underground communities that work for societal and cultural change. To suggest that preaching is resistance is to invite members of religious communities to oppose the occupying power of evil in our world and to place their lives in the stream of those who are working for change. When individuals and communities decide to be God's revelation in the world, their alliances and loyalties must shift; the coalitions they build will drastically change; and justice must be the criterion through which all their theology is forged.

Weeping, confession, and resistance are not only descriptive metaphors for the act of preaching, but the movement and process of these realities create a homiletical methodology. Sermons need to be constructed in such a way that individuals and communities experience the forms of oppression we are trying to address. Illustrations and language call people to *weep* and passionately feel. Sermons also need to be crafted in ways that adequately *confess* the truth of the oppressions. Bold speech and realistic examples enable people to understand with clarity and insight. And, our proclamations need to be shaped in ways that evoke *resistance* and action. Invitations and powerful narratives empower people to respond and to act.

PREACHING:
THE TASK OF THEOLOGICAL INTERPRETATION

In the spring semester of 1989, Mark Kline Taylor, Associate Professor of Theology and Culture at Princeton Theological Seminary, and I taught a class together called "Theological Interpretation for Contemporary Preaching." The intent of that class was to enable present and future preachers and religious educators to identify some of the most critical theological issues at stake in the problems of handicappism, ageism, sexism, heterosexism, racism, and classism. We spent one entire class session in theological reflection and discussion about each of these expressions of evil in our midst. We then spent the following session listening to two preachers attempt to address the issue directly in their sermons. Each preacher was asked to pay particular attention to traditional theological positions, constructs, and arguments that serve to undergird and perpetuate this particular form of violence and oppression, and attempt to weave that theological critique or insight into the sermon. It was a difficult, demanding class. There I saw preachers begin to face in new and deeper ways the radical evil in their own lives, in the church, and in the world. I also experienced preachers struggling to be the kind of theologians the church desperately needs in order to move our communities from comfortable distance to weeping, from denial to confession, from complicity to resistance. This kind of preaching is a sign of hope for the church and world.

The Limits and Challenges of the Task

The pages that follow are primarily focused on the act and vision of preaching, but I hope they will contain disturbing and encouraging words for all religious people who take the task of being working theologians seriously. This book is also written from a white, North American, Protestant woman's perspective, but I hope that it will point to areas of common human and religious concern. I am aware, however, that the evolution of my social and theological consciousness has been fundamentally shaped by the realities of social location. I am white; I am a woman; I am a feminist; I am a middle-stratum, North American person; and I continue to choose the Christian church as my primary religious community. My evolution has been just as fundamentally shaped by my not being a person of color, by my not having any discernible disability, and by my not being poor. The pages that follow will be honest only if they convey as clearly as possible the tremendous tension and struggle I feel as I live my life, and do my work, between the experiences of oppression and the experiences of privilege. The particular perspectives and analyses that each of us brings to the theological task and to the craft of preaching can only enrich and deepen our collective work.

These pages and this homiletical and theological naming are offered as an example of the struggle to be a more responsible theologian and preacher. I hope these pages contain insights that will help all of us whose life work is making connections between the realities of our world and the language of our faith, all of us who know that violence and suffering are of an overwhelming magnitude, and all of us who are committed to looking critically at the dimensions of Christian theology that undergird and perpetuate this web of radical evil.

Preaching as Redemptive Activity

My hope is that this book will help preachers become more politically and socially aware and more theologically responsible in a world caught in a web of radical evil. But I have a clearer, deeper hope. I believe that contemporary preaching needs to be an expression of our redemptive activity in the world. In these pages I am not attempting to deal with the question of theodicy, the theological endeavor of trying to reconcile evil with the goodness of God. This is a central theological concern within the Christian faith, but this is not the focus of my work. I seek to give glimpses into what preaching as redemptive activity might look like in a world of pervasive evil. In the act of preaching there is the possibility that preacher and community together might express their most life-giving passions, their most honest truth telling, and their most courageous resistance. When this passion and truth and resistance stand in faithful opposition to the oppression and suffering of humanity and stand firmly rooted in a fidelity to life, this is redemptive activity; this is saving activity.

The chapters that follow are intended to invite us to see our preaching as redemptive activity and to help preachers and communities together discern the varied ways they can resist the violence of radical evil. Chapter 1, "Revelation Confronts Denial," focuses on handicappism. I am using the word *handicappism* to denote the systematic denial, domination, and oppression of persons with disabilities. Chapter 2, "Embodiment Challenges Marginalization," focuses on ageism. I am using the term *ageism* to refer to the systematic denial, domination, and oppression of older adults. Chapter 3, "Breaking Silence Exposes Misogyny," focuses on sexism. I am using the word *sexism* to designate the systematic denial, domination, and oppression of women. "Grace Transforms Condemnation," chapter 4, focuses on heterosexism. I am using the term *heterosexism* to denote the systematic denial, domination, and oppression of lesbians and gay men. Chapter 5, "Conversion Uproots Supremacy," focuses on white racism. I am using the term *white racism* to refer to the systematic denial, domination, and oppression of people of color. Chapter 6, "Crosses Reveal Privilege," focuses on classism. I am using the word *classism* to designate the systematic denial, domination, and oppression of people because of their economic condition.

I begin each of the first six chapters by naming the type of violence to be discussed. In each of those chapters I follow that naming with a section called "Radicalizing Moments." These describe some of my own moments of *weeping*. The experiences I examine and reflect upon in those sections are encounters that moved me from varying degrees of awareness to passionate feeling and understanding. Beginning with concrete experiences of oppression and suffering is always the starting point of the liberation theologian and preacher. These experiences are so powerful they claim our weeping and our passion.

Following each section of radicalizing moments, there are pages of *confession*. If confession is radical truth telling about our individual and collective lives, then it is important to name and understand the realities of our social and political life as fully as possible. It is essential that preachers understand the particularities of oppression and violence adequately enough to speak with clarity and insight. I consider the depth and breadth of the preacher's social analysis to be indicative of how seriously that preacher approaches confession. The social analysis portion of each of the chapters is intended to aid the education and awareness of preachers and communities so that they might speak confessionally and truthfully about the violences we face.

In the final section of each chapter, I raise theological issues that are important for preaching and that are pertinent to each expression of violence and oppression. Part of our *resistance* to evil must be work that is theological in nature and content. Critiquing theologies of the cross that justify and condone human suffering of every description is an act of resistance. Suggesting that persons with disabilities know and experience God in ways able-bodied persons do not is an act of resistance. Participating in the redemptive work of breaking the silences surrounding rape, incest, and woman battering is an act of resistance. Preachers and communities participate in resisting evil as they critique and uproot theologies that undergird it and seek to build new theologies that bring embodied justice into the world. The magnitude of human suffering beckons us to move from our places of "standing at a distance." In the spirit of redemptive preaching, where weeping, confession, and resistance are interwoven, I offer the following sermon in hope that it will illumine the intent and challenges of the words that follow.

✧ STANDING AT A DISTANCE ✧

A Sermon on Luke 23:44–49

*This sermon was preached on Good Friday, 1990,
in the Princeton United Methodist Church.*

The scriptures of our faith tell us:

There was darkness.
There was tearing.
There was crying.
    And breath ceased to be.

A centurion was shaken and changed by the obviousness of innocence.

A crowd of distanced spectators became a mass of wailing humanity.

And in the deepest places of our heart and spirit we know the horrors these words won't ever touch.

There was screaming.
There was bleeding.
There was breaking.
    And life was strangled from one who seemed to be the
    essence of life.

Soldiers and onlookers laughed and taunted, viewing death as entertainment. The mob violence was seen in all its obscene madness. And *all* withdrew to ease the pain, to calm the terror, to deny the horror.

"But all his acquaintances, including the women who had followed him from Galilee, stood at a distance, watching these things" (23:49).

Here is a death that is ugly, a death that tries to strip away all human dignity, a death that crushes the spirit, a death that threatens to silence life itself.

It is a death too horrible to stand beside, too enraging to embrace, too terrifying to walk into and touch.

It is a death we know we cannot bear, and so we view with compassion those who drew themselves apart, and are quietly grateful for the ones who did not abandon him altogether.

And yet here is the death of one who was the bearer of life to so many, and who drew himself so close to all. Here is *Jesus* painfully, devastatingly alone.

"But all his acquaintances, including the women who had followed him from Galilee, stood at a distance, watching these things."

We know all too well this *standing at a distance*. For many of us it is not just something we do during life's most demanding moments or when we are afraid; it has become for many of us a way of life.

In a world where pain and despair are so evident not only in the far corners of our globe but in our own lives and in our homes, it seems strangely natural to seek a distanced place to stand, to claim our right to a refuge of denial, to rage against a call to constant vigilance.

But somewhere in the midst of our denial and rage there is the painful awareness that we must be willing to touch death, to fully know life.

And frequently in our distanced places there is the beckoning truth that crucifixions must be *taken hold of* and stopped, and it is this stopping that will have saving power for us all.

And yet far too often (like "all his acquaintances, including the women who had followed him from Galilee") we who look to the example of Jesus for an understanding of radical love and for the gift of hope and life *stand at a distance, seeing all these things.*

I went to see the Names Project Quilt in November of 1988 in Washington, D.C., a living, growing memorial to the thousands of people who have died from AIDS. At 7:10 A.M. the quilt began to be unfolded, and from 7:10 in the morning until 6:00 in the evening, names were read: Mike Belt, Michael Collins, Lynn Carter, Leroy Estrada, Katie Mitchell, Lee, Stephen, Tom, my brother . . . , those without a hand to hold.

As you walk around the quilt you see lovers weeping, running their fingers over the names of those they have loved. You see families standing in silence. You overhear friends telling stories. You see thousands of others looking, searching for names, searching for a tangible sign that death has not had the final word. All who make this quilt, all who work to display it, all who come to see it — they look for redemption in the midst of this modern-day crucifixion.

It is a death that is ugly, a death that tries to strip away, a death that wants to crush, a death that threatens to silence life itself.

It is a death too horrible to stand beside, too enraging to embrace, and too terrifying to walk into.

But for many, it is a death that has already been *taken hold of,* a death that has been tasted and touched, a death that has been lived daily.

But many of us stand at a distance and see these things.

It is like so much of life. Many of us convince ourselves that it does not touch our lives, our loved ones, our homes, and so we feel no compelling drive to touch it, and certainly no call to *take hold of it.* Yet in the more honest moments of our lives we know once again that we lose the fullness of life when we cannot or will not touch the fullness of death.

But how do we move from standing at a distance to becoming one who *takes hold of* this crucifixion?

If you have ever imagined or known a child dying in your arms, you can move closer to parents who stand weeping at this quilt.

If you have ever fought to hold onto the life or presence of a lover, you can come closer to those who run their hands over treasured names.

If you have ever known the pain, the rage, the sorrow of senseless dying, you can come closer to those who quilt these panels of names so that the power of life is redeemed and people are remembered.

And if you can come closer, you can *take hold of* this crucifixion and work to stop it. The fliers that accompany this quilt say: "Turn the power of the quilt into action!"

The message and mandate that surely accompany our faith carry a similar message: We must turn the power of crucifixion into action, into a love that is so radical and so interwoven with the fabric of suffering that crucifixions cease to be. This is what it means to be Christlike; this is what it means to *pick up our crosses:* We pick them up and we take hold of them so that some day there will be no more crosses on which we crucify life.

Beverly Harrison, a visionary ethicist of our day, reminds us:

> Jesus' death on a cross, his sacrifice, was no abstract exercise in moral virtue. His death was the price he paid for refusing to abandon the radical activity of love — of expressing solidarity and reciprocity with the excluded ones in his community. Sacrifice, I submit, is not a central moral goal or virtue in the Christian life. Radical acts of love — expressing human solidarity and bringing mutual relationship to life — are the central virtues of the Christian moral life.[1]

When we stand at a distance we observe and perpetuate sacrifice; when we take hold of crucifixions and stop them, we become bearers of life.

In recent months I have taken a particular interest in Guatemala, an amazing country rich in cultural diversity. It is a place of great natural beauty. And it is a place of great human beauty, for 60 percent of the people of Guatemala are descendants of the great Mayan Indians.

But Guatemala is a place of death as well. Five percent of the population owns 90 percent of the land, and the indigenous people must fight for their very existence. In a powerful book called *Death and Resurrection in Guatemala*, Fernando Bermúdez shares a story that epitomizes the everyday crucifixions that permeate this land:

> One day the army appeared in a small village in northern Guatemala. The captain read five names of beloved villagers ... and demanded that relatives of these five men execute them. ... The army would return to see that the execution had been carried out the

next day. They promised to destroy the entire village, and surrounding ones, if this demand was not fulfilled.

As soon as the army left the village people formed into groups to decide what to do. The response was unanimous,... "We will not do it." But when the five brothers who were to be killed took the floor, they stated, firmly: "Brothers and sisters, go ahead and carry out the order. It is better for us to die than for thousands to die." The people began to weep. The members of the five families were speechless.

Here is the description of what followed:

It was about four in the morning when the march to the cemetery began. The whole population of the villages took part, men, women, and children. The five condemned persons headed the great procession. All walked in silence, except that you could hear people weeping. They were experiencing in their own flesh the sorrow of Good Friday.

They came to the cemetery. The graves were dug, and the people formed a large circle. The five catechists took their places in the center. One of them prayed.... All the people prayed with him. Another said, "We're going to die, but don't worry, we're going to be with God. It's all right to kill us. If we're not killed, our children, our wives, our relatives, and the whole population of these villages will die. Go ahead and kill us." Another said, "I only want to ask you one favor. Help my children." Another tried to speak and could not.

The terrible moment of crucifixion arrived. The relatives of the five drew their machetes. The five catechists felt the pain and anguish of death in their flesh. The executioners felt it in their souls. The martyrs were hacked to pieces, and their blood covered the earth, mingled with the tears of the witnesses. All were weeping, some fainted. Here was a mountain of suffering. One of those present went out of his mind.[2]

The witnesses who recounted these events said: "We remember them with holy reverence, because it is thanks to them that we are alive today."

Here is death that is ugly, that strips away, crushes, and threatens life itself.

But here is not sacrifice as an end in itself; here is not a romanticized cross. Here is the taking hold of crucifixion on behalf of a community; here is a walking into death so that life might be preserved for others.

As long as there are crucifixions, let them be on behalf of life, but ultimately let them cease to be.

But many of us stand at a distance and see these things.

We tell ourselves it is only a small country of struggling peasants. We convince ourselves the politics are beyond our understanding and the situation does not touch our lives, and so we are not compelled to touch it. And yet we know that distancing from death diminishes our humanness, and each of us longs to move from standing at a distance to become one who takes hold of this crucifixion.

And we try to imagine our children dying of starvation and violence daily; and we try to move closer.

And we struggle to imagine daily terror, exploitative work, lifelong poverty, and cycles of preventable disease; and we try to move closer.

And we face, even though we want to deny, our own country's economic and political support of Guatemala's army of terrorism and our own complicity in the annihilation of a people; and we try to have the courage to move closer.

And if you can come closer, you can take hold of even this crucifixion and work to stop it.

When we stand at a distance, we observe and perpetuate sacrifice. When we take hold of crucifixions and stop them, we become bearers of life, redemptive agents.

There was darkness.
There was tearing.
There was crying.
There was screaming.
There was bleeding.
There was breaking.

And all withdrew to ease the pain, to calm the terror, to deny the horror.

"But all his acquaintances, including the women who had followed him from Galilee, stood at a distance, watching these things."

Revelation Confronts Denial—
HANDICAPPISM

TRANSIT

When I meet the skier she is always
walking, skis and poles shouldered, toward the mountain
knee-swinging in worn boots
over the path new-sifted with fresh snow
over greying dark hair almost hidden by
a cap of many colors
her fifty-year-old, strong, impatient body
dressed for cold and speed
her eyes level with mine

And when we pass each other I look into her face
wondering what we have in common
where our minds converge
for we do not pass each other, she passes me
as I halt beside the fence tangled in snow,
she passes me as I shall never pass her
in this life

Yet I remember us together
climbing Chocorua, summer nineteen-forty-five
details of vegetation beyond the timberline
lichens, wildflowers, birds,
amazement when the trail broke out onto the granite ledge
sloped over blue lakes, green pines, giddy air
like dreams of flying

When sisters separate they haunt each other
as she, who I might once have been, haunts me
or is it I who do the haunting
halting and watching on the path
how she appears again through lightly-blowing
crystals, how her strong knees carry her,

how unaware she is, how simple
this is for her, how without let or hindrance
she travels in her body
until the point of passing, where the skier
and the cripple must decide
to recognize each other?

— Adrienne Rich[1]

Handicappism is the systematic denial, oppression, and domination of people with disabilities. To focus on the reality of handicappism is to confront the able-bodied community with its responsibility for and its complicity in the oppression of people who have disabilities. Handicappism comprises the structures, attitudes, theologies, and blatant forms of discrimination that limit, render invisible, exploit, and violate people who have disabilities.

Handicappism exists within religious communities. It is perpetuated by the inaccessible buildings where our communities worship, the condescending attitudes we often exhibit, and the haunting absence of people with disabilities from ministries in our churches and synagogues. In the United States, we have all been conditioned by a culture that tends systematically to structure people with disabilities out of the mainstream of our society, and thus out of most of our lives. Isolation and invisibility are common experiences for people with disabilities. Church communities are also isolated from the human giftedness of people who have disabilities. Our culture and our religious communities are incomplete because of this. Why is it not shocking to religious communities that people with disabilities are either silent or absent in our common life? Why is it not angering that the theological insights and religious convictions of people with disabilities come forth from so few of our pulpits? Why is it not amazing to us that our outreach or evangelism committees seldom speak about the people who have been driven away from our churches by structures that do not accommodate their needs and by attitudes that destroy human dignity? These are harsh questions to ask of ourselves, but the denial in many of our churches is an even harsher truth for people with disabilities. We are all impoverished by the denial of the very existence of people with disabilities and by the repression of their particular religious perspectives, gifts for ministry in the world, and contributions to our evolving faith communities.

Focusing on religious communities and specifically on the preaching and teaching ministries that happen there, the pages that follow seek to address the oppression of handicappism in our midst. I continue to believe that relevant preaching ministries today are built with a keen sensitivity to human differences. Preachers must not speak in response solely to the needs and concerns of their own congregations, but must also address the needs and concerns of all God's people. How shall we preach when so many strands of the human community are not represented or present in our collective life? How can we work for change as preachers and congregations, so that persons with disabilities are empowered to speak out, feel that our churches are responsive enough to make their distinctive needs and desires known, and feel invited to add their wisdom to the transformation of our churches and synagogues into more inclusive communities?

RADICALIZING MOMENTS

My own awareness of this issue has been slowly growing over the past fifteen to twenty years. I remember my education beginning some eighteen years ago when I was the dean at a week of summer camp that took place on a rugged portion of land in southern Ohio. The site was virtually inaccessible in every way. One of the counselors decided to bring her two daughters, Barbara and Kay, who had cerebral palsy. Both of these young women used wheelchairs. I vividly remember pushing Barbara's wheelchair into our "home in the woods," seeing Kay and Barbara lifted onto a flatbed truck for a late night hayride, and watching fifth and sixth graders push them in their wheelchairs down a very steep hill to the lake for worship. In these moments I felt terror and awe in the face of their vulnerability and trust. I remember them dancing in their wheelchairs, speaking of their Christian faith, and laughing out loud at meal times. In these moments I felt warmed by our common humanness. For an entire week a group of adults and youth were immersed in a relationship that left all of us changed. I felt invited into a new world, a world that compelled me to take human difference as seriously as I had tried to take human sameness. We learned many things, and *access* became a real, concrete issue for the entire camp community, and lack of access became a form of oppression we all experienced.

My understanding of the oppression of people with disabilities has been growing actively since that camp experience long ago. I have known that this oppression involves not just active discrimination against people with disabilities, but a denial of their very existence. The violence of denial became clearer to me during the spring of 1989. In preparation to deal with handicappism in a session of the class "Theological Interpretation for Contemporary Preaching" at Princeton Theological Seminary, I went to three major libraries in Princeton, New Jersey, looking for pictures of adults with disabilities. I was looking for pictures depicting disabled adults in various common activities: working in settings of various kinds; relating to family members, friends, and lovers; enjoying the beach; spending time with children; creating music or art; grocery shopping; demonstrating convictions in political and social action. In nearly two weeks of looking for such pictures, I found none.[2] Librarians seemed puzzled at the request. The only pictures I could locate were in the children's section of the public library. This reality painfully suggests that seeing children with disabilities is acceptable to the able-bodied community, but seeing adults with disabilities as vital, whole human beings is beyond the comprehension of the able-bodied community. It is shocking to ponder the assumptions that are at the heart of such denial. This expression of denial suggests the lives of millions of people are meaningless and insignificant. This is denial at a very ugly level.

NAMING AND UNDERSTANDING THE VIOLENCE

The very language we use to describe the societal oppression of people with disabilities is crucial.[3] The books that I have read focusing on people with disabilities and the conversations I have had with members of the disability community are teaching me a new language. In a previous book I consistently used the term *differently abled,* and in some ways I am still drawn to this description as one that points to difference, but has no inherent judgment within it.[4] However, I think there are very particular realities, concerns, and issues related to disabilities that a phrase like *differently abled* obscures.

The literature in the field uses the word *disability* most frequently. Perhaps this is emerging as the most acceptable and unifying term. It is important to remember, though, that people with disabilities strongly affirm the right of all persons to choose how they will speak of themselves and their lives. I am coming to understand the word *disability* as a descriptive term. In legal terms it is one's incapacity or inability to act.[5] As my consciousness continues to be raised, I grow in my belief that a person lives with a disability, but a person is not handicapped; nor does a person have a handicapping condition. These labels situate the problem or experience of limitation solely within the person herself or himself.

There are realities associated with disabilities that are life enhancing and positive as well as difficult and challenging, and it is important to acknowledge and understand these varying realities. I believe that being *handicapped* is an experience of oppression that is the direct repercussion of living with a disability in a world that is unwilling to address the needs, gifts, and very existence of people with disabilities. I understand that many people use the term *handicapped* to refer to physically limiting realities, but I am choosing to use it as descriptive of the kind of passive and active oppression that the larger society inflicts upon people with disabilities. While speaking about the impact this kind of oppression has on the lives of people with disabilities, Victoria Lewis clearly addresses the issue of responsibility:

> When you can't go to the same movies or parties as everyone else because there's no ramp; when you can't attend after-school activities because there's no sign language interpreter; when you can't read the same books as your friends because they're not in braille; or when no one will take the extra time to understand your speech, it can really get hard to feel good about yourself. It's hard but not impossible, because none of those things are your fault.[6]

This analysis and naming make claims upon the able-bodied world and call for our response as a society and as a religious community. It is an environment of discrimination or oppression that causes a disability to become handicapping. A person who is blind, in the context of a community where appropriate educational resources are provided, cannot see but has no handicap. When that same person seeks to attend a school in which there are no Braille learning materials, she or he may now be handicapped, not by a disability, but by the environment and community that do not provide appropriate resources for adequate education. These are important distinctions in language. Language can limit and reduce people, as surely as it can affirm and empower. People who have disabilities are often not seen as the whole, vital human beings they are; nor are their lives understood in all their fullness. There is a profound difference between seeing a person *as* a disability, and seeing a person who *lives with* a disability.

The Christian church is painfully quiet about disabilities. Religious communities need to become aware and responsive. "The statistics provided by the World Health Organization for the 1981 Year of Disabled Persons... show that the 500 million people in the world who suffer from a physical or mental disability are among the most oppressed, marginalized, and poverty stricken in our societies."[7] There are churches and religious communities that are actively involved in confronting this form of human oppression. Even though they seem to be the exception, they are an important witness to the larger church. There are churches committed to making every part of their buildings and every aspect of their programs accessible. Ramps and elevators, sign language interpreters, and Sunday morning bulletins and newsletters in Braille are tangible symbols of inclusiveness and justice. The presence of curriculum materials designed for persons who have special learning needs and the creation of educational programs and church camp experiences that sensitively work to integrate the able-bodied community and the disability community are an inspiration and challenge to the larger church.

Within the Christian church the level of understanding and education about disabilities is limited and inadequate. Even in contexts where pastors, seminary students, and religious educators speak openly about other forms of oppression, handicappism is seldom mentioned. In local churches and national denominational offices handicappism is often not a priority issue. If discussed at all in our religious life, it often is in relation to *access*. This is a beginning, but the church also needs to address its oppressive theology and its unwillingness to be an inclusive community at every level of its life.

In addition to the issue of access, any adequate analysis of handicappism attempts to address an ever-widening set of complex questions and issues. Not only do persons with disabilities face blatant discrimination in relation to access; they also face economic, cultural, and political oppression. Unemployment and economic hardship are major problems within the entire disability community. Even in the midst of growing awareness and action, the particular needs and concerns of the disability community are underrepresented in the educational and political processes in this country. People with disabilities are relationally disenfranchised by the able-bodied community's isolating attitudes, narrow stereotypes, and fearful denial of the sexuality and wholeness of each person.

Christian persons are called to confront the fact that in many ways the Christian church has provided a theological foundation for these expressions of discrimination and denial. Particularly as preachers, we need to take a fresh and critical look at our theological assumptions and affirmations. This theology has often been a source of pain and oppression. Individual preachers and various church communities suggest that all people must *hear* the word of God to be saved, must *come into sight* in order to be faithful to the gospel, must *stand* in order to participate in the community's liturgical life, and must *intellectually grasp* concepts and doctrines of the faith in order to be mature religious persons. All of these assumptions exclude vast numbers of people from our common life. As preachers who preach from texts about healing miracles, we fail to ask ourselves how the words and messages of our proclamations might be experienced by persons with disabilities. Much of our theology and preaching has created a portion of the foundation upon which oppression and denial thrive.

How shall we as preachers deepen our understanding and critique of handicappism in order to preach a word that seeks to liberate the human community from such oppression and denial? What worlds do we need to enter and what stories do we need to know to honor the rich human diversity represented within the disability community? What exclusive language needs to be changed, and what theological affirmations need to be challenged? We can begin with a closer look at the disability community itself. As we contemplate our preaching ministries anew, these stories, confrontations, and reflections may call us as preachers to weep, confess, and resist.

THE PARTICULARITIES OF DISABILITIES

One of the responsibilities of preachers and congregations alike is to educate ourselves about the real lives of people in the disability community. We need to understand the impact and nature of various disabilities. We need to understand the subtle and blatant experiences of oppression that people with disabilities face, and we need to be more knowledgeable about the complex issues involved.

As I move into the particularities that follow, I want to acknowledge a point of tension. I have chosen to include within this chapter aspects of the lives and experiences of persons who are deaf. It has been an important education for me to learn that there are vast differences between persons who once were hearing and became deaf later in life, and those persons who have been deaf from birth. I understand that many persons who have always been a part of Deaf culture and community do not consider deafness to be a disability. (On the capitalizing of the word *Deaf,* see p. 25 below.) Culturally Deaf persons have their own language (American Sign Language), their own culture, and their own community. I understand that including discussion of culturally Deaf persons in this chapter may be controversial and debatable, but I still think the inclusion is important.

Even if the Deaf community does not consider deafness to be a disability, from the perspective of our larger social reality, *all* people who do not hear are oppressed by structures and attitudes that limit and deny. The reality of the culturally Deaf person and the reality of the person who has become deaf later in life are both denied in most of our religious communities. I am in no way trying to deny the identity and self-naming that emerge from Deaf culture; rather I am continuing to focus my attention on the forms of oppression that render certain people in our culture invisible. If the dominant culture continues to view deafness of all kinds as a disability, then the consequences of this attitude and labeling must be addressed within the larger oppression of what I am calling handicappism.

Persons with disabilities are as varied and different as people without disabilities. One woman expresses it this way:

> So many factors influence how we experience our disabilities. Money. Degrees of mobility. Family relationships. Community structures. Cultural/ethnic/racial backgrounds. Whether our dis-

abilities are progressive or stable; whether they're visible or hidden; whether they're life-threatening; whether they're clearly diagnosed or mysteries to Western medicine; whether they cause us pain; whether they break up regular sleeping and eating patterns; whether we grew up with them or they were caused by disease or accident later in life.[8]

If the church seeks to be in relationship with all the human community, then a part of our task as religious persons, theologians, and preachers involves educating ourselves about the full reality of disabilities. In the midst of such diverse disabilities, there perhaps is still a common thread of experience, the everyday experience of denial and oppression. Katherine Corbett and Victoria Lewis say it simply: "The only basic common ground among them is the common discrimination faced by all persons with disabilities, for there is always difficulty."[9]

Understanding particularities is a process of education and consciousness raising. The stories that follow are an invitation to all of us to open our buildings, our lives, and our communities to different worlds of humanness. These worlds will make claims upon our resources, our privileges, our power, and our worldviews.

The Birthing of a New Day

"On March 1, 1988, a rally was held on the Gallaudet University football field to convince the students, faculty, staff, alumni, and board of trustees that the Gallaudet community believed it was time for a change, time for a deaf president. It was the beginning of a chain of events that would focus national attention on deafness and Gallaudet and bring about a historic change."[10]

Gallaudet University is located in Washington, D.C. In all its history, from 1864 when the university was established until March 1988, there had never been a Deaf president of this predominantly Deaf institution. Before the historic protest, there were twenty-one members of the board of trustees, but only four members were Deaf.[11] Until this moment, hearing people had maintained primary leadership and power in this Deaf university. Unquestioned domination sparked the protest at Gallaudet. However, what really gave rise to the courageous revolution were the pride and vision of the Deaf community. It was this community's identity and unified strength that forged a transformation.

On March 13, 1988, history was changed. Dr. I. King Jordan was selected president of Gallaudet University, the first Deaf president of this prestigious Deaf institution. President Jordan expressed the significance of the moment in these words: "I agree that it is a new day. All of us who have an interest in the rights and empowerment of disabled or minority people have benefited from the events of that week in March. The ramifications of what the students and their supporters achieved during the week will continue for years."[12]

While this story about Gallaudet revealed many things to our world, two seem particularly important: First, the Deaf community has strength, vision, and clarity of identify as a definable people; and second, the cultural and linguistic oppression and domination by the hearing community continue. Both revelations are important to the church and to the larger society.

This historic event confronts the hearing world with a different world of humanness that cannot be ignored. It is a world that hearing people are not a part of, do not belong to, and will never know. This truth must be spoken clearly and consistently. When taken seriously and faced by persons who hear, it is a truth that frightens us and disorients our own safe world. It is easier to push this truth aside. How is it that Gallaudet, a predominantly Deaf institution, could have been in existence for 124 years before the selection of a Deaf president took place? How is it that only one hearing person, Dr. Laurel Glass, on a board of trustees with seventeen hearing people and four Deaf people, supported Dr. Jordan?[13] How is it that Dr. Elizabeth Zinser, the first choice of the board before the protest, could be elected president of Gallaudet University without a working use of sign language?[14] The students of Gallaudet compelled the world to look at the dominance of the hearing world and its profound denial of the competence and strength of the Deaf community.

As the Christian church opens itself to look at dominance and denial in the reality of handicappism, it is challenged to look at the very nature of human difference. When portions of the human community and the church cease to dominate and deny, individual people and whole communities become able to encounter more fully the truths of those differences. The public event at Gallaudet gave greater visibility to the Deaf community as a distinctive community unknown to most people within the United States and around the globe.

The Distinctive World of Sign

Within the growing literature about deafness and the Deaf community, there are two particular books that have deepened my understanding of language and culture. In *Seeing Voices: A Journey Into the World of the Deaf,* Oliver Sacks analyzes the nature and significance of sign language.[15] Sacks, a hearing person himself and a professor of neurology at the Albert Einstein College of Medicine in New York City, focuses his reflections on the indigenous language of Deaf communities. Located in the United States, he gives primary attention to American Sign Language, the indigenous language of the Deaf community in this country and in parts of Canada. This choice of focus is important. Signed English may be the known and preferred language of many people who have been hearing at some time in their lives, but it is not the natural language of those people who have always been deaf. To direct one's attention to American Sign Language is to attempt to break the total domination of English as an imposed oral language. This does not negate the reality that English is important to deaf persons, for English is the language of reading and writing. However, it is to attempt to honor the primary language of the Deaf community.[16] Within a larger discussion of linguistics, Sacks speaks about the distinctive nature of Sign:

> The single most remarkable feature of Sign — that which distinguishes it from all other languages and mental activities — is its unique linguistic use of space. The complexity of this linguistic space is quite overwhelming for the "normal" eye, which cannot see, let alone understand, the sheer intricacy of its spatial patterns.
>
> We see then, in Sign, at every level — lexical, grammatical, syntactic — a *linguistic* use of space: a use that is amazingly complex, for much of what occurs linearly, sequentially, temporally in speech, becomes simultaneous, concurrent, multileveled in Sign.[17]

This not only suggests that Sign is a different language, but that it is distinctly different from all languages known to human beings. This language distinction is one of the cultural components that gives the Deaf community its identity and worldview. If the hearing community in the church took seriously this profound cultural difference, individuals and communities would not only need to learn a different language, but a language that is fundamentally different in type and nature from anything we have ever known.

Sacks's analysis of Sign not only educates the hearing world to the structure and movement of this language, but it sensitizes us to the unique capacities and proclivities of a community whose cognitive style and worldview are visually and spatially oriented: "To be deaf, to be born deaf, places one in an extraordinary situation; it exposes one to a range of linguistic possibilities, and hence to a range of intellectual and cultural possibilities, which the rest of us, as native speakers in a world of speech, can scarcely even begin to imagine."[18] Hearing communities within the church, and outside, have difficulty grasping this difference. However, this does not free us from the responsibility of finding ways to be in solidarity with the Deaf community as it struggles for its own liberation; nor does it free us from addressing the oppressive structures and attitudes within the hearing community that hinder that liberation.

The Shaping of a People

A second important book, *Deaf in America: Voices from a Culture,* continues to reveal the world and culture of Deaf people. In the introduction, Carol Padden and Tom Humphries give an explanation that has informed my writing and thinking:

> Following a convention proposed by James Woodward (1972), we use the lowercase *deaf* when referring to the audiological condition of not hearing, and the uppercase *Deaf* when referring to a particular group of deaf people who share a language — American Sign Language (ASL) — and a culture. The members of this group reside in the United States and Canada, have inherited their sign language, use it as a primary means of communication among themselves and hold a set of beliefs about themselves and their connection to the larger society. We distinguish them from, for example, those who find themselves losing their hearing because of illness, trauma or age; although these people share the condition of not hearing, they do not have access to the knowledge, beliefs, and practices that make up the culture of Deaf people.[19]

This book gives an inside view of Deaf culture. It weaves together important historical information, stories from the lives of Deaf people themselves, and insights into the changing consciousness of the community.

The primary issue in the book that interests me as a theologian and preacher is the strength of Deaf culture and the cultural endurance of Deaf people, who constantly must live in a world that is not their own. In the beginning chapters of the book, Padden and Humphries help us understand the unfolding development of Deaf children. Out of their distinctive cultural patterns, Deaf children are sensitized to difference. "At age seven, Helen can detect subtle differences in movement contours between native or very fluent signers and those who have learned the language relatively recently; she knows that inexperienced signers often distort circular movements or add wrong movements to signs."[20] The clear difference between a Deaf child's development and the development of many hearing children is that very soon these *differences* are no longer without judgment. A Deaf child soon moves from thinking "I am me" to "I am different." This difference is soon perceived as inferiority. This movement in understanding and discernment of the world is a part of the early experience of oppression.

This is not, however, just an experience of oppression or victimization; it also becomes an opportunity to strengthen self-identity, to clarify the roots of one's cultural connections, and to hold tenaciously to the enduring values of one's own people. These are amazingly difficult lessons to be learned by young Deaf children, and there is much to be learned from Deaf families and cultural communities that make this possible. This living within one's own culture and language, while existing in the midst of a world that is "other," is the experience of all minority people who live in worlds dominated by realities that are not their own. This is cultural imperialism. How do theologians and preachers disengage from and critique this kind of denial? How do we let such difference inform our thinking and our work?

The research that I have referred to about the Deaf community focuses exclusively on the world of the culturally Deaf. Persons who are hearing impaired or have lost their hearing later in life do not share Deaf culture, often communicate with signed English instead of American Sign Language, and still participate in the culture of the hearing world. Many persons live between two worlds. They do not belong to the Deaf community and they no longer have access to the world of hearing. This can be a very isolating and painful place of existence, and is indeed the situation of millions of people.

I have given particular attention to Deaf culture because it is an identifiably strong community, and a community that most of the hearing world denies and oppresses. The world that this community reveals to the church is one of vast difference in language, self-identity, and worldview. This world of humanness is a profound challenge to preachers and religious communities.

The Larger World of Disabilities

The world of disabilities is multifaceted and complex. Until recently there have been very limited written resources about the lived realities of persons with disabilities. Six books in particular are very useful in raising our collective consciousness (full bibliographic information for each is given in the Notes):

- *All Things Are Possible,* by Yvonne Duffy.

- *Disabled, Female, and Proud!: Stories of Ten Women with Disabilities,* by Harilyn Rousso.

- *No More Stares,* by Ann Cupolo Carrillo, Katherine Corbett, and Victoria Lewis.

- *Sinister Wisdom 39: On Disability,* edited by Elana Dykewomon.

- *With the Power of Each Breath: A Disabled Women's Anthology,* by Susan E. Browne, Debra Connors, and Nanci Stern.

- *With Wings: An Anthology of Literature by and about Women with Disabilities,* edited by Marsha Saxton and Florence Howe.

These books have two primary things in common: They are solely about women with disabilities; and they are composed of the actual words of the women themselves. Through interviews, poetry, personal reflections, letters, and telephone conversations, various women across the lines of ethnicity, class, sexual preference, and age express their experiences of being women with disabilities. Feminism and the woman's movement in general have obviously become part of the impetus for so many volumes about women and disabilities. The nature of all these volumes makes them primary source material for a broader exposure to the complex world of disabilities and a clearer understanding of the oppression women and men encounter in the midst of a world designed for able-bodied people. The volumes reflect a keen awareness of the interconnection of the structures of oppressions. Each volume reflects an awareness of the inseparableness of sexism and handicappism. In a chapter entitled "Disability, Sexism and the Social Order," Debra Connors offers a stinging critique of the present system as she suggests that *disabled women* is exactly the term that describes the oppression of women with disabilities:

> Sexism and able-ism work in concert to disqualify us from vast areas of social life. Our unique set of barriers is further compounded by discrimination based on our race, age and sexual preference. Objectified as women and as medical, social work and charity cases, disabled women have been deeply invalidated as human beings. We have been disabled by our society. No euphemism will change this.[21]

There is no adequate way to appreciate the worlds of these women without reading their full stories. The stories are varied and reflect distinctive differences. In these volumes, more than two hundred women confront us with powerful, articulate voices and words — words of anger, of hope, of perseverance, of vitality, and of activism. As I read story after story, I was painfully confronted with my own limited understanding of, and exposure to, the wide range of human disabilities. How do we preach in congregations where people are living in silent worlds of chronic pain and illness? As preachers and pastors, how do we minister in hospitals and institutions where persons experience abuse from both the ignorance and intentional exploitation of medical personnel? If we more adequately understood the way persons who are blind experience their world, how might the content of our sermons change? And how would our liturgical expressions and our sermons be transformed if we seriously responded to the special needs and gifts of persons with mental disabilities?

It is time for the church to listen to the disability community, to sensitize our ministries and our theologies, and to educate ourselves about how we can be open and just communities of faith. In respect and admiration for the distinctive insights, confrontations, political analyses, spiritual truths, and clear convictions of women with disabilities, I think it important for them now to speak for themselves. Included here are the voices of black women, white women, lesbians, and older women:

- *The voice of a woman who uses a wheelchair states forcefully:*

  people smile and say hello to me. very different from when i'm able to walk, and am thus just another dull nonentity. i don't know how to feel about this. it seems similar to the ways adults often treat children, looking down on those of us below their eye level. it makes me feel incompetent, not fully a person. yet it is hard to dislike friendliness.[22]

- *The voice of a woman with multiple sclerosis is very clear:*

  What I hate is not me but a disease. I am not a disease. And a disease is not — at least not singlehandedly — going to determine who I am, though at first it seemed to be going to.[23]

- *The voice of a woman with Hodgkin's disease speaks a difficult truth:*

  A disease and its treatment can be a series of humiliations, a chisel for humility.[24]

- *The voice of a woman with a learning disability demands what is just:*

  It has not been easy for me to find my place in society as an LD adult. It took hard work, self-discipline, and positive thinking. I had to demand the training that was needed in each situation.[25]

- *The voice of a woman with an environmental illness (immune system dysregulation) confronts us with the work we need to do:*

  We get tired of doing all the work. If a womon [sic] indicates you're making her sick, ask if she needs you to move away, and how far. If you're at her home, offer to shower with safe products. If you smoke, be aware that smoke is highly toxic and more and more people are becoming sensitive to it.[26]

- *The voice of a woman who is blind claims her own rights:*

  Had I not had a history of political activism, in civil rights for blacks and in opposition to the Vietnam War, I might not have been so ready to fight for my rights as a person with a disability. I realized I would have to take the energy I had put into social change for other people's benefit and use it to benefit myself and other disabled people.[27]

- *The voice of a woman who is quadriplegic advocates her own community:*

  My main interest is bringing information to the black community, because we don't have it — especially not black people with disabilities. We don't have access to things like getting a wheelchair or to health and other needed services.[28]

- *The voice of a woman who has progressive rheumatoid arthritis affirms life:*

  Pain is a constant in my life, always has been. But in the interest of living, the pain became tolerable. And I've thought that was the prize — LIVING.[29]

- *The voice of a woman partially paralyzed from polio addresses sexuality:*

  Although there have been a number of articles in various medical and nursing journals discussing whether or not Differently Abled women are able to have babies, there has been virtually nothing about birth control. Our fertility and its regulation is one more facet of our sexuality usually ignored by the professionals who are supposed to be rehabilitating us.[30]

- *The voice of a woman who is mentally disabled exposes a silent hierarchy:*

  Probably the lowest on the general hierarchy of disability, set up by the able-bodied society and mirrored in the disabled community, are those individuals labelled mentally ill or mentally retarded.... Frequently considered to be "better off" in institutions, we are often drugged up, locked away, shocked out of our minds, and totally rejected by both the able-bodied and otherwise-disabled communities.[31]

These excerpts suggest only a few of the complex questions raised by these women's stories. As each woman speaks her own story, one becomes increasingly clear about the distinctiveness of each person's needs, worldview, and experienced reality. A person who uses a wheelchair experiences very different issues of access than a person who is Deaf. The sexual needs and physical concerns of persons who experience paralysis are distinct and varied. Within the particularity of each disability, there are distinctive challenges and joys in the experience of raising children. Some of these women have disabilities that are less visible, and that reality creates its own particular set of issues and challenges. Some of these women face multiple levels of oppression because they are women of color, poor women, older women, or lesbians. If the church is ever to understand the realities of disabled persons' lives, individually and collectively, then we must begin to *listen*, to *read*, and to *know* the unique particularities of those individual lives.

Most of the volumes cited above include the stories of women who live with chronic illness and pain. This is an important inclusion, for it portrays a realistic view of the vastness and magnitude of disabilities. Chronic pain and illness are as unaccommodated and denied in our society as are those factors commonly defined as disabilities. These stories are the stories of women struggling to confront the oppression of social structures, social attitudes, and social denial. These voices and words confront the church, and point the church toward transformation.

PREACHING REVELATION

Theological literature reflecting on handicappism or on the experiences of people with disabilities is limited. Literature about disabilities is primarily comprised of historical accounts; sociological, psychological, or linguistic approaches to, or analyses of, disabilities; and descriptive accounts of disabilities in the form of personal narratives. Although there is minimal material that addresses theological or religious questions, the stories and reflections from the lives of persons with disabilities raise enormous theological questions for the task of preaching. I have chosen to cluster my theological reflections in two sections in the pages that follow. The first section will raise a variety of theological issues that seem critical for hearing and able-bodied people to consider if they desire to build a theology of responsiveness and solidarity with persons with disabilities. The second section will focus on *revelation* as a primary theological issue that emerges in relation to persons with disabilities and the oppression against them. I believe that all human beings are made in the image of God, and thus are distinct revelations of God's nature and activity in the world. I also believe that persons with disabilities know and experience distinctive aspects of God's revelation that can be named and articulated only by them. How we know God, what ways we experience God in the midst of human life, and how we become the human face of God — all these seem critical and poignant issues.

Questioning Assumptions

We need to look critically at our use of hearing and seeing imagery, the exclusively oral nature of the preaching act, and some of the unquestioned hermeneutical principles that have guided our biblical interpretations. These critical questions will guide us into alternative images, new methods of proclaiming, and sensitized hermeneutics. We need to reflect upon the implications of some common assumptions we are making in preaching.

Seeing and Hearing Imagery   We can begin by looking at a key text from scripture:

> Then the disciples came and asked him, "Why do you speak to them in parables?" He answered, "To you it has been given to know the secrets of the kingdom of heaven, but to them it has not been given. For to those who have, more will be given, and they will have an abundance; but from those who have nothing, even what they have will be taken away. The reason I speak to them in parables is that 'seeing they do not perceive, and hearing they do not listen, nor do they understand.' With them indeed is fulfilled the prophecy of Isaiah that says:
>
> > 'You will indeed listen, but never understand,
> >   and you will indeed look, but never perceive.
> > For this people's heart has grown dull,
> >   and their ears are hard of hearing,
> >   and they have shut their eyes;
> >   so that they might not look with their eyes,
> >   and listen with their ears,
> > and understand with their heart, and turn —
> >   and I would heal them.'
>
> But blessed are your eyes, for they see, and your ears, for they hear. Truly, I tell you, many prophets and righteous people longed to see what you see, but did not see it, and to hear what you hear, but did not hear it." (Matt. 13:10–17)

Countless texts throughout scripture contain seeing and hearing imagery. In a very fundamental way, seeing and hearing the truth of God remain central descriptive images for affirming faith in the Christian community. This usage leaves me with serious questions as I approach such ancient texts for preaching. I am confronted with questions I never before raised and realities I never considered. As the consciousnesses of preachers are raised by the distinctive experiences of all persons, they will need to reflect sensitively on the use of language and imagery closely connected to disabilities.

A starting place for preachers might be simply to ask ourselves, "How would a person who is deaf, or a person who is blind, interpret and understand this passage from Matthew?" Even as we ask ourselves that important question, it is not difficult to understand the offense of such a text. I have heard countless preachers use hearing and seeing language without showing any conscious connection between the language and its ability to wound, offend, and stereotype. Preachers also use images about walking, running, and standing with little awareness of the reality of limited mobility for many people. Many times preachers do not make the connection, but as communities with growing awareness, we need to help each other toward that end.

It is not just the language of the text that offends, but the message. The implications of the text are clear no matter how much work one does to place it in its historical context, or to understand its function in the early teachings of Jesus. Those who do not see and hear cannot understand. Those who do not see and hear are indifferent. Those who do not see and hear have a dull heart. Those who do not see and hear should turn to be healed. *Those who do see and do hear are blessed.* I understand the symbolic nature of Jesus' language, and as a person who sees and hears, I can personally relate to and appreciate the images of seeing and hearing as ways people discern truth and faith. I also understand that *seeing* in this passage does not relate to physical seeing, but spiritual seeing. Even so, the implications of the text are ultimately oppressive for people who do not physically see or hear. Also, even if we substitute *understand* in all those places that seeing and hearing imagery appear, we face the issue of how those who have mental disabilities come to faith, or participate in a life of faith. Preachers can continue to preach from these verses, but if we desire to be inclusive and sensitive, we must practice new thinking, new naming, and a dramatic reworking of the text. In *Bread Not Stone,* Elisabeth Schüssler Fiorenza articulates the challenge clearly when she says: "Such a process of naming transforms our metaphor of Scripture as 'tablets of stone' on which the unchanging word of God is engraved for all times into the image of bread that nurtures, sustains, and energizes women [and men] as people of God in our struggles against injustice and oppression."[32]

The Word of God　As a preacher and homiletician, I struggle with many questions about the very task and act of preaching. When preachers attempt to shape a theology of solidarity with persons who have disabilities, particular questions immediately surface. Preachers *speak* the Word of God, and *preach* the Word of God. Preaching is an important and valued oral event in the life of religious communities. In the midst of that affirmation, I find myself wondering: What does this mean in the Deaf community? Where is the Word of God, and what is the Word of God for those who do not hear? What does the act of preaching mean in a predominantly Deaf congregation?

These questions have tremendous implications for the future of our preaching ministries. Perhaps it is time for us to take a serious look at the exclusively *spoken* nature of proclamation, and open our sermons to visual and kinesthetic dimensions we have not previously considered. "And the Word became flesh and lived among us,... full of grace and truth" (John 1:14). The words of John do not say the Word was spoken among us, full of grace and truth. The Word is incarnate and embodied, and comes to us in spoken word, healing touch, prayerful act, iconoclastic action, and silent presence. As proclaimers of the Word, have we forgotten the many forms of its expression? The spoken art of preaching is an important ministry. However, can it not be deepened and enriched by making connections to our other senses? This connection will not simply enhance the aesthetics of preaching, or deepen its effectiveness as a communications act, but will strengthen the inclusiveness of our proclamations.

Guiding Hermeneutical Principles Liberation theologians from a variety of perspectives agree that scripture texts have served liberating as well as oppressive purposes in the history of our church and world. Through a variety of methods and from very distinctive perspectives, hermeneutics asks critical questions of the text in order to understand it, appropriate it for our lives, and proclaim it more faithfully. Liberation theologians, and persons who preach from that perspective, know that the principles of interpretation one uses greatly affect the messages one proclaims.

As a pastor and preacher, I have wondered for a long time how persons with disabilities experience and understand many of the healing stories in the Gospels. As a homiletician, I wonder what hermeneutical principles guide persons with disabilities in interpreting scripture.

When I read the account of Jesus healing a paralytic (Matt. 9:1–8), I want to explore basic definitions and connections: What do members of the disability community say about the nature of *healing* in human existence? From the perspective of a person with a disability, what critique might be offered about the implied connection between sinfulness and disability? Who are the *crowds* today, and what might be their reaction?

When I read the account of the woman who was healed from a flow of blood that had lasted twelve years (Mark 5:25–34), I want to expand my understanding: What insights about life and faith do persons have who have lived with chronic, long-term illness? What human interactions, moments of seeking, or experiences of presence bring healing? What voice might this woman have if she could speak through a contemporary woman?

When I read the account of the Gerasene demoniac (Mark 5:1–20), I want distinctive insights. From the varied perspectives of persons with disabilities, I want to know how this man who lived among tombs is understood. From the perspective of persons who have mental disabilities, I want to ask: Was this man as misunderstood, isolated, and feared in his own day as countless persons with mental disabilities are to-day? What realities and life experiences torment those who have mental disabilities?

The Christian church, and all religious communities, desperately need the particular hermeneutical principles and insights that can only be articulated from persons with disabilities. These reflections will deepen our experiences of these texts and transform the preaching that seeks to illumine them.

Honoring God's Revelation

One of the theological issues at stake in dealing with the oppression of handicappism and the giftedness of persons with disabilities is revelation. George Stroup commenting on revelation says, "Traditionally when Christians have attempted to explain what they know about God and how they have access to that knowledge, they have appealed to something called 'revelation.' "[33] Revelation is about God's self-disclosure and how persons experience that disclosure. For centuries the Christian community has articulated and affirmed a clear connection between preaching and revelation. Even though proclamation is only one of several ways the human community experiences God's self-disclosure, it has been a very important, central form of revelation in the church's life.

In this regard, I find myself asking several questions. First, what is the fundamental difference between the Word of God *signed,* and the Word of God *spoken.* From what little I understand about Sign, I would guess the difference must be great. If the spatial language of Sign is simultaneous, concurrent, and multileveled, does it reveal radically different dimensions of God to the human community than does the linear, sequential, and temporal language of speech? Second, what is the form or nature of revelation in the life of a person who is both blind and deaf? Third, are there distinctive forms of God's revelation that are revealed in the lives of people with disabilities that are not revealed or experienced in the lives of able-bodied people? Stroup says, "Revelation yields not the solution to a problem, the answer to a difficult question, but the unveiling of a mystery."[34] What do people with disabilities know about the mysteries of God? This question takes me beyond my reflections on the pastoral, theological, and homiletical responsibilities of the hearing and able-bodied community, and into areas of revelation known from the perspective of persons with disabilities.

Revelation: The Nature of God In an article called "The Good News!" Mary Weir, a member of the Deaf community, proclaims: "In the beginning, God freely created all people in God's image: yellow, black, white, brown; women, children, men; deaf, able-bodied, paralyzed, retarded. All together are made in God's image. Each is unique, without any one, God's image is incomplete. All of God's creation is blessed as very good."[35] This is a very powerful theological affirmation. No part of creation is superior to another. No part of creation is inferior. What is *normal* is the created nature and shape of each being. What is *natural* is the distinct giftedness of each creature. This does not suggest that some disabilities are intended by God, or that human beings do not have a responsibility for certain behaviors that bring disabilities into other persons' lives. What this suggests to me is that all creation is blessed and claimed by God as worthy and good.

Not only does Weir affirm the goodness of *all* creation, and the incredible uniqueness of each person, but she shocks us with a suggestion that God is incomplete without each one of us. Much of traditional Christian theology teaches us that God is untouchable, transcendent, and wholly other. Yet we also affirm that we are made in God's image. If indeed we are made in God's image, then Weir is correct in asserting that God is not complete without each one of us. To experience the radical nature of this affirmation, one has to restate it in another way: God is yellow; God is black; God is woman; God is deaf; God is paralyzed; God is retarded; God is child. This God is not wholly other, removed, and distanced from our experience. God is a part of our experience, intricately interwoven with each of us while being so much more than any one of us.

Women from vastly different perspectives and religious communities are challenging and transforming traditional Christianity with new imagery for God. This theological naming comes from renewed attention to ancient female imagery for God within scripture itself, and female imagery that emerges from within women's diverse human experience. Liberation theologians from Latin America urge the church to see God as poor and oppressed. Many womanist, African-American, and African liberation theologians urge us to see God as black. One of the challenges of the disabilities community will surely be to suggest that God is paralyzed, blind, or deaf.[36] At some very basic level, if we cannot consider this possibility, we cannot affirm that all human beings are made in the image of God. Our understandings of God, and thus our theology, must change or our affirmations of faith are contradictory and inconsistent.

Revelation: The Nature of Human Existence   The human community has much to learn about the very nature of human existence from persons who have disabilities. Persons with disabilities not only *experience* and *name* God in ways that expand God for us all; they also *embody* a presence and human reality that disclose/reveal God to the rest of the human community in distinctive ways.

Prudence Sutherland, a member of the disability community, in an article entitled "Backlash!" says:

> Disabled people, however, are in a different position. Nature, not an unjust social order, has made us dependent upon able-bodied people — and that will always be the case. Suppose all our demands were suddenly met? A job for every disabled person; every building and all transportation accessible; unlimited, free attendant care. A disabled person would still need a non-disabled person to get out of bed in the morning.[37]

This reality makes the nature of human existence quite distinct for many people with disabilities. Sutherland is clear about human interdependence and is not seduced by societal claims about independence or confused by personal claims of rugged individualism. For many people with disabilities the myth of privatized living is not only shattered, but has never existed. As people with disabilities speak about limited mobility, attendant care, institutionalized living, and daily threats of death, the myth of total independence is exposed for the lie it is. The cultural myth of individual control becomes absurd. The reality of limitation also challenges the Christian church to look critically at its own theology that states that it is more blessed to give than to receive, more righteous to do the loving act than to be the recipient of that loving act. A woman writing from within the disability community expressed it this way: "Can the church not bless my receiving as sacramental as much as your giving, i.e. your helping me?"[38] Perhaps persons with disabilities will shape a new theology of receiving that will change us all.

What do persons with disabilities know about the interdependent nature of creation and community? I assume that human beings who understand and experience life in such interdependent ways will reveal rich dimensions to us about God's interdependence with all creation.[39] What do persons with disabilities know about human vulnerability? What do persons with disabilities know about the loss of control and how that reality shapes and influences the human person? What do persons with disabilities know about unending anger and frustration? I am not intending to romanticize vulnerability, interdependence, or loss of control; rather I want to point us to the reality that persons with disabilities confront the entire human community with radical worlds of difference.

Debra Connors says: "It is unpardonable in an individualist society to fail to be 'self-sufficient.' Our society values a false sense of independence which results in pain and a sense of worthlessness for women and men whose capabilities have been ignored and whose potential has been uniformly underdeveloped."[40] The disability community confronts us with truths about human existence: our mutual interdependence, our human vulnerability, our embodied humanness, all realities that much of the able-bodied community wants to deny.

Douglas John Hall suggests that there are four aspects of our basic human condition that can produce suffering: (1) loneliness — a sense of incompleteness; (2) limitation — a sense of what one cannot do; (3) temptation — a sense of trying to exceed the limits of our humanness; and (4) anxiety — the threat of nonbeing.[41] This is one able-bodied person's understanding of those qualities that make for humanness and that also lead to pain and suffering. They seem descriptive of my life experience, but as a theologian, preacher, and human being, I long to hear members of the disability community critique and elaborate on these observations about basic human existence. From what I have come to understand, I believe that there must be qualities inherent in the lives of persons with disabilities that are categorically different from these universally assumed qualities. Or are the understandings and experiences of these qualities of human life simply different? What are some of the fundamental realities of being a person with a disability that bring pain and suffering, and instill wonder and joy?

The Creation of a New Theology

In response to handicappism, hearing and able-bodied preachers and religious communities need a theology of solidarity and responsiveness. We also await the kind of theological reflection that can be done only by persons with disabilities. The evolution of this theological reflection is in a nascent state and will require the church's commitment of resources and energy if it is to develop more fully. The kinds of new theologies that are emerging from within the disability community will enrich and challenge religious communities around the world. The vision and struggle of persons with disabilities are revolutionary. When movements locate their work within a struggle toward liberation and situate their praxis within resistance against injustice, they are calling for transformation. I hope this community's individual and collective theologizing will shape a different anthropology, a distinctive theology of embodiment, a critical scriptural hermeneutic, and a new understanding of God. This new theology will surely deepen our understanding of God's revelation and broaden our experience of God's disclosure.

✦ 2 ✦

Embodiment Challenges
Marginalization—AGEISM

INVESTMENT OF WORTH

You value the earthen vase —
each crack applauded
for authenticity,
a slave's Freedom Quilt —
hand-pulled stitchery
a rare tale relinquished,
Victorian silver hair pins
with filigreed flowers
delicate as unconscious.
A collector of ancients
quite proud of your tastes
but scornful of
curled brown leaves
slight gray webs
parched desert soil
of a woman
turned and tuned to her ripening,
whose life is dear
as a signed first edition,
whose death as costly
as a polished oak bed.

— Terri L. Jewell[1]

In our day aging has become a frequent topic of conversation and re-search. Age-related demographics in the United States reveal that a quiet transformation is taking place in the very nature and composition of our nation. These figures and statistics shatter many of our unquestioned myths and stereotypes and have become one of the most effective ways to communicate quickly what is transpiring. In *Agewave*, Ken Dychtwald paints a vivid picture of the changes that are sweeping across this country:

Now, in the late 1980s, there are more than 30 million Americans over 65 — some 12 percent of the population — and this group is increasing by nearly 6 million every decade. In the last two decades, the over-65 age group has grown more than twice as fast as the rest of the population. In the last hundred years, while the population of the country has multiplied 5 times, the population over 65 has multiplied 12.5 times. In July of 1983, the number of Americans over the age of 65 surpassed the number of teenagers. We are no longer a nation of youths.[2]

These changes are influencing and changing every facet of our personal and social reality. These changes provide tremendous opportunities and possibilities for vital ministries in our religious communities. "Aging is not just a social issue but a major force for change."[3] It is challenging to ponder how we might shape preaching ministries in response to the metamorphosis happening around us. Preachers will need to sensitize themselves to the complex issues surrounding age, aging, and ageism by turning their attention to older adults in a new way. We will need to draw from gerontology, sociology, psychology, theology, and religion in order to develop a new consciousness about the giftedness of older adults and the violence of ageism. In recent years the field of gerontology has expanded and gained increased recognition. Age-related books, journals, and professional symposiums reflect a deepening commitment to the integration of religion and aging. Growing numbers of religious communities, churches, temples, and denominational agencies have developed policy statements about, and programmatic responses for, a ministry with older adults. Even though it has become increasingly acceptable to speak about *age* and *aging*, it is still not fashionable to speak about *ageism*. It is painfully difficult for the human community to focus its attention and action on ageism. Age and aging are areas of medical, social, and religious investigation and inquiry. Ageism is the systematic exploitation and oppression of those in our society who are labeled and deemed to be old. Even though age and aging are topics of growing awareness and interest, *ageism* as an issue of injustice is frequently met by denial, resistance, and hostility. To speak of ageism is to focus conversation and research on our larger society and its prejudicial attitudes and dehumanizing structures.

The focus of the pages that follow is clearly on ageism. Age and aging scholarship may inform a critique of ageism even when this is not the primary emphasis. Older adults are marginalized by social structures and attitudes that discriminate, exclude, and oppress. We are a people who deny the natural aging process, our universal human finitude, and the reality of death itself. To focus primarily on ageism is not to suggest that all older adults can be reduced to people who are victimized and oppressed. Rather it is to address those attitudes and social structures that continue to inhibit fullness of life for those in our society who are older.

Richard Kalish, in "The New Ageism and the Failure Models: A Polemic," speaks about a kind of new ageism that he feels is present in the philosophy and critique of many advocates of the elderly. He believes that most of the models formulated to address issues related to ageism are fundamentally failure models. He raises serious questions about the validity of literature that remains focused solely on the injustices of ageism. In a critique of Robert Butler's book *Why Survive?* he says, "This book has served effectively to rally the sympathetic and persuade the dubious that the plight of *the* elderly requires remediation. But what accumulative effect does this book, and its kindred media and political writings and speeches, have on older persons?"[4]

I deeply disagree with Kalish's position. It is important to note that Robert Butler's *Why Survive? Being Old in America*, published in 1975, was one of the most thorough and confrontational books about the violences of ageism. The book describes and analyzes the unmet needs and critical concerns of older adults and exposes countless violations. Older adults do not need to be protected from the fullness of this kind of documentation. Those who consciously and unconsciously support these oppressive structures need to be confronted with the fullness of our social reality. Kalish ends his critique of a new ageism by suggesting that "we can refocus our attention on the later years as opportunities for flexibility, joy, pleasure, growth, and sensuality."[5] These words seem naive when faced with statistics from the 1986 U.S. census, which revealed that 31 percent of all black persons, 22.5 percent of all Hispanics, and 10.7 percent of all whites who are sixty-five and over are living below the poverty level in this country.[6] His words are also elitist in the face of the reality that 19.7 percent of all women over eighty-five years of age live in poverty.[7]

The repercussions of poverty on older adults are immense. Housing and medical care are perpetual problems, and it is estimated that 25 percent of all suicides happen within the population of older adults.[8] These statistics represent the lived experiences of millions of people in this country. If all older adults could know the promise of joy, pleasure, flexibility, and sensuality, instead of just the struggle for survival, then I would gladly abandon a focus on the injustice and oppression of ageism.

RADICALIZING MOMENTS

I have experienced the pain of ageism in the lives of people I love, and in my own life. I have experienced the structural marginalization that slowly disempowers older adults, isolates them in nursing homes, and takes control of their lives. I have experienced fear and oppression in attitudes that will not allow people to speak of their own death, that assume that older adults lack vital sexual lives, and that stereotype all older adults as conservative in their social and political views. I have experienced profound age segregation in our common life, and a lack of understanding about friendships and intimate connections that exist across generations. The events and relationships described below have made me more aware of ageism and its many forms of stereotyping, silence, segregation, and marginalization. Learning how to discern and name these moments in our own lives is an essential part of our theological and homiletical task.

When I was a teenager, my Aunt Bessie and Uncle Tom both died. For me, they were very much like grandparents. Aunt Bessie was active in the church and community almost all her life, yet her later years were lived in isolation in a nursing home. Sometimes her physical care was adequate; sometimes it was not. It was difficult to get honest information about her daily condition from the staff. Aunt Bessie died in that same nursing home while I was the only one in the room with her. When it became clear to me she was dying, I called the nurses. They tried to force me to leave, but I remained until she died. The sterile room and the mechanical human interactions diminished the profound sacredness of the moment. In those final moments it was as if Aunt Bessie and I had no right to be together and no protection for the special bond we shared. This was frightening and angering. I have never blamed family members for her isolation and her dying in a nursing home, but to this day it still feels tragic.

During my Uncle Tom's terminal illness there were times of hospitalization. I will never forget one visit. Several family members were present. He began to talk about dying, and each time he tried to speak someone quickly silenced him with assurances that he was fine and that he would get better. This happened more than once, and finally he gave up trying to communicate to us his feelings about wanting to die. To this day I have regretted what happened there. To be silenced about one's own death seems like one of the harshest denials imaginable. The fear and denial in that hospital room were very human, but also very violent.

When I was a pastor at Epworth United Methodist Church, I grew to love two older couples. In the life we shared together during the early years of my ministry, they became my constant teachers about aging and ageism. They allowed me into their lives in some very intimate ways, and for four years we touched each others' lives deeply. I learned more than I could say about the joys and the heartaches of aging and ageism from these four people. I spent hours with one of the couples, Martha and Forest Smith, as they struggled with painful decisions about prostate cancer. This was a constant part of their life for several years. I remember many profound conversations about life and faith with them, and I remember conversations about the specific pain and fear of life changes related to Forest's illness. The frank conversations we had about the fullness of their relationship, including the vitality and meaning of their sexual life, will remain with me forever. They understood their life together as sheer gift, and they lived with a sense of strong vocation. Together we walked through each stage of their decisions. The grace and clarity of their individuality, as well as their togetherness, taught me a great deal about love and commitment.

Another couple, Al and Mildred Wallace, struggled with the debilitating results of a stroke. Even though I knew them before this happened, most of the intimacy of our relationship developed in a nursing home where Al was living after the stroke. I remember extraordinary conversations with them about family, faith, work, and the challenges of life. I remember so vividly Al's tears of frustration as he tried so hard to regain strength and mobility. I remember becoming aware of the conditions of his life in the nursing home: no privacy, very little control over any aspect of his daily activity, and the profound loss of his preferred home. I gained new insight about loss and control as holidays and birthdays happened and Al and I would scheme together about what gifts he wanted to buy Mildred. I also remember with awe Mildred sitting by Al's bed for hours every single day. Mildred and Al taught me some very profound lessons about fidelity, loss, presence, and persevering strength.

All of life is a mixture of this kind of pain and joy. All older adults will know the natural repercussions of aging. For disenfranchised older adults, these natural repercussions are magnified by the unnecessary violence of ageism. In an ageist society that isolates most of us from the richness of human experiences, we lose the chance to know the joy of strong love, the hope of fidelity, the satisfaction of shared companionship across ages, and the beauty of mutuality within relationships that transcend tremendous age differences.

NAMING AND UNDERSTANDING THE VIOLENCE

The kind of aging-terminology we use in our preaching and in our ministry will convey our underlying convictions and assumptions. In the literature that focuses on age, aging, and ageism, there is no consensus about language. There is also no consensus about language when older adults speak about themselves. Some of the literature refers to adults who are fifty and above as "older adults" or "older women and men." Some of the literature refers to these same persons as "elders" while other works simply say "those who are old." Some writers use the term *the elderly* while others speak about "aging persons" or "senior citizens." These references are important although many times the designations seem very arbitrary. Naming the particular age that determines when one is an older adult, a senior citizen, or an elder is just as arbitrary. Older adults, like other oppressed people, have had the power of naming stolen from them. As the movement against ageism among older adults themselves becomes stronger in this country, they will surely instruct the larger society about their preferences.

In the midst of this ambiguity, and with some reservation, I have chosen to use the term *older adults* as the primary descriptive language in these pages. This designation feels less romanticized, less pejorative, and less idealized than many of the other terms. In several places I use the word *old* when I am trying to expose the labeling and oppressive actions of the larger society. All our language about age and aging will continue to be somewhat distorted because the prior judgments our society has made about what constitutes old age reflect a very distorted and segmented view of human life.

Maggie Kuhn, who convened and founded the Gray Panthers in 1972, says, "Agism is the notion that people become inferior because they have lived a specified number of years."[9] In some ways this definition may seem far too simplistic, but it points accurately to the irrationality of an ageist society. Ageism is irrational because it is a form of violation and oppression built on false stereotypes and myths and constructed with denial and fear. All people are aging from birth to death, not just those persons who are sixty-five and older. All people face human finitude and limitations, not just those persons who experience some of the limiting realities of older adult life. Ageism is built on the belief and practice that old people are fundamentally inferior. Ageism is the process of dismissing older adults, relating to them as if they do not exist. Ageism is the process of treating older adults as if they were children. Ageism is the process of disenfranchising older adults, controlling them as if they are powerless.

I have come to believe that the term *marginalization* accurately portrays the attitudinal and structural ramifications of ageism. Marginalization has become the way our society attempts to push older adults to the periphery of our social institutions, to the margins of economic power and humanizing communities, to the edges of our interpersonal and family structures, and to the outer limits of life itself. In the United States, ageism and its subsequent marginalization stem from a complex set of understandings and structures within our particular society. It is to some of those understandings that I want to turn first, then offer a critique of several structural injustices that are a part of our larger social reality.

Ageism: Attitudes and Understandings

Our culture has lost a foundational understanding of the larger *life span* and of the fact that all people are aging. Our society has a very distorted and segmented way of understanding human life itself. Maggie Kuhn challenges us again when she says:

> All are born of seeds, grow, and mature, bear flowers, fruit, prog-
> eny, wither and die, and in the process replenish the earth. Our
> own aging should not be feared or denied. It identifies us with the
> whole created order and with our Creator. But in our competitive
> profit-centered society we have violated the essential wholeness of
> the life span, and chopped it into segments, each quite separate.[10]

In our culture the "essential wholeness" of our human life span has been obscured by age-segmented understandings and praxis. Instead of seeing childhood, adolescence, and adulthood as aspects of a single life, we view these stages of growth as almost taking on a life of their own, unrelated to past and future. We are enculturated to cast aside each prior stage of development and enter fully into the present moment. All too soon we forget the child and adolescent we have been, or we cannot conceive of the older adult that we will soon become. "We not only tend to deny the real existence of old men and women living in their closed rooms and nursing homes, but also the old man or woman who is slowly awakening in our own center."[11] When childhood is cut off from adult-hood, we lose the power and hope of memory. When adolescence and adulthood are divorced from childhood, we lose the power and hope of dreaming. Both memory and hope are essential parts of the human journey. "This combination of memory and anticipation is no less true for the aged than for any earlier time of life. The only difference for those who are old is the relatively limited amount of chronological time they may anticipate."[12]

All ages are connected and interwoven in the fabric of one's com-plete life journey. The drive to separate and segment life does not lead us toward integration and wholeness, but brings us alienation, isolation, arbitrary restrictions, and stifling expectations. I share my daily life with very few older adults or children. This is typical for countless adults in our society. Age segregation is portrayed in our culture as natural and normal. In contrast, the ministries of our churches should call us back to the universal truth of essential wholeness.

Confronting Stereotypes and Myths   Struggling against ageism also in-volves confronting the stereotypes, myths, and illusions that perpetuate it. Stereotyped understandings of an age group are precisely what seg-mented theories of the life span rest upon.

Statistics about longevity in this country shatter myths about limited years of retirement living and reveal the composition of the older adult community. "At the turn of the century there were only a few hundred thousand Americans over 85; today, there are 3.3 million, and it is estimated that there will be close to 20 million by 2050."[13] Accurate information about longevity pushes us to look critically at our assumptions about vocation and vision in the later years of life. Many people will live fifteen to twenty-five years after retirement. How will the worship and preaching ministries of our religious communities support the spiritual lives of older adults as they continue to live their visions of justice, care, and love in the world? What special ministries might older adults initiate within our faith communities? How will we speak to the special needs of life transitions and retirement?

Present information about the health and mobility of older adults breaks many of the stereotypes and myths about frail, dependent older people.

> The great majority (68 per cent) of persons over 65 consider themselves in "good" or "excellent" health compared to others their own age and report that they are able to carry out their daily activities without any serious impairment. Eighty-five to 90 percent are able to manage independent living in the community, and another 2.4 million are healthy enough to remain semi-independent — if supportive services and appropriate housing are available.[14]

Our sermons and our ministries need to portray older adults as pictures of strength, resourcefulness, and endurance. Through ministries of word and action we need to call our congregations into conscious advocacy of the special kind of assistance that is needed for older adults to remain independent in the community.

Statistics about work and retirement clearly counter our stereotypes about lack of productivity and increased leisure among older adults.

> While 12 percent of all people 65 and over are employed, a much higher 18 percent in the 65–69 age group are working. And it should be added that 8 in every 10 mature citizens who are working have no intention whatsoever of retiring. Sadly, among the majority who have retired, a substantial 37 percent said they did not stop working by choice — they were forced to retire.[15]

These honest reflections about retirement and work need to be seriously heard as we look critically at forced retirement and limited possibilities of work for persons as they grow older. Many of the attitudes and structures of our society make it impossible for older adults to work for economic gain and for vocational fulfillment. The proclamations from our churches need to speak to this injustice.

An important step in confronting ageism is to confront and dismantle the stereotypes and myths that fuel it. These stereotypes and myths
negatively shape the attitudes and understandings of children, youth,
and adults, and give rise to the prejudices that undergird ageism.

Ageist Myths: Families, Women, and Religious Communities   Ageism does
not just perpetuate stereotypes and myths about older adults; it also
gives all of us a distorted view of the social reality in this country. A
very common assumption among white, middle-class Americans is that
a large number of older adults are institutionalized. The stereotype un-
derneath this assumption is that most families abandon older family
members to the care of institutions. Some resources suggest that only 5
percent of all persons sixty-five and over reside in institutions.[16] Across
this nation, it appears that family members are significantly involved in
the support of older adults.

> Slightly over half (51 percent) of the 17.2 percent of the elderly who
> require support services receive all of their needed care from fam-
> ily and friends. In most areas, relatives and friends provide the
> vast majority of the care received by the functionally impaired el-
> derly in the community. In Massachusetts, for example, if one were
> to total up all of the hours of light housework support provided
> during any seven day period, 77 percent would come from infor-
> mal sources. For meals, the informal provide 87 percent of the total
> supports, for shopping the estimate is 90 percent and even for per-
> sonal care, 74 percent of all support hours come from family and
> friends.[17]

The dissemination of this kind of information can break a powerful
myth in our society.

It is important to add to these revealing statistics the rather shocking
truth that most of this informal care is given by women who are daughters, sisters, and friends of the older adults. This effort has an enormous
social and economic impact on middle-aged and older women in our
society. It is estimated that as many as 17 percent of women between
the ages of forty and forty-four have children under the age of eighteen living at home, while at the same time 97 percent of those same
women have parents over the age of sixty-five.[18] We obviously live in an
era when adult women are still raising children by the time their parents
have become older adults. This reality makes for an incredibly complex
set of familial responsibilities for women.

As preachers and religious communities, our ministries might do
well to reflect more understanding and support for women, across ethnic and class lines, who are so faithful in the care and support of family.
Our ministries might also reflect a much deeper social and theological

critique of a social system that continues to make basic relational and familial care so thoroughly dependent on women. This clearly reveals the connection between ageism and sexism. For many of the women who become caregivers for older family members there is tremendous economic loss: "According to a variety of studies, between 12 and 28 percent of caregiving daughters leave the work force to provide care. These women often lose salary and benefits, retirement pensions, social networks, and work satisfaction. Caregiving responsibilities also may compel some women to remain unemployed."[19] One can easily begin to see how middle-aged women who are the primary caregivers of older adults later become a part of the astonishingly high percentage of older women who are living in poverty.

Poverty in the late years is fundamentally linked to one's participation in the labor force at earlier years of life, one's level of employment and benefits, and the continuity of one's working years. In addition to women providing a great deal of informal care for older parents, daughters are also the family members most likely to have older parents living with them. "When aging parents live with offspring, eight out of ten are mothers, and two-thirds of them are living with a daughter."[20] There is a myth that working women are less involved in family life today and less committed to the relational fabric of our society. Even though I believe the relational expectations of women have always been a deep part of the oppression of sexism in our society, and a change would be justified, this change does not indeed appear to be happening. Most women simply maintain multiple levels of relational responsibility while working in the labor force of this country. This information reveals the intersection of ageism, sexism, and classism in an obvious way.

One final myth that flows from ageism has produced a distorted view of religious communities. In many of the Christian churches of which I have been a part, there is still a marginalizing assumption made about older adults. Many people still believe that older adults *receive* from our religious communities more than they give. Many believe the church is *in service* to this age-segmented population, not in ministry with them, and we hold fast to a myth that older adults in our religious communities are the most *narrow and conservative*. These assumptions abound even though older adults often underwrite a very large portion of the budgets of many of our churches and synagogues, support the entire worship and programmatic life of our congregations, and provide vital and creative leadership. Rabbi Kerry Olitzky reflects on the empowering and prophetic witness of older Jewish adults in his own life of faith, and in the larger community's collective life:

Aged Holocaust survivors facing impending death have taught me how to live with hope. Elder scholars who sit at the study desk day in and day out have taught me how to let the text sing through me. Older teachers have taught me the joys of teaching even the Hebrew alphabet amidst the wonderful innocence of childhood. And pioneer social activists have taught me that there are struggles yet to be fought.[21]

Not only do older adults support and undergird the ministries of most of our religious communities, but their religious understandings, spiritual wisdom, and prophetic visions often transform those of us in ministry with them. Far too few preachers see older adults as these kinds of sources of wisdom, insight, and faith. Our preaching would surely change if more of their stories were heard, more of their truths were integrated in our lives, and more of their gifts were cultivated and nourished. Blaine Taylor, in a book about a local church ministry by and with older adults, reflects on his own growing awareness of the false nature of myths and stereotypes. "The majority of those over sixty-five supported our efforts to open up the church, to risk using the building, to serve the poor and the young, to seize chances to serve the neighborhood, and to become more active in mission."[22]

Individuals, groups, and social institutions in this country are diminished by ageist stereotypes and myths. Our religious communities, where high percentages of older adults invest their lives, ought to lead the prophetic and visionary process of breaking these lies that bind us. Ageism is a form of violence that primarily oppresses and marginalizes older adults, but ultimately ageism's violence touches us all.

The Violence of Dismissal   At the heart of ageism and its marginalization is dismissal. The first step in this dismissal is labeling: Aging is problematic, and older adults are problems. This understanding of age, aging, and older adults has only recently dominated this country. It is a relatively new phenomenon. Naming the historical evolution of this attitude would be lengthy, but John Lindquist explains the evolutions in these words:

> Throughout most of history the aged have been the controlling force in society. Industrialization destroyed that power. They lost control of the land when factories replaced agriculture. They lost control of education when schools replaced their wisdom. They became obsolete when technologies made better goods at a faster pace. The coming of the Boomers increased the pace of change. Their numbers turned our heads in their direction. They were the market, the votes, the new communicants. They became our new guides.[23]

As the values and contributions of older adults have gradually been replaced by the values and controlling forces of youth, there has been deep and violating dismissal. Individuals, organizations, and institutions within our society often see older adults more as problems to be taken care of than trustworthy resources of creativity and passion. This dismissal not only is indicative of the personal and collective attitudes in our culture, but also, consequently, has become a necessity in our economic and political life. "Old people have become the raw materials for gerontological research and such growth industries as nursing homes and retirement villages. Old age has been declared a problem so that our gross national product will grow."[24]

This is a clear example of societal understandings and structures intersecting and becoming utterly dependent on each other. Aging has become big business in the United States, and this booming business is fundamentally dependent on labeling age and aging a problem. In response to that problem a range of public and private services have emerged. Many of these services have improved the everyday lives of older adults, but this truth should still not obscure the fact that economic interests are at stake in such developments. The church needs to hone a much more sophisticated critique of the intersection of, on the one hand, age, aging, and ageism, and, on the other hand, the mushrooming development of responding services.

Age is not the problem; ageism clearly is. Aging is not necessarily problematic simply because there are some distinctive needs and concerns associated with the process of aging in later years. Older adults are not problems; rather the problems are the cultural, religious, and societal understandings that dismiss and marginalize them.

Ageism: Social and Political Structures

Prejudicial attitudes, false myths and stereotypes, and labels are only a part of the violence of marginalization. Ageism is structured into the very social and political fabric of our nation. Four aspects of the ageism reflected in our social structures seem critical. These are the attitudes and actions regarding: (1) older women; (2) housing; (3) medical care; and (4) nursing homes and home care. These four aspects of ageism clearly reveal the connecting points of racism, sexism, and classism. Economics is what these four aspects of ageism have in common.

Older Women: Majority of the Older Poor   An undisputed fact in the research is that women form the largest percentage of older persons who are poor. It is true that women live longer than men in our society, but women of each of every age are poorer than men of that same age. When women are removed from the labor force during their later years, this inequity continues to show itself in devastating proportions. Today 72.4 percent of the elderly poor are women, even though women are only 58.7 percent of all elderly. Put another way: 15.2 percent of women sixty-five years or over — that is, two and a half million women — live below the poverty threshold compared to 8.5 percent of elderly men. The poverty rate significantly increases to 19.7 percent if women over the age of eighty-five are considered.[25]

Robyn Stone gives us a larger framework in which to analyze the reality of poor older women:

> In order to understand why women are more likely than men to be poor in old age, it is important to recognize that the economic status of elderly persons depends upon their lifelong marital and family obligations and their employment history. Paternalistic customs and laws that encouraged female dependency, the division of labor between genders with women as primary caregivers, and labor market discrimination are important determinants of gender differences in poverty among the elderly.[26]

While certain economic conditions of many older adults have improved in recent years, these changes have not improved millions of older women's lives. Many more women than men will live their older years in poverty and will live many years alone. Many more older women than older men will be institutionalized at some point during their aging process and will be the victims of violence and abuse in our nation's towns and cities, nursing homes, hospitals, and private homes. This is not to suggest that the structures of violence and marginalization do not have a profound impact on men. However, women in greater numbers and for greater numbers of years will be affected by the injustice of ageism.

Women and men of color are significantly more vulnerable and exploited in the aging process than white men. Even though his statistics are dated, Robert Butler provides helpful information about the intersection of racism, classism, and ageism:

> The percentage of aged blacks living in poverty is twice that of aged whites. Forty-seven percent of all aged black females have incomes under $1,000.... The American Indian elderly suffer from a much lower life expectancy than blacks or whites; their average length of life is estimated at 44 years, so comparatively few survive to old age. Mexican-American elderly fare little better; for example in Colorado their life span is 56.7 years compared to 67.5 for other Colorado residents.[27]

The realities behind these statistics have not significantly improved. If anything, they have become increasingly oppressive. These figures challenge the naive assumption that Social Security, Medicare, and Medicaid have improved the living conditions of all older adults. Many women and men of color in this country do not live long enough to benefit from some of the changes that have been instituted in recent years. And even though older white women's life expectancy has increased over recent years and their general economic conditions have improved, millions of them still live in poverty.

The church's ministry in addressing the interrelated injustices of sexism and ageism is critical. The involvement of religious communities in the struggle for employment and equitable wages for women in the present will diminish the poverty of future generations of older women. Most of our religious communities have large numbers of older women. How might we empower them to be their own advocates in the political arenas of this country? As preachers, what will be our response to the distinctive needs, insights, and life conditions of older women and older persons of color?

Housing In a day and age when homelessness across the age span is an enormous issue in this country, it is no surprise that older adults experience housing problems in their own distinctive way. It is true that many older adults own their own homes. It is also true that many older adults are homeless or live in substandard hotels, crowded boarding homes, mobile home parks, and housing that is run down and dangerous. Poor older adults live in both rural areas and urban areas. It is estimated that two-thirds of the nation's substandard housing can be found in small rural towns and villages where there is often no plumbing or electricity. Retirement communities are often more expensive than many older adults can afford; older adults who desire to buy a home often have difficulty obtaining a mortgage; and there simply is not enough public housing to accommodate the tremendous need. The same economic realities that have put millions of people homeless on the streets of our towns and cities have caused severe problems for older adults as well.[28]

Medical Care Adequate and available health care is an additional problem for older adults. "The average income for the elderly is between 50 and 60 percent of that for the general population but medical bills at age 65 are three to four times higher than when the older person was younger."[29] At a time when a person's medical needs are increasing, an older person's economic power is continually decreasing. There are many older adults who simply do not have any kind of adequate health care, while many others have health care that is only minimal.

John Lindquist gives us a realistic picture of the medical needs of older adults when he says:

The elderly make disproportionate use of medical care facilities, compared to those under age 65. Approximately 18 percent of them were hospitalized in 1981, compared to nine percent of those under age 65. They stay in the hospital longer (10 days on average, compared to 7 days for younger Americans), and visit doctors more often (six visits per year compared to four). Various federal (Medicare), state (Medicaid), and other (insurance) programs, cover only 67 percent of their medical bills.[30]

There is much discussion today about whether the larger population *will* provide for the basic needs of older adults. For me, the question is *how?*

Religious communities could become increasingly involved in the issues of housing and health care. The concrete conditions of the lives of older adults are tremendously affected by whether or not we become advocates in the shaping and changing of public policy. The everyday well-being of older adults increases when religious communities decide to strategize about housing alternatives and advocate preventive, holistic medicine. Preaching, as confession and invitation, might play a vital role in the inspiration of our local communities.

Nursing Homes and Home Care   Millions of older adults receive care within their own homes and millions also reside in institutional facilities such as nursing homes. The quality of care in these settings is of major significance to the health and well-being of older adults. Nursing home care and other types of institutionalized care have received more public attention in recent years than care within the home. We are coming to understand, however, that millions of older adults receive some form of home care. Perhaps the reason most Americans know so little about home care is that the realities surrounding this social service are appalling. In an article entitled "We Care for the Most Important People in Your Life: Home Care Workers in New York City," Rebecca Donovan describes the breadth of home care in that city and the general oppression of home care workers. On an average day in New York City, more people are cared for in their homes (59,554) than in nursing homes (36,072).[31] Donovan describes the characteristics of these workers: "Nearly all home care workers (98 percent) are women, and 96 percent are either Black or Hispanic. Almost half (46 percent) are immigrants. Most have come from the Caribbean islands, especially Jamaica, the Dominican Republic, and Haiti."[32] These workers have no assured job continuity, no chance for promotion, no legal or economic protection, and no medical coverage. "Although home attendants are key workers in the health care industry, they cannot obtain medical services for themselves and their families. . . . As a group, these workers have no coverage for 92 percent of the health problems for which they receive treatment."[33]

Even though lack of medical coverage and unavailability of health care are critical problems, equally problematic are the conditions in which these women work and the low salaries they are paid. Older adults who need care are not to blame for this exploitation; rather the fault resides in a social and economic system that devalues social services and defines aging as big business within our larger capitalist economy. This situation is a prime example of the interstructuring of sexism, racism, and classism in our common life.

Nursing homes are a related issue. There are many quality nursing homes across our country, but in recent years the American public has been shocked by growing reports of abuse within some nursing homes. Within all the literature on nursing homes that I have read, the most enlightening were a booklet and an article that confronted churches, synagogues, neighborhood communities, family members, and friends with our responsibility for quality of life in nursing homes. David Oliver offers a different perspective than many of us have considered:

> Every time I read about some kind of nursing home scandal, or read a government report criticizing the quality of care provided in homes, or overhear a family member, student, clergyperson, or other, wax righteous over the deplorable conditions of nursing homes in general, and/or a local home in particular, I get sick to my stomach. This feeling is more intense when I hear members of a church/synagogue/parish carry on in the same fashion. This aggression, often produced out of personal guilt, is misplaced. There are no enemies here, only ourselves.... What bothers people most about nursing homes is the perceived extent to which the people living there are treated. And how are they treated? They are denied the most important thing which makes life a drama. They are denied our continued fellowship, friendship, and continued encounters which make life the exciting enterprise that it is. We are the problem, but we put the blame elsewhere.[34]

Our total absence in these care facilities contributes to a part of the isolation and loneliness that abide there. These facilities are intended to provide extended care; they are not able to provide a holistic and healthy life. James Anderson, in his booklet about improving long-term nursing home care, goes to the heart of the problem when he says, "There is just no way to write a check and simply buy quality of life for another human being."[35] Until the responsibility of nursing home care is embraced by the larger community of which we are all a part, these facilities will often be dehumanizing forms of marginalization.

PREACHING EMBODIMENT

As a pastor I can easily see the devastating repercussions of our religious communities' ageist assumptions, our age-exclusive ministries, and our absence of advocacy for the rights and dignity of older adults. As a preacher I know the subtle and blatant violations caused by our illustrations regarding employment, our perpetual emphases on that which is young, our narrow views of vocation, and the condescension of our naming and labeling. In the face of these realities, three particular theological issues seem critical to me in a preaching agenda that seeks to struggle against ageism. All three issues cluster around the reality of our embodied human existence. The issues are these: affirming embodiment, accepting finitude and death, and celebrating incarnation. We are embodied people. Our human condition is limited and finite, and we all will die one day. The miracle of incarnation is that God is revealed in each of us, regardless of gender, ethnicity, age, or physical condition. These three theological issues illuminate truths about our basic humanness, truths that many of us want to ignore or deny. A part of what gives rise to the attitudes and structures of ageism is the denial of these truths.

Important questions that might shape a preaching ministry faithful to the task of eradicating ageism might be: How can we speak of, and interact with, older adults in such a way that we do not encourage the violence of disembodiment? How can we speak of, and interact with, finitude and death in such a way that we do not encourage fearful disengagement, deny the real experience of those who are dying, and negate the real human limitations of all people? How can we celebrate with our proclamations and our actions the reality of God's incarnation in the lives and ministries of older adults?

Affirming Embodiment

Christian persons often affirm a belief that we are created by God in our entirety. Our bodies and our spirits are gifts from our creator. However, we also stand in a tradition that has proclaimed some very devastating messages about the evil and sinful nature of our bodies.

Much of our society seeks to distance itself from the joys and the limitations of physical embodiment and values the spiritual realm of life more than the physical. Philosophy and theology that relegate the body to the realm of evil persist in dominating religious thinking and practice. We often abandon our bodies because we believe they are not good. Even though as religious persons we may affirm that God has created us as good, and that all creation is a gift of God's graciousness, most of us find it difficult to proclaim these truths about our bodies. We know that we encounter the world, each other, and ourselves through our bodies, yet we have been taught and conditioned to believe that our spirits can and should transcend our embodied reality.

The split between body and spirit is a dualism that has been with us for a very long time. James B. Nelson calls this split "spiritualistic dualism."[36] Even though the ancient Hebrews, our ancestors in faith, had a much more integrated understanding of body and spirit, and celebrated human sexuality as a gift from God, the dualistic philosophy of Greek culture has dominated Christian theology and practice for centuries. This split between body and spirit not only does violence to our human interactions but also has given rise to an exploitation of the body and the earth.

Splitting the body from the spirit has a profound impact on our social relations. Separating body and spirit creates a disembodied way of relating to all the material realities of our world. Devaluing the body leads to repressed sexuality, stifled sensuality, and an attitude that bodies (people) are disposable. Given these realities about much of our public and private life, ageism should not surprise us. Aging is a process inseparably related to the body. We project onto older adults our deepest disdain for the nature and functioning of the human body. Carter Heyward connects this failure to embrace the body as sacred goodness with the violence of our day: "This becomes clearer to me as I ponder with others the extent to which *all* evil, that is, the malicious violation of creation itself — human beings, plants, animals, air, water — seems rooted in our failure to know and to take seriously the holiness of the body."[37]

Physical deterioration and mobility losses are a universal part of the aging process. All human beings face this natural part of the process of life, but many are not able to accept its inevitability. Our bodies scare us. "They exhibit defect, vulnerability, change, decay. They bear intimations of our own mortality."[38] For many people the aging process of older adults represents embodiment at its most uncontrollable and painful level. For many older adults the same ambiguity about the body that has been present throughout their lives surfaces in distinctive ways in later years. Many older adults say they feel *betrayed* by their bodies as those bodies become less mobile and impose limits on life. Others speak about their bodies as a kind of enemy to be conquered during the aging process. This feeling is not limited to older adults, but seems to be a common human experience. "Most of us know the feeling of being ashamed of our body, the wish to extricate ourselves from our body, even the hate of our body."[39]

When we hate our bodies, it is easy to feel that they are the enemy and that the way to escape them is to transcend them spiritually. This reaction is one reason why so much of the literature on aging reflects a very disembodied theology. Older adults are encouraged to disengage, to go inward and let go. Even though these dimensions of life can be a part of a healthy spirituality in older adult years, I am disturbed and angered by the constant suggestion of disengagement and disassociation. It is suggested that the real task in the second part of life is the inner quest. Many believe the primary life task of older adults is to disengage and to enter into a time of reflective activity and introspection. Others say, "Old Age harvests the work of a lifetime." Some writers emphasize the important role of maintenance in the on-going work of older adults.[40]

Disengagement, letting go, maintenance, introspection, and embracing the inner quest are all important dimensions of human spirituality. These particular dimensions may indeed speak in some profound ways to the particular life needs of older adults. Reviewing the quality and meaning of one's life through introspection and reflection can be healing and powerful. It is equally clear that maintaining friendships, tending connections with chosen groups and communities, and nurturing family ties are essential for quality life in later years.

I have two major problems with the images of disengagement and introspection. They disembody older adults with a spirituality that often suggests that the body must be increasingly transcended in order that one's inner, spiritual life can flourish. They suggest that life in many ways is over, and maintenance, reflection, and life review remain. The older years of one's life are a harvest, but surely they are a planting as well. These images are subtle. They violate the fullness of what older adults experience and the richness of what they contribute to our common humanity.

Some aspects of the current spirituality and theology of aging suggest a spirituality of compliance. While the larger societal violences of disengagement and marginalization are being forced on the lives of older adults, spiritual mentors suggest that acceptance of this oppression is a part of their spiritual task. I think this moves into the realm of theological and spiritual violence. These images can easily relegate older adults to a life of the past and convey strong messages that the material realities of their daily embodied existence are unimportant. It is important that preachers and communities understand and not be deceived by a spirituality of aging that flows from a theology of disembodiment and disengagement.

Older adults can neither be reduced to body nor reduced to spirit. Preaching ministries need to help religious communities shape a theology of aging that affirms and embraces older adults not only as spiritually wise and serene elders, but also as passionate lovers, angry activists, and struggling human beings. To overspiritualize the daily existence of older adults is to contribute to the loss of their embodied wholeness, and when human beings lose their embodied selves they lose their capacities to connect and relate to the larger world. "But if we abandon the body, we sacrifice our feelings, and with them our capacity for self-expression and relatedness to others."[41] Ultimately, this is a part of what the violence of marginalization involves, the annihilation of feelings, self-expression, and relatedness. To confront such violence, our preaching ministries will have to be extremely attentive to the kind of theological and spiritual assertions about embodiment that come forth from our proclamations.

Accepting Finitude and Death

Our society's *denial* of finitude and death is a very intricate and profound part of ageism. Human beings are limited. Human beings die. It is painful and difficult for much of the human community to accept these realities about our human nature. Images of individual strength, autonomy, and control are everywhere. These images form and shape our society's self-understanding and philosophy of life. These images and understandings are so fundamental to our everyday existence that they leave us ill-equipped to cope with or accept human limitations, losses, and death. In an article on disengagement theory, W. Paul Jones makes some very valuable and clarifying connections between our society's denial of aging and our denial of death. He says:

> It is of deep significance that we hide and disguise not only corpses but our own feelings and questions. In fact, even direct language statements about death and dying are regarded as crude, to be replaced by euphemisms. And so, we are compelled to conclude this: Disengagement focused on death and its symbols is a life stance which in being acted out finds expression as ageism.[42]

The aging process is different for each individual, but the universal human truth of aging is that we all will experience increasing limitations, multiple losses, and death. These experiences are not all that aging is, but they are a part of what aging involves for most human beings. What the aging process, and thus older adults themselves, represent, then, is the epitome of what most of us are taught to avoid and deny. "In a society seemingly unable to succor us against deep feelings of loneliness, dispensability, and fragility of living, it follows inevitably that the elderly become symbols of myriad deaths to be avoided even in the mind."[43]

In addition to a denial of our own human limitations and finitude, *fear* is central to ageism and marginalization. Fear, like hatred, sparks violence. While most human beings in this country do not hate old people, many of us fear them. We fear what they represent; we fear seeing ourselves in them; and in their presence we fear our own limitations and losses. We segregate older adults; we remove them from sight; and we punish them for embodying the realities that terrorize us. Henri

Nouwen's *In Memoriam* is a book about his mother's death. I will never forget how I felt when I read the following section:

> It slowly dawned on me that she who had followed every decision I made, had discussed every trip I took, had read every article and book I wrote, and had considered my life as important as hers, was no longer. Little by little I became aware that mother, although far away, had always been part of my wanderings, and that indeed I had viewed the world through the eyes of her to whom I could tell my story. I began to feel that the airport, the limousine, the long trip to my apartment and all the other small inconveniences had become emptier, less meaningful, even somewhat absurd, because the ever-present dialogue with her had suddenly come to an end. Even so, I still found myself thinking: "I should write her about this," or "She will love to hear that story when I come home for Christmas," only to realize that she would never again read my letters or hear my stories. What is the value of my trips, my lectures, my successes and failures, my struggles and joys, when my stories remain hanging in the air?[44]

These words gave expression to some of my terror about emptiness, meaninglessness, and death. I return to them often when I am in need of something that will express the depth of existential fear I possess about loss and death.

I do not believe that Nouwen's words are intended to idealize parenting or parents. Nor is it my intent to portray parents as adults with no unique individual identity apart from the children they nurture. It is my intention to suggest that many of us are terrorized by the losses we associate with aging and death. Without attentive, conscious awareness of our own terror, it becomes a part of the ageism within us and around us. "Ironic though the truth be, *it is our own fear of death* that results in the often brutal isolation of the very dying person whom we 'love.' Indeed, it is usually the *family* who create for dying persons 'a process marked by loneliness, irrelevance, and an absence of awareness.' "[45]

The church has much work to do in relation to the denial and fear of death. The ministries of our religious communities could begin to address the feelings of aloneness that often reside in those who are dying. We need to learn how to listen to and honor their life reflections. We need to learn how to refrain from giving answers that trivialize. We also need to listen sensitively to the terror of emptiness and loss in those who remain. We need to break the prevalent illusions in our culture and in our religious communities that somehow we can cling to life and possess it. "Much violence in our society is based on the illusion of immortality, which is the illusion that life is a property to be defended and not a gift to be shared."[46] Life is a gift to be shared, and many older adults come to realize this in ways that are difficult for younger people to understand. Many older adults are ready to die, but we who remain cannot let go. Many older adults are clear about the meaning of their lives and feel peaceful in their dying process. It is often we who remain who struggle against death.

This refusal to let go of life can be seen in the use and abuse of medical technology. We have learned to prolong the physical lives of people, but we have not learned how to listen to and acknowledge a person's request to die. Countless questions about the appropriate use of technology in prolonging life remain unresolved in our society. These are serious theological and ethical questions. Religious people need to honestly examine their attitudes about death as they wrestle with them. In an article about biomedical ethics in the future, three experts in the field of medicine and health say:

> Hopefully by the year 2000, our society will have come to grips with the inevitability of death. Up until this time, we seem to have confused our efforts at prolonging dying with our quest to prolong life. It seems to us that we have replaced the natural death process with a system driven by both death-delaying technology and a death-delaying social ethic.[47]

How will we preach in a day when life-support systems prolong dying in an effort to prolong life? How can we preach in such a way that we empower people to face the natural process of death? Preaching about death helps us better understand life. And if we preach about the true depths of life, not illusions, we will learn better how to die. "The preaching about life ought always include life leaning irreversibly towards death. So that one is prepared for death by life."[48] The preaching moments in our religious communities could be experiences in which the giftedness of life is eternally proclaimed and the goodness of death is honestly acknowledged. If preaching could be more honest about the lived realities of older persons and less biased by our own denial and fear, it might be a powerful source of healing and hope.

Another aspect of theologizing about finitude and death deeply influences our preaching ministry. Many preachers are so focused on the meaning and possibility of eternal life that they do not know how to theologize *with* people about some of the deepest dimensions of life and death. We ultimately do not know what to say in the face of such a final ending. What is ultimate about a person's life? What is eternal? Instead of struggling with persons to articulate their own theological affirmations about ultimacy and eternity, we far too often offer shallow pictures of eternal life. Joseph Sittler, in a very insightful article on aging, critiques traditional preaching about eternal life. He says:

How can we ever use the word "eternal" about something whose substantial interior meaning is temporal and passing? And yet the scriptures do use the word, "eternal life." I am shocked by the fact that I have seldom heard a sermon about the meaning the term has in Scripture. I never in my own parish heard my own pastor talk about the meaning of eternal life, and therefore, by not talking about it, or not unfolding the biblical use of the language, we permit people to carry on this partly secular and partly banal notion that eternal life means the same as some lovely country club after death. This is disobedient, bad biblical teaching and reprehensible preaching.[49]

He goes on to speak about the use of the notion of eternal life in scripture and about the unclear and somewhat ambiguous discussions Paul puts forth in Thessalonians and Corinthians. Paul's final affirmation is that whether we die or whether we live, we are God's. We have the same relationship to God in death as we do in life. Sittler powerfully challenges us: "We must disabuse our people of these strangely secular, materialistic and worse, utterly egocentric notions of eternal life, and teach them that the doctrine of eternal life means that if you are in Christ, and Christ in you, you now and forever participate in the deathless life of God."[50]

This is the kind of theology we need in contemporary preaching about finitude and death. The promise of participation in the deathless life of God is a promise that offers an assurance that is unspeakable. This is the kind of theological affirmation I hope a pastor or friend will offer to me as I am dying. This is what I would hope we could also say to each other while living.

Celebrating Incarnation

Several years ago I found a children's illustrated story entitled *Wilfrid Gordon McDonald Partridge*.[51] It is the story of a mutual friendship between a small boy named Wilfrid Gordon McDonald Partridge and a ninety-six-year-old adult named Miss Nancy Alison Delacourt Cooper. Miss Nancy is Wilfrid Gordon's "favorite person" of all the older adults who live in an old people's home next door. Wilfrid Gordon and Miss Nancy spend lots of time together; he tells her all his secrets. One day Wilfrid Gordon overhears his parents talking about Miss Nancy, saying she is a "poor old thing" because she has lost her memory. Wilfrid Gordon asks what a memory is, and his father tells him it is something you remember. During the next few days, Wilfrid Gordon spends time with several of the other people in the old people's home and asks them the question, "What's a memory?" He receives a variety of answers: A memory is something warm; a memory is something from long ago; a memory is something that makes you cry; a memory is something that makes you laugh; and a memory is something as precious as gold.

Wilfrid Gordon then returns home to look for memories for Miss Nancy. Out of his own life he gathers up a box of shells he found long ago, a puppet that always made everyone laugh, a medal of his grandfather's that made him sad, his very own precious football, and a warm egg from the hen house. He returns to see Miss Nancy. As they visit he hands her each item one by one. The warm egg reminds her of bird's eggs she found long ago. One of the shells causes her to remember a trip to the beach when she was just a girl. The medal brings back the memory of her brothers going off to war and never returning. As she looks at the puppet she remembers her sister laughing with a mouth full of porridge. And when she picks up the football she remembers the day she met Wilfrid Gordon and all the secrets they told each other. "And the two of them smiled and smiled because Miss Nancy's memory had been found again by a small boy, who wasn't very old either."[52]

This story celebrates the transforming power and possibility of incarnation. Incarnation celebrates that God becomes flesh and dwells among us. Incarnation celebrates the way we know and experience God in the life and touch of another. As Miss Nancy listens to Wilfrid Gordon's secrets she becomes a touch of God's grace and love. As Wilfrid Gordon evokes and shares Miss Nancy's memories he becomes the embodiment of God's redemptive power. Wilfrid Gordon is not just a child to be dismissed — he is a cherished conversationalist; and Miss Nancy is not just an old woman to be disregarded — she is a cherished confidant. God comes to us in the embodied reality and presence of each other.

A preaching ministry that celebrates incarnation will seek to articulate the distinctive ways God is present and embodied in the lives of all people. God is known to us in the lives of older adults in the same human ways God is known to us in infants, in adolescents, in children, and in middle-aged adults. Older adults are wise, but they are also playful. The lives of older adults teach us about loss, but they also reveal to us unknown strength. Older adults show tremendous strength, and reflect awesome vulnerability. Can we not say the same for people of each and every age across life's span?

A preaching ministry that celebrates incarnation will not dismiss, romanticize, or generalize the ways older adults make God manifest in their individual lives and in our world. It will articulate and boldly proclaim the truth of these manifestations of God, and celebrate them as distinctive and amazing incarnational gifts.

✧ 3 ✧

Breaking Silence Exposes Misogyny— SEXISM

WHAT DOES IT TAKE?

1

The martyrs they give us
have all been men
my friend, she traces her life
through them   a series of assassinations
but not one, not
one making her bleed.

This is not the death of my mother
but my father
the kind one/the provider
pressed into newsprint
in honest good will.

*If they took **you***
I would take to the streets scream, BLOODY MURDER.

But the deaths of our mothers
are never that public
they have happened and before
we were not informed.
Women do not coagulate into one
hero's death; we bleed
out of many pores, so constant
that it has come to be seen
as the way things are.

2

Waiting
my mother's dying
was not eventful.
Expecting it

I put a hole in my arm
no TNT blast
but a slow excavation
my nails, in silent opposition
digging down to the raw part
inside the elbow.

If they took **you**
I would take to the streets
scream, BLOODY MURDER.

What does it take to move me?   *Isn't the* **possibility**
your death   *of your dying*
that I have ignored   *enough?*
in the deaths of other women?

—Cherrie Moraga[1]

Sexism involves the systematic denial, exploitation, and oppression of women. As the hierarchical gender structuring of personal and social reality, sexism assures and secures male domination. As with other forms of systematic oppression, sexism is defined and critiqued from very different perspectives. What we believe to be the root of sexism will determine the nature and strategies of our resistance.

Some believe that sexism can be understood solely within the framework of economics. This understanding of sexism suggests that if forms of economic exploitation were to cease, the exploitation of women would end. Others believe that sexism is built upon biological differences that account for the structuring of society according to gender roles. This analysis of sexism suggests an equal valuing of gender differences would terminate the exploitation and oppression of both women and men. Still others believe that sexism is socially constructed male dominance, a dominance that is central to patriarchy and male supremacy. This analysis suggests that only a transformation of the entire fabric of gender relations will stop the violent exploitation of women worldwide. I locate my commitments and my analysis with those women and men who believe that male domination is socially constructed and that sexism has to do with the attitudes and structures that secure this domination.

The Christian church contributes in significant ways to the structuring of male domination within our culture. The church's idealization of marriage relationships, traditional family patterns, and the institution of motherhood serves to reinforce male dominance and female subordination. The church's theology also contributes in a very direct way to gender inequity. Preachers are often primary voices that idealize dominant/subordinate gender relations and uncritically proclaim theological affirmations that continue to secure male supremacy. Religious communities, and preachers in particular, need to look at the distinctive violence of sexism and give voice to the specific repercussions of this domination in the lives of women.

RADICALIZING MOMENTS

Being a woman with all the attendant fears and limitations that accompany that reality in our society, I find that it is extremely difficult to recall and identify clearly specific radicalizing moments in my awareness of sexism. In many ways I feel that I have spent a lifetime growing into a deeper awareness of women's oppression, a greater understanding of my own complicity in the violence of sexism, and the kind of analysis that might lead to fundamental social transformation.

I have vivid childhood memories of being told that playing ball, shooting marbles, and climbing trees were activities for boys. I remember being "coached" by adults at church camp to make myself *lose* in co-ed sports. I can remember wondering if I would ever "walk right," be feminine enough, or learn to be passive in such a way as to be acceptable. From my early years of being a teenager until the present moment, I can never remember a time I have not been afraid of being raped. I remember always being confused by the responsibility young girls seemed to have for everything from controlling male sexuality to forming the right combination of characteristics to *win* a husband. Even though my biological family encouraged a great deal of dignity and expression in my childhood and teenage years, the overwhelming female reality into which I was enculturated was subtle but persistent submission. I now understand that women must work a lifetime to understand fully the myriad and complex ways this submission is woven into their lives.

Even though most of my radicalizing moments had to do with a gradual awakening about sexism, I do recall the experience of trauma and shock in the early years of my ministry when I read Kathleen Barry's book *Female Sexual Slavery: From Prostitution to Marriage, the Landmark Study of All the Ways Women Are Sexually Enslaved.* She asserts that women around the world are sexual slaves. Even though I wanted to dismiss her argument, it rang frighteningly true. "Female sexual slavery is present in *all* situations where women or girls cannot change the immediate conditions of their existence; where regardless of how they got into those conditions they cannot get out; and where they are subject to sexual violence and exploitation."[2] The breadth of her study and its shocking exposure of female sexual traffic, the role of prostitution in male supremacy, the politics of rape and marriage, and the exploitation of girl children around the globe left me devastated. To this day I can still remember going into the living room of the home in which I was raised and saying to my mother, "Mom, it isn't just that the world discriminates against women, it *hates* women." I can also recall the horrified look on my mother's face. This is surely a truth that every mother wants to deny, especially to her daughter. Reading this book was a turning point in my life. It was one thing for me to image a world in which men actively discriminated against women, excluded them, and even occasionally exploited them. It was a very different reality for me to image a world in which men hate women and actively seek to dominate and exploit them. This realization was like a plunge into an abyss, and became a moment in which I knew the world would never be the same.

NAMING AND UNDERSTANDING THE VIOLENCE

Misogyny: The Hatred of Women

For many women and men the magnitude of sexism is so devastating that silence and denial are tempting escapes. Even the word *sexism* distances and abstracts the everyday oppressions of women from our consciousness and emotions. Sometimes the realities of sexism are described as the oppressiveness of patriarchy, the destructive limitations of androcentric values, philosophy, and theology, or the rampant devaluing of women's reality. These are a part of the truth of sexism, but these words do not speak strongly enough. The terrifying truth that surfaces over and over again in the texts of our day, and in the lives of women and men, is *misogyny*. Misogyny is the hatred of women. This is what is at the heart of male domination and female subordination. Misogyny remains the only name for me that does justice to the magnitude of this violence. Leonard Schein, in an article entitled "All Men Are Misogynists," speaks honestly about misogyny as a socially constructed reality in men's lives.

> For men to become fully human, to liberate ourselves from forced sex roles, and to really understand ourselves, one of the first things we must deal with is our hatred of women. We have to understand the origin of our misogyny and the full significance of the fact that we live in a patriarchal society. Patriarchy's foundation is the oppression of women. The cement of this foundation is the socialization of men to hate women.[3]

This is the kind of honesty and accountability that is essential in the lives of men and women if misogyny is to be faced and resisted. How can religious communities encourage and nurture such honesty?

Misogyny has myriad faces. Misogyny is at the heart of exclusive, male God-language and imagery. Misogyny is at the center of many women's daily experiences of degradation. Misogyny creates relational isolation in men, and suffocating need for affirmation in women. Misogyny makes men subjects and women objects and contributes to a world where objectification and needless exploitation are justified and protected.

Because misogyny is so multilayered it sometimes leaves preachers and specific religious communities immobilized in their naming and resistance. As preachers we have an opportunity and responsibility to give specificity and concreteness to the face of misogyny. Misogyny as expressed in the physical and sexual violence against women is *named* in the world with terms and phrases like sex colonization; femicide (the killing of wives); men possessing women; sexual violence; the secret trauma; and the politics of rape.[4] Misogyny is *experienced* in the lives of female children and women as incest, battering, rape, sexual harassment, pornography, and constant fear. Even though the attitudes and structures of denial are deep and strong, I find these expressions of violence impossible to ignore.

Male Domination as Social Norm

If misogyny is the hatred of women, male domination is the lived reality of misogyny. Gender inequality and male supremacy are built on the structures of domination. Male domination is a system of power that renders women inferior to men, and is constructed from a basic domination/submission understanding and structure of gender relations.

Male domination equals power. Andrea Dworkin suggests that male domination and supremacy involve seven dimensions of power:

1. Basic to male-supremacist ideology is that men have a self and women lack it.

2. Male power involves the use of physical strength against others less strong or those without the sanction to use strength as power.

3. Male power is the capacity to terrorize and involves the use of self and strength to inculcate fear *in* a whole class of persons and *of* a whole class of persons.

4. Male power is the power of naming, a power that enables men to define experience, to articulate boundaries and values, to decide what can and cannot be expressed, and to control perception itself.

5. Men possess the power of owning, including the lives of women and children.

6. The power of money is distinctively a part of male power.

7. Men possess the power of sex, for sex manifested in action, attitude, culture, and attribute is the exclusive property and province
   of men.[5]

Male dominance is dependent on men exercising their control and
power over women with whatever means necessary. Violence often becomes the means within which men create, maintain, and expand their
male dominance.

Two important dimensions of human experience enable domination
to continue without critique or question. Within the lives of men the process of objectification takes place so thoroughly that women are seen
as no longer fully human. If men believe that women do not have a
self, are biologically and socially inferior, can be reduced to property
that can be owned, and have corrupting and engulfing power in their
lives, then it is not difficult to see how men systematically learn to view
women as objects. Leonard Schein says, "As our consciousness develops
its picture of women as inferior, we then objectify our dominant position and their subordination. Psychologically, we objectify the people
we hate and consider our inferiors (another example of this process is
its extension into racism)."[6] There is such distancing in the process of
objectification that *use* and *abuse* seem normal and natural.

We all know that this objectification is deeply wrong. Objectification
is at the heart of abuse and violence. Understanding it helps us clarify
some of the structures of enculturated masculinity that lead to inexplica-
ble violations. Objectification is part of what allows grown men to rape
three-year-old female children with no understanding of the violent victimization involved. It is part of what allows millions of men to beat and
batter women while believing that they have a perfect right to demand
obedience and submission. It is also a part of what allows husbands
to rape their wives while totally denying any violation. It is crucial for
men to understand the evolution of objectification in male thinking and
experience. A primary task for men within our religious communities
will be the difficult work of deconstructing a worldview and a relational
framework that allow for this kind of violation of women and female
children.

The second dimension of human existence that allows male dominance to continue is the way women become male-identified under
male supremacy. Many women are unable or unwilling to acknowledge
and name male domination as a personal and social reality. I do not
believe that women are simply insensitive to or unaware of the oppression of women and the violence expressed against women. Rather, male
power is so thorough that women's lives and sense of self have been
colonized. For many women male identification is a primary means of
survival.

Male identification is the act whereby women place men above women, including themselves, in credibility, status, and importance in most situations regardless of the comparative quality the women may bring to the situation. Through male identification, women automatically acknowledge men's authority, word, and actions.... The inability of women to put themselves in the place of a woman victimized is ultimately a denial of self living in the conditions of colonization.[7]

Women in a male-dominated world become more male-identified than female-identified. There are severe repercussions for women who step outside male identification. The violence women witness and experience is a powerful silencing and compromising agent. Many women live under the illusion that male identification and female submission will render them safe from the most blatant violences of male domination. Beverly Harrison exposes that illusion in women's lives when she says: "But as the massive, sustained, and universal patterns of violence toward women in this and other societies make clear, rage toward women lies just beneath the surface of all of our social relations and our institutional life. Women's 'weakness' is, often, women's unnamed terror of this reality."[8] In order to resist sexism and male domination many women must face and address their terror and the kind of male identification that flows from that fear.

Fundamental to any preacher's understanding of sexism will be a thorough understanding of the objectification of women by men and the compelling power of male identification among women. Any religious community committed to feminism and to resisting sexism will have to address these two issues within the individual lives of women and men, and in the relations of our communal life together.

Listening to the Voices of Women

Women and men who preach need to turn their attention to the voices of contemporary women who are the bearers of some very painful, horrible truths. Voices of confrontation and truth always make their claims upon us. Several things need to happen within the lives of preachers and within our religious communities if we are to respond to the truths around us. Religious communities need to find the unjust violence against women as compelling as our silence. For many women, this will mean facing fears about male violence and facing their own complicity in male domination/female subordination. For many men, this will mean facing the relinquishment of their own unquestioned power. All of us need to find places within ourselves and our communities where male domination is named as a violation of mutual right relation, and male violence no matter what the explanation or justification is declared wrong. We also are called to shape communities where gender equality and mutuality are created and where power is something known and shared by women and men alike. This will require preachers to face their deepest fears about the very nature and structure of their human relationships.

We are challenged to envision a new world of gender relations even in the face of the structural force of male dominance. We are invited to imagine a world where gender differences are acknowledged and honored, but gender hierarchy is abolished. This envisioning is difficult, for male domination and gender hierarchy are so fundamentally woven into the fabric of our personal and social reality that we cannot imagine a different world. We know that women's lives depend on our courage and ability to envision and create this different human reality.

Women are courageously breaking the silence that has rendered their realities, their truths, and their life experiences invisible and meaningless. Doing so is a theological and religious act. As women's silence continues to evolve into speech, and women's invisibility is transformed into visible presence, the human community is faced with the fact that women find it difficult to survive within male domination and supremacy. "Women have been deprived not only of terms of our own in which to express our lives, but of lives of our own to live."[9] Women are speaking and resisting because they long for and demand the right to have lives of their own. For many men who have not only possessed the terms in which to express their lives but their lives themselves, this existential truth may seem unbelievably foreign. It is essential that men accept this truth as truth, without trivialization, defense, or denial, if they are to understand the truths of women's voices. For women it is essential that we not allow the belief that our lives are an exception to the violence, the hope that violations will never touch us, and the fear that they already have, to keep us from hearing these truths as well.

Violence and Terror: Enforcing Male Domination

For a very long time I wanted to believe that male violence against women was extraordinary and unusual. There are still moments when I want to believe that women who experience the violence of rape, daughters who experience the abuse of incest, and wives who experience the battering by a husband are rare in situation and circumstance. I no longer believe that any of these things are true. Male violence is blatant among us in its breadth and intensity. It crosses boundaries of ethnicity and class, and terrorizes every corner of the globe. For preachers in this country there are three particular manifestations of this male violence that I want to examine.

Rape, Woman Battering, Child Sexual Abuse

By focusing the central section of this chapter on rape, woman battering, and child sexual abuse, I hope that preachers might see more clearly some of the specificity of sexism. These expressions of violence are urgent and life-threatening, and in many ways reveal the evil side of misogyny most clearly.

Many religious communities acknowledge the reality of sexism, but few are willing to probe its most violent dimensions. The church remains painfully silent about these particular expressions of violence. Even though there is increasing documentation of women turning to pastors for help, many pastors and preachers continue to deny the existence of violence against women within their congregations and within the larger social sphere.[10] It is unusual to hear a preacher directly confront issues of battering, rape, and incest, or to witness preachers confronting the patriarchal underpinnings of such violence. To raise issues about violence against women is painful and terrifying.

Joy Bussert in a book about battered women says,

> Although we can talk in safe generalities about equal opportunity and affirmative action, and although we can theologize around the issue of women's ordination and women's role in the church, when we raise the issue of whether or not a woman ought to be beaten in her own home, we focus the male-female question in a very dramatic and poignant way in the minds and hearts of many people.[11]

Preachers are often unwilling to ask these kinds of dramatic questions that unearth the foundations of patriarchy.

Rape, incest, and woman battering are forms of sexual violence. They are forms of violence first and foremost, but within our social structures of male domination and subordination, they are also expressions of sexual violence. Catharine MacKinnon in her analysis of sexuality in our society suggests that sexual violation *is* in fact a form of sexual practice, and urges us to see the complexity and truth of this statement within our lives. In summarizing much of the research that has been done with men who have acted violently with women, she asserts that their acts of violence are indeed sexual. In speaking about such men she says: "It is sex *for them*. What is sex except that which is felt as sexual? When acts of dominance and submission, up to and including acts of violence, are experienced as sexually arousing, as sex itself, that is what they are.... Violence is sex when it is practiced as sex."[12]

For many women and men who have worked hard to separate the categories of sex and violence in hopes that the violence against women will be more fully recognized, this statement confronts and asks us to look at language and definitions again. It is important that we see rape, child sexual abuse, and woman battering as intricately linked with eroticism and sexuality in a culture where gender inequality and male domination exist. In a system of male domination and female subordination, violation and control of the powerless (women and children) are a part of what is sexual. "Because the inequality of the sexes is socially defined as the enjoyment of sexuality itself, gender inequality appears consensual. This helps explain the peculiar durability of male supremacy as a system of hegemony as well as its imperviousness to change once it exists."[13] In light of this analysis *sexual violence* seems the most appropriate descriptive term.

All forms of violence against women, all forms of sexual violence, serve to reinforce male domination and gender hierarchy. Male supremacy demands control and fear for its maintenance. As shocking as it seems, in a system such as this, rape becomes the behavioral expression of sexuality and ultimate conquest. "Female sexual slavery, in all of its forms, is the mechanism for controlling women through the sex-is-power ethic, either directly through enslavement or indirectly using enslavement as a threat that is held over all other women. This is the generalized condition of sex colonization."[14]

One of the most startling aspects of the literature dealing with rape, battery, and incest is that most men believe that acts of sexual violence are their prerogative.

> Patriarchy divides males and females into dominant and subordinate castes on the basis of gender and polarizes human sexuality and personality into masculine and feminine dimensions. This division eroticizes power and aggression in men. As a result male sexual functioning operates as the *instrument* of women's oppression and enforces male rule.[15]

In a culture in which strict gender hierarchy and male domination are sanctioned, there is tremendous confusion between sexuality and sexual violence, between healthy, mutual sexual activity and abusive acts of terror. This confusion and mystification obscure and minimize the daily violations in women's lives. Sexual violence is not sex; nor is it sexual activity primarily. It is violence that is sexual in nature. Violence has become eroticized to the point that it is very difficult for many people to distinguish between sexual violence, sex as violence, and violence as sexual activity.

Marie Fortune, director of the Center for the Prevention of Sexual and Domestic Violence in Seattle, Washington, has done important work on the issues of sexual violence. She suggests that there are several erroneous beliefs that encourage the confusion between sexual activity and sexual violence:

1. Anything that employs the sexual organs must be primarily sexual in nature.

2. The source of a man's sexual response is external and somehow beyond his control. He is not responsible for what he does with that response.

3. The widely accepted "romantic love ideal" requires a dominant-subordinate relationship between two people.

4. Men have the prerogative to impose their sexuality on others regardless of others' wishes.[16]

The assumptions behind these beliefs are extraordinary. Any act, no matter how violent, that involves sexual organs is primarily sexual activity. Men have no ethical accountability for any expression of their sexuality. Superiority and inferiority are central dimensions to the creation and maintenance of all love relationships. And men's sexuality and sexual activity function in a way completely independent from the feelings or wishes of another human being. "Male sexuality begins to appear predatory in nature, i.e., it takes what it wants when it wants it without regard for the consequences to others."[17]

Sexual violence must be analyzed and understood within this context of firmly held beliefs about power, conquest, the eroticism of violence, and prerogative. Clarity about these violating beliefs and practices also helps us understand the root nature of change that must take place in order to stop the violence.

Rape In the past two decades statistics about rape have become more public in the United States. A conservative estimate suggests that one in every three women will become a rape victim sometime during her life. Rape crisis hot lines and centers are an assumed part of our society. Even though these services are crucial, why are we not shocked at their presence among us? Why are our religious communities not outraged about the magnitude of this violence? And why do preachers continue to be so conspicuously silent?

Society has been challenged to broaden its definitions and its understandings of rape. Two contrasting definitions of rape convey the changes in definitions within the past ten years:

The law defines rape as sexual intercourse with a female, not the wife of the perpetrator, accomplished without the consent of the female.[18]

Although legal definitions of rape vary from state to state, the most comprehensive definition refers to forced penetration by the penis or any object of the vagina, mouth, or anus against the will of the victim.[19]

The second definition of rape is broader and more comprehensive. Within this new definition, the law finally recognizes wife rape, which prior to this change was a legal impossibility. The change also acknowledges the rape of men by men, and the rape of men or women by women. Broadening the definition of rape is a very significant breakthrough. We can distance ourselves from the reality of rape if we hold on to the notions that rapists are strangers to the women they rape and that rapes happen primarily as violent attacks in dark streets and alleys. We must face the fact that these stereotypes are simply not true. Rape exists in the lives of preachers and in the homes of people we know. Rape is interwoven into every aspect of our personal and social relations: so much so that throughout the literature acknowledged rapists articulate that the only difference between themselves and other men is that they have been caught and publicly exposed. This is a powerful indictment about the prevalence of sexual violence and our society's denial.

Redefining rape compels us to look into the hidden places of our lives and into the places of our common life where rape is frequent.

Only 90,434 rapes were reported to U.S. law enforcement agencies in 1986, a number that is conservatively believed to represent a minority of the actual rapes of all types taking place. Government estimates find that anywhere from three to ten rapes are committed for every one rape reported. And while rapes by strangers are still under-reported, rapes by acquaintances are virtually nonreported. Yet, based on intake observation made by staff at various rape-counseling centers (where victims come for treatment, but do not have to file police reports), 70 to 80 percent of all rape crimes are acquaintance rapes.[20]

In recent years the American public has been confronted with the prevalence of acquaintance rape. Most women who are raped are raped by dates, friends, lovers, and husbands.

Two extensive research projects were completed in recent years related to acquaintance rape and rape in marriage. One was entitled "Ms. Magazine Campus Project on Sexual Assault," funded by the National Institute of Mental Health.[21] The study was completed in 1985. The project was a scientific study of acquaintance rape on thirty-two college campuses within the United States. There were 6,159 responses, from 3,187 women and 2,972 men. The average age was 21.4 years, and most of the students were single. They represented widely different cultural, ethnic, and racial backgrounds.

In one year 3,187 women reported suffering: 328 rapes (as defined by law); 534 attempted rapes (as defined by law); 837 episodes of sexual coercion (sexual intercourse obtained through the aggressor's continual arguments or pressure); 2,024 experiences of unwanted sexual contact (fondling, kissing, or petting committed against the woman's will).[22]

Another research project conveyed equally shocking statistics about acquaintance rape, more specifically rape within marriage. In a sample of 644 married women surveyed in San Francisco in 1978, 87 or 14 percent were victims of at least one completed or attempted rape by their husbands or ex-husbands.[23]

Because marital rape is still one of the most hidden and silenced arenas of violence against women, these statistics probably reflect a very conservative percentage. Because women have been considered the property of men in marriage, marital rape has been thought inconceivable. When rape was narrowly defined as sexual intercourse with a female other than one's wife, marital rape was literally impossible under the law. If we have come to understand rape as forced penetration, then legally there is a new precedent for holding husbands accountable for raping wives. The impact of rape in marriage is devastating for many women:

> Many women who are raped by their husbands do not perceive that they are victims of rape.... Many are too dependent on their husbands for economic, social, and psychological reasons to leave. One solution for these women is not to see forcible intercourse as rape. Another more common adaptation is to give up the right to say no, and to be always sexually available, regardless of her wishes.[24]

Regardless of the circumstances, if sexual activity is against a woman's wishes, it is sexual violence. This violence is never justified by the sacred relationship of marriage or the trusted relationship of friend or lover. The research tells us that the impact of acquaintance rape and marital rape is at least as severe and detrimental as that of stranger rape. In addition to the sexual violence itself, basic relational trust is often shattered, and a woman's sense of self is severely damaged. "When you are raped by a stranger you have to live with a frightening memory. When you are raped by your husband, you have to live with your rapist."[25] In addition, acquaintance and marital rape victims receive even greater blame and ostracism. Somehow, it is as if they are responsible for the violence done to them. Our religious communities work hard to deny this truth about women's experience of violence within marriage.

> The lack of public awareness about the reality of marital rape can be ascribed largely to the secrecy surrounding the problem, a secrecy maintained by most parties to the problem — victims,

abusers, and the public at large. Victims are ashamed. Abusers help to keep them quiet and intimidated through threats, emotional blackmail, and a kind of "brainwashing" that makes the victims feel that they are to blame. The rest of us feel awkward, uncomfortable, and helpless to do anything, so we choose not to ask and not to hear.[26]

Before rape will be something we can face fully and faithfully, both women and men must be willing to indict these actions that occur in the American bedroom and home, as well as in unknown places in our streets. This will be a difficult task for preachers who have unfortunately often blessed the heterosexual bedroom and home regardless of the circumstances.

Woman Battering   It is estimated that in the United States a woman is beaten by a man every eighteen seconds. Wife assault is so widespread that many people believe that half of all wives will experience some form of inflicted violence during their marriage, regardless of ethnic or socioeconomic status. Police receive more calls for help from victims of domestic violence than from victims of any other kind of serious crime. Battered husbands or male partners are estimated to be a fraction of 1 percent of the total number of battered spouses or partners.[27]

Battering is a serious expression of sexual violence, and, like rape, it primarily violates women. It may seem strange to think about woman or wife battering as sexual violence, but I am compelled by the literature to consider battering, along with rape and incest, as an expression of male dominance and sexuality. This usage calls for a very different understanding of sexuality, as noted by Catharine MacKinnon in her analysis of sexuality within a culture of male domination:

> The term *sexual* refers to sexuality; it is not the adjectival form of *sex* in the sense of gender. Sexuality is not confined to that which is done as pleasure in bed or an ostensible reproductive act; it does not refer exclusively to genital contact or arousal or sensation, or narrowly to sex-desire or libido or eros. Sexuality is conceived as a far broader social phenomenon, as nothing less than the dynamic of sex as social hierarchy, its pleasure the experience of power in its gendered form.[28]

There is a danger in this shift of definitions. Women and men have struggled very hard to have woman and wife battering seen first and foremost as an expression of violence. However, I believe that the force involved in battering women is deeply connected to male gender and sexuality in our culture. If gender is socially constructed, like our understandings of masculinity and femininity, then male aggression often is an expression of that masculinity and a dimension of masculine sexuality.

If we feel ourselves wanting to deny the connection, we might ask ourselves some very serious questions: Why are battered women also often subject to rape? Why do so many men force women to have sex after a beating? Why does violence begin or escalate during pregnancy? Why do so many men speak about intense jealousy when they explain their reasons for battering?[29] All of these questions suggest that there are many hidden and complex connections between male sexuality and battering.

I am equally persuaded that the term *domestic violence* does not adequately describe the reality we face. If only a fraction of 1 percent of the victims of domestic violence are men, then *wife battering* and *woman battering* are much more truthful terms.

As with rape, woman battering cuts across all segments of the American population. Although many men in our culture are socialized to exert violence and force and to use their power to maintain domination, there appear to be some identifiable characteristics of men who batter. Joy Bussert describes those characteristics as an unusual anxiety about their own masculinity, an inability to express happiness and anger, and a total dependence on the women they batter.[30] Added to these characteristics are Lenore Walker's assertions that men who batter are unusually possessive and jealous and are often from homes and families where violence was inflicted on them as children.[31]

Just as there are myths, stereotypes, and misunderstandings surrounding rape in American culture, there are equally destructive illusions and myths that shroud woman battering from our consciousness and indignation. Lenore Walker has identified twenty-one myths that perpetuate our silence around this issue. Seven of these myths seem particularly important in understanding men's justification and society's denial:

1. The battered-woman syndrome affects only a small percentage of the population.

2. Battered women are masochistic.

3. Middle-class women do not get battered as frequently or as violently as do poorer women.

4. Minority-group women are battered more frequently than Anglos.

5. Battered women are uneducated and have few job skills.

6. Battered women deserve to get beaten.

7. Battered women can always leave home.[32]

These myths are simply not true. Research shows that woman battering is a widespread phenomenon, perhaps touching at least one-third
of all American homes. No woman enjoys being battered or beaten.

Battering cuts across all class and ethnic distinctions even though
poorer women and women of color are more likely to come in contact
with community agencies and resources than women with economic
resources that allow them to remain more private. Not only do battered women represent a range of educational levels, from elementary
grade through doctorates, but also they are homemakers, psychologists,
business women, and corporate executives.[33] Many women find themselves unable to leave home because of economic dependency, learned
helplessness, responsibility for children, and fear of escalated violence.[34]

All these myths are a part of a cycle of blaming the victim, imply-
ing that women have ultimate responsibility for the violence. "Victim
provocation theories leave sexist behavior and ideology unquestioned.
They keep us scrutinizing the victim's behavior and, as a result, remove
responsibility from the man, the community, and the social structures
that maintain male violence."[35] It is essential for religious communities
to look critically at the myths they hold about woman battering, and for
preachers to ask ourselves why denial is so thoroughly rationalized in
our culture.

As regards woman battering, two critical theological and pastoral issues are at stake for religious communities: the idealization of the family,
and the privatization of marriage. The Christian church continues to uphold and defend the institutions of family and marriage at the expense
of women. Both of these institutions are central to the maintenance of
male control. "The door behind which the battered wife is trapped is the
door to the family home."[36] Until our religious communities regard the
lives of women as being as important as the myth of the all-American
family, wife battering will continue and be deemed a necessary and important sacrifice. The maintenance of family never justifies the abuse
and violation of women within it. Until we no longer regard the lives
of women as the property of men, the battering of wives, dates, and
lovers will continue. Preachers need to lead the way in shaping new understandings of family and marriage. We need to articulate and commit
ourselves to the kind of relational ethics that will no longer ignore, justify, and condone woman battering in any circumstance or situation. In
our sermons we need to paint powerful alternative pictures of mutuality
and gender equity.

Child Sexual Abuse   Some statistics suggest that one out of every four
females under the age of eighteen will be sexually abused by someone
well known to the child. The American Humane Association found that
girls made up approximately 87 percent of the child victims of sexual

abuse, and that 75 percent of the offenders were household relatives, friends, or neighbors known to the child.[37] Even though in the past two decades child sexual assault has become a topic of increased knowledge and concern in this country, there remains a great deal of silence and denial.

Child sexual abuse takes many forms. "Pornography is probably the largest procurer of children for sexual slavery."[38] Children around the globe are kidnapped and sold into illegal prostitution.[39] Further, although we have probably come to focus most upon incestuous abuse of children, extrafamilial sexual abuse is common.

Mary Winters, in a guide for clergy and laity about sexual and domestic violence, broadens our understanding of child sexual abuse by differentiating and articulating its expression: "Sexual abuse of children (also called child molesting) may be *nonphysical;* indecent exposure, obscene telephone calls, peeping toms, or child pornography. *Physical sexual abuse* is genital or oral stimulation, fondling, or sexual intercourse, including incest and rape."[40] When we define child sexual abuse, it is essential that we remain very clear about the victims. The victims are not adults; they are children. As with rape and woman battery, cases of child sexual abuse involve high incidents of blaming the victim. It is astonishing that any adult might seriously believe that children are responsible for their own sexual abuse. "Children, by definition, cannot give or withhold consent when approached sexually by an adult because they are immature, uninformed, and usually dependent on the adult. Consequently, they lack the real power to resist. Therefore, any sexual contact between an adult and a child is abusive."[41] Blaming the victim is so rampant among us, even in relation to child sexual abuse, that our understandings about responsibility are oftentimes distorted.

In 1989 in a lecture in New Mexico, Laura Davis said about accountability: "Even if a child is naked, throws herself on her father's lap, and says she wants to have sex, it is still the adult's responsibility to name this as inappropriate behavior, and to assure that the encounter ends."[42]

There are indications that child sexual abuse has increased in recent years. Because of the hidden nature of the abuse it is difficult to judge just how much more widely reported it is, and how much more it has increased. Diana Russell asserts that incestuous abuse before eighteen and extrafamilial child sexual abuse before fourteen have quadrupled between the early 1900s and 1973.[43] She suggests several factors that may contribute to this increase:

1. Child pornography and the increased sexualization of children.

2. A sexual revolution in attitude and practice within our country that encourages sexual activity among children.

3. A backlash against sexual equality and a reassertion of male control with children, who have less power than adult women.

4. Untreated child sexual abuse in the lives of boys, who later grow to be men who become sexually abusive themselves.

5. The increase in stepfamilies, for there appears to be a higher percentage of stepfathers who are sexually abusive in the lives of girl children than biological fathers.[44]

There are also strong connections between men who batter and men who sexually abuse children. "Just as there is a high statistical incidence of boys who witness fathers battering their mothers growing up to become batterers themselves, so there is a high incidence of fathers *and brothers* having incest with female children in those families where the father is a batterer."[45] As much as we might want to separate rape, woman battering, and child sexual abuse, they are a part of the web of male sexual violence that is denied, encouraged, and vehemently condoned in a culture of male domination.

It is long overdue that religious people, and preachers in particular, look around themselves to *see* the pain and abuse inflicted upon the lives of girl children and the resultant effect in adulthood. As devastating as it is to recognize, some of the greatest confrontation needs to take place in the trusted relationships within families and friendships. The truth we know about child sexual abuse, and violence of all kinds, is that the *trust* has already been shattered and the relationship already broken. Our pretending this is not so changes or restores nothing. The breaking of silence and the calling to accountability hold promise for recovery and transformation.

PREACHING: BREAKING SILENCE

New theological naming involves the work of critique and deconstruction, but it also creates and bodies forth new understandings of religious meaning. As a result of women's naming, I have come to understand *breaking silence* as an essential theological concept in a theological agenda that would resist male domination. Breaking the silence of the violence that engulfs women's lives is a redemptive act that declares that the lives of girl children and adult women are holy and sacred and that violence is a distortion of our human relations. I want to turn now to a fuller exploration of breaking silence as the primary theological concept that might inform preaching ministries struggling against sexism and male domination.

There are three dimensions to this act of breaking silence that place it in the realm of saving, transforming activity. Breaking silence stops the cycle of violence, demands individual and community accountability, and begins the process of restoration and healing.

Stopping the Cycle of Violence

The cycle of violence must stop if there is ever to be movement toward justice and wholeness. When people break out of this silence, it is not just that they are responding to the individual, private lives of victimized women; they are also calling the entire structure of male supremacy into question. To break the silence about male violence is to stop the concrete behaviors that reinforce and maintain male domination. The church knows that this is true at a conscious and unconscious level, and thus it too often backs away in silence. This silence can be broken in many ways.

When a woman decides to leave her home and seek the safety of a woman's shelter, the silence of her oppression is broken. In that same act the silence and denial of male violence are shattered if only for a moment. This impulse to reach out for help is a movement toward life. When a girl child decides to tell a family friend that her father is sexually abusing her, the silence of her abuse is broken. In that same act the silence and denial of destructive family privacy and distorted male sexuality are shattered if only for a moment. This impulse to tell is a movement toward life. When a woman decides to press charges against an acquaintance who has raped her, the silence of her domination is broken. In that same act, the silence and denial of male ownership and supremacy are shattered if only for a moment. This impulse to hold accountable is a movement toward life.

These impulses toward healing, accountability, and transformation are movements toward a healthy sense of self, relationality, and community. The impulses come from a desire for survival itself and an end to violent abuse. They are faithful, saving acts. "Therefore, Christianity is not only a life of proclamation of the saving act of God in the past, but also a life of participation in and with the sanctifying grace of God in the present."[46] For women and men to break the silence and denial surrounding violence against women is to participate in the work of sanctification.

Marie Fortune believes that breaking the cycle of violence involves truth telling, deprivatization, deminimization, and protection for the vulnerable. Cycles of violence are broken as helping professionals acknowledge the breadth and depth of the violations that have occurred, expose the violence to public scrutiny, listen to and believe the stories of victims, and become advocates for protection for those who are at risk.[47]

Religious communities and preachers have much to learn from

women and men working in direct human services with women who are victimized by violence. They understand with absolute clarity that the first step in responding to violence is to stop it. Women working with battered women's shelters respond *first* to the safety of the woman who is in danger. Psychologists and social workers respond *first* to the safety of children who are sexually abused. Women advocates who work directly with women who have been raped respond *first* to the immediate safety and needs of the woman who has been raped.

What makes this redemptive work so shocking for some is that it places girls and women in positions of ultimate importance and priority. The safety and lives of women are more important than the sanctity of marriage and the prerogatives of male sexuality. The safety and lives of girl children are more important than parental power and the privacy of the family. These are radical shifts in power and priority. The church should be deeply disturbed that most of the concrete services in this country that respond directly to violence against women have been created by women's advocacy groups outside the church. Pastors and preachers need to be confronted with the fact that these groups are literally saving people's lives because they are responding to the violence in women's lives in ways the church is not.

The literature suggests that when preachers are bold and clear in their sermons about issues related to woman battering, rape, or incest, women do come forward to speak with them in an attempt to break the silence and the violence. Even with full awareness of this truth, countless preachers remain painfully silent and participate in the church's larger denial. Or worse yet, preachers and pastors urge women to return to the cycle of violence. Not only blatant insensitivity keeps many preachers silent, but also much of our traditional theology encourages denial in a very insidious way.

Some of our traditional understandings of sin have provided a firm foundation on which silence and denial have thrived. In an article entitled "Evil, Sin, and Violation of the Vulnerable," Mary Potter Engel begins to construct a new understanding of sin from the perspective of a theology of liberation from sexual and domestic abuse. She explores four dimensions of a new understanding of sin that contribute to a liberating theology in response to violence against women, three of which are particularly relevant to breaking the silence surrounding violence. She renames sin as *distortion of feeling*, as *betrayal of trust*, and as *lack of care*.[48]

Christian theology has suggested that it is sinful to be angry and resistant. Human beings are to be self-sacrificing, slow to anger, and always loving. This definition of sin and its implications for righteous human behavior leave victimized women blaming themselves for the violence inflicted upon them. Women believe that if they had been more self-giving, less angry, and more loving, violence would not have occurred. Our traditional understandings of sin have robbed women and men of the power and impact of righteous indignation and healthy anger. Our Christian theology has traditionally stressed passive acceptance of the conditions of one's life. Anger and resistance are the epitome of sin.

In defining sin as a distortion of feeling, Engel makes two important theological moves. She shifts responsibility to perpetrators who distort and shatter right relation, while simultaneously encouraging women to express anger, indignation, and resistance in their own lives in ways that help terminate the violence. Engel also begins to develop an understanding of sin that is corporate in nature. The moral indifference of preachers and religious communities is named as the sin of distorted feelings. This understanding of sin compels preachers and religious communities to break into the cycle of violence and demands that we respond with outrage and resistance. "If all of us were to speak and act out against sexual and domestic abuse with the righteous indignation of the prophets, we would no longer be colluding in an oppressive system of violence."[49]

Christian theology has also suggested that sin has to do with the prideful arrogance of disobedience and self-love. These understandings have kept women and children silenced in their own victimization, and have kept preachers and religious communities believing that this suffering is necessary and righteous. Women are particularly vulnerable to an understanding of sin that suggests that all human beings have "crosses to bear." For many women and girl children violence and abuse become those totally justified crosses. "The central image of Christ on the cross as the savior of the world communicates the message that suffering is redemptive. If the best person who ever lived gave his life for others, then, to be of value we should likewise sacrifice ourselves."[50]

Women have been encouraged to love others at total expense to self, and dimensions of Christian theology have provided the moral and ethical underpinnings for such total self-sacrifice. Here again, Engel makes two very helpful theological moves. She suggests that sin is the act of betraying trust, not the act of disobedience. She also shifts the definition of sin from self-love to a lack of care. As an attempt to empower women who are victimized by violence she encourages women not to participate in the sinfulness of allowing the boundaries of their own self to be disregarded and violated. "Rather than speak of sin as pride or self-love to victims, we should speak of it as distortion of the self's boundaries."[51] Through both suggestions Engel helps us to understand that the sin of perpetrators is the betrayal of a trusted relationship, and the sin of women caught in the web of violence is a willingness to participate in their own victimization.

These understandings empower women and men to break out of

the web of violence. They also shift our understanding of sin away from self-loathing and self-denial and direct us toward encouraging women to develop a sense of self-love and a genuine sense of power that will make them less vulnerable to the domination and abuse of male violence. Engel's new theological naming enables us to transform our understandings of sin in such a way that many levels of silence can be broken. The distorted apathy and silence of society toward violence within trusted, known relationships can be broken, as well as the apathy and silence toward violence perpetrated by strangers.

Preachers have an opportunity to break the silence surrounding violence at many different levels. When we speak directly about woman battering, domestic violence, incest, and rape in our proclamations, we break the silence of denial. Our theological work breaks silence also as we rework aspects of traditional understandings of sin that perpetuate violence and proclaim liberating definitions that mobilize the Christian community's resistance. With new understandings of sin, preachers might be more fully empowered to break the silence of popular moral indifference, the silence of justification and betrayal in the lives of perpetrators, and the silence of women's conditioned complicity and powerlessness.

Individual and Community Accountability

One of the profound repercussions of silence and denial is the privatization of the violence. As long as the church continues to believe that violence happens to isolated individuals in the privacy of homes, bedrooms, and darkened streets, individuals and whole communities are never held accountable. Pastors and preachers participate in this privatization. "Out of arrogance, embarrassment, ignorance, or feelings of helplessness, pastors often give the impression that violent control of women and children is sometimes a necessary part of family life and must be accepted."[52] Far too often instead of preachers empowering individuals and communities to become increasingly responsive and accountable about violence, they accept the status quo with a haunting indifference. How might preachers move individuals and communities toward greater accountability?

It is not just the church's traditional theology about sin and suffering that has contributed to male domination and female oppression. There are deep, permeating strands of Christian theology that define females as fundamentally inferior human beings. The church's theology has often reduced women to objects as surely as has the larger society. Carole Bohn describes and critiques this web of dehumanizing theological assumptions about the superiority of males and the inferiority of females as a theology of ownership.[53] In examining the account of creation in Genesis 2 and 3 she describes the theology that flows from it in this way:

> Man's authority to rule over woman is traced to God's intention in this account from Genesis 2 and 3. . . . Throughout history, laws of various societies have attempted to limit the extent and means of man's control, but the underlying message, built into the words and structures of religious tradition, remains constant. By God's design, women and children are subject to men.[54]

By its very nature, a theology of ownership keeps violence not only privatized and hidden, but also theologically condoned. If men *own* women and children, and are their moral, emotional, and physical superiors, this not only serves as a rationale for silence, but becomes a justification for men to indeed *control* that which they own. This theology of ownership contributes in a significant way to the silence and denial of churches and preachers.

Part of the power and distortion of patriarchy and male domination comes from their ability to structure lies into human consciousness and social structures. No human being owns another human being. No theological concept or belief justifies violent domination. Preachers must be very attentive and sophisticated in our critique of every aspect of Christian theology that suggests male domination is the natural order of creation. Dismantling this theology of ownership is in many ways an essential move toward individual and community accountability. It is not enough to simply respond to the violence itself; we also need to critique the underlying theology that helps to perpetuate it. Bohn critiques mainline denominations' pronouncements against violence that are devoid of deconstructive and constructive theologizing about the root causes. "While they call their churches to some sort of action, they do not challenge their institutions' historic stance toward and complicity with the problem. They are pragmatic attempts to confront the problem of domestic violence; yet they are primarily band-aids designed to alleviate a symptom."[55]

She goes on to suggest three concrete steps that must be taken to dismantle a theology of ownership. First, religious communities must begin to make connections between the personal and the political. There must be a shift from seeing acts of violence and the need for healing as individual matters to seeing violence and healing as communal and systemic matters. "It means that pastors, along with all other care-givers, will have to move out of the study and into the community to demand justice and participate in healing."[56] Second, religious communities must abandon any theology of ownership if they are ever to move from viewing domestic violence as a private issue to seeing it as a public concern. They must be willing to critique and abandon all accounts of creation that serve to condone and justify a system of violating gender relations. Third, pastors and preachers must seek to develop a concept of responsible adulthood.[57] The church needs to lead the way in developing theologies that challenge all understandings of dominant/subordinate relationality. Mutuality, accountability, and interdependence must be nurtured and given value. Violence in human relationships might continue to exist, "but such actions would be considered aberrations of adulthood, an unacceptable loss of impulse control, and would be subject to the scrutiny and judgment of religion and society."[58] Dismantling the complex and multilayered dimensions of a theology of ownership is an enormous theological and homiletical task. These assumptions keep preachers and religious communities unable and unwilling to call for greater individual and community accountability. At present, violence is silently accepted as normative in human life. Until violent behavior is seen and confronted as a profound distortion, there can never be corporate responsibility.

Restoration and Healing

Holding an individual accountable for violence done is a redemptive, saving activity as surely as the act of stopping the violence itself. A part of breaking silence involves directly confronting those who are perpetrators. Holding persons accountable is a critical part of our saving, redemptive work in the world. Preachers are in an important position within the church to call for the kind of confession and reparation that make for justice. Perpetrators of violence are held accountable when they are asked to acknowledge the violation that has occurred, when repentance and transformation are actively engaged in, and when some form of restoration of those harmed is enabled.[59] As mentioned earlier, a part of developing a theology of responsible adulthood might involve preachers explicitly and implicitly deepening the entire community's commitment to an accountability that involves just restitution for the victim and redemptive transformation for the offender.

The need for restoration and healing also demands that preachers and religious communities move beyond an intellectual understanding of violence into the heart of this pain and terror. Until every man can sensitively imagine what it means to live daily with the fear of being raped, and until every woman is "moved by the deaths of other women,"[60] the silence of male violence will not be broken and the magnitude of women's pain and fear will never be fully exposed. Restoration and healing call each of us into compassionate imagining and embodied resistance.

While writing this chapter I made two calls trying to locate the most recent statistics about woman battering and rape. I was given the number of a center in Washington, D.C. After I dialed the number, a woman answered the phone. I said, "Hello, my name is Chris Smith." The woman on the other end of the line asked, *"Are you safe?"* I could not speak for a moment; then I answered, "Yes." I asked my question, thanked her for her work, and hung up the phone. For a few moments I wept uncontrollably. My awareness was fundamentally changed by that woman's question. Until the people of God can feel and experience the power and pain of that one question, we will never find the courage to confront the misogyny that engulfs all of our lives in perpetual cycles of violence.

✦ **4** ✦

Grace Transforms Condemnation — HETEROSEXISM

A LITANY FOR SURVIVAL

For those of us who live at the shoreline
standing upon the constant edges of decision
crucial and alone
for those of us who cannot indulge
the passing dreams of choice
who love in doorways coming and going
in the hours between dawns
looking inward and outward
at once before and after
seeking a now that can breed
futures
like bread in our children's mouths
so their dreams will not reflect
the death of ours;

For those of us
who were imprinted with fear
like a faint line in the center of our foreheads
learning to be afraid with our mother's milk
for by this weapon
this illusion of some safety to be found
the heavy-footed hoped to silence us
For all of us
this instant and this triumph
We were never meant to survive.

And when the sun rises we are afraid
it might not remain
when the sun sets we are afraid
it might not rise in the morning
when our stomachs are full we are afraid
of indigestion

when our stomachs are empty we are afraid
we many never eat again
when we are loved we are afraid
love will vanish
when we are alone we are afraid
love will never return
and when we speak we are afraid
our words will not be heard
nor welcomed
but when we are silent
we are still afraid.

So it is better to speak
remembering
we were never meant to survive.

—Audre Lorde[1]

Condemnation seems like the most fitting word to describe the astonishing violence perpetrated upon lesbians and gay men. To describe the oppression of gay men and lesbians as an experience of *invisibility* and *silence* is to mask the aggressive nature of the violence. Lesbians and gay men are not simply made invisible in the social fabric of our nation and in the community life of most of our churches, they are actively excluded, harassed, and persecuted. The relational and social values and experiences of gay men and lesbians are not simply silenced; they are judged inferior, deviant, and sick. This kind of condemnation is condoned and justified by many of our religious communities.

There is a kind of righteous judgment that flows from the pulpits of this land that ought to be of major concern for every thinking, sensitive person. In the name of the Christian gospel the everyday lives and rights of gay and lesbian persons are actively violated. Lesbians and gay men are denied their civil rights; they are excluded from ordination in most of our mainline churches; and they are physically and emotionally attacked on public streets, in the privacy of family homes, and in the professional offices of homophobic lawyers, psychologists, social workers, and business persons.

Through its theologies, biblical interpretations, and sexual ethics, the Christian church is one of the primary institutions that provide a foundation for social and ecclesiastical oppression of lesbians and gay men. Religious communities are being called to face their own condemnation and fear. This challenge comes from lesbians and gay men who are making claims upon the church, urging it to critique its theology, open its ecclesiastical structures, and compassionately transform its preaching, pastoral, and liturgical ministries. To look honestly at the church's role in the condemnation of lesbians and gay men is to be a part of the transformation of the social fabric of our world.

The starting point for our naming and understanding the oppression that flows from condemnation and fear is critical. Contemporary religious scholars, pastors, and preachers differ tremendously in their naming of the problem. Some consider homosexuality itself the problem and look to scripture, Christian tradition, and ecclesiastical authority as sources for clarity and judgment. Others consider the actual oppression of gays and lesbians to be the problem, and turn to those same traditional sources for reconciliation and compassion. Still others consider the problem to be rooted in the impact of patriarchy. For these persons, the distorted relations of heterosexism and homophobia are the fundamental problem. Their analysis turns not only to scripture, tradition, and ecclesiastical structures for a critique of power, male domination, disembodied sexuality, and gender inequality, but also to the prophetic lives of gays and lesbians themselves in the historical context of our day.

Not only does the naming of the problem vary among religious persons, but also approaches and responses to the problem are equally diverse. Letha Scanzoni identifies four basic responses by Christians to homosexuality: condemnation, change, celibacy, and commitment.[2] The first three approaches reject homosexuality at various levels of essence and behavior. These approaches call for the continual judgment of both homosexual persons and their actions, the total conversion and change of gay and lesbian people, and celibacy as the only moral and ethical choice for a person of homosexual orientation. The fourth response suggests that committed, monogamous relationships that are analogous to heterosexual marriage are acceptable and morally right between persons of the same gender.

Even though there are distinctive ways to describe the responses of Christians to the lives and reality of gay and lesbian people, there is pervasive similarity in judgment and condemnation. In an article about various approaches to homosexuality among Protestant, Catholic, and Jewish communities of faith, Robert Nugent and Jeannine Gramick, drawing from James Nelson's categories in *Embodiment*, describe four prevalent ways of approaching the issue of homosexuality:

1. The rejecting-punitive view sees both homogenital expression and the homosexual condition/orientation as sinful and prohibited by God.

2. The rejecting-nonpunitive position rejects homogenital *acts* but not homosexual *persons*. Homogenital acts are condemned as contrary to human nature.

3. The qualified acceptance position holds that although a homosexual orientation including, in some cases, genital expression can be an acceptable way of living out the Christian life, it is still somehow inferior to heterosexuality.

4. The full acceptance position holds that homosexuality is part of the divine plan of creation, that homosexual people are present as a sign of the rich diversity of creation, and that homosexual expression is as natural and good in every way as heterosexuality.[3]

It is important to note that in both Scanzoni's and Nelson's analyses, most of the approaches religious people take toward homosexuality are punitive and unaccepting. Most of these approaches take homosexuality as the problem to be addressed, rather than the social structures of human community that produce heterosexism and homophobia.

An understanding of these approaches to homosexuality is important and revealing. There are many good books and articles that carefully examine the relationship between natural law and homosexuality, the relationship between scriptural interpretation and ecclesiastical attitudes, and the Christian tradition's evolving views about sexuality, procreation, and gender relatedness.[4] All of these approaches assume that homosexuality and lesbianism are problems to be illumined, understood, and addressed. Many times these approaches further the cause of justice for gay and lesbian people, and this is important. However, the way I name, address, and analyze the problem is quite different from these approaches.

I do not see homosexuality as the problem that needs to be addressed. In contrast, I see the church's condemnation of lesbians and gay men as the major pastoral and theological problem. This condemnation gives rise to specific concerns:

- the church's blatant justification of its condemnatory behavior toward lesbians and gay men;

- the root causes of the violence that plagues the everyday lives of gay men and lesbians, and the diseases of hatred and fear that diminish us all;

- the ways preachers might deepen their own analyses and broaden their critique of heterosexism and homophobia;

- the ways that preachers might respond with prophetic and visionary words and actions to the distinctive needs of this exiled community.

RADICALIZING MOMENTS

My awareness of the oppression of lesbians and gay men has been growing for a very long time. However, several very particular personal and professional experiences have deepened and broadened my political analysis, my passion and rage, and my commitment to the eradication of this violence.

In 1975 I was interviewed by the Board of Ordained Ministry in the United Methodist Church for deacon's orders. I had finished my first year of seminary and was eligible to become ordained as a deacon. This is the first of two ordinations that happen in my denomination. The interview went very well, but I will never forget the final question of the day: "If you become a minister in our conference, would you vote to ordain homosexuals?" I paused for a very long time, not because I was unsure what I felt, but because I knew this question could cost me my ordination. The man who asked was well known for his condemnation of gay men and lesbians. I finally responded: "I am a woman struggling for my own place in the Christian church, and for the rights of women to be ordained. As a part of an oppressed group of people I could not possibly vote against another group of oppressed people struggling for their place and rights as well." The man looked at me and said, "I do not agree with your position, but can clearly understand why you stand where you stand." I was unanimously approved and ordained deacon within a few months after the interview.

I am grateful for the connections that I was already making between sexism and heterosexism, the oppression of women and the condemnation and oppression of lesbians and gay men. I still feel anger when I think of the power of his intimidation. I had to speak my convictions in a very controlled and calculated manner for fear my support would exclude me from any possibility of being ordained. That experience deepened my understanding of power and its ability to evoke fear and compromise, the strength of male control in asserting what is ethically right and wrong, and the dominating condemnation of heterosexuality.

In August 1987, the national United Methodist Clergywoman's consultation took place in Great Gorge, New Jersey. The consultation is often a healing time for many clergywomen. Liturgical celebrations and preaching are inclusive and creative; the strong and vital gifts of clergywomen are alive and present in workshops, plenaries, and informal conversations; and the vision of a very different Christian church permeates the event. Yet even in the midst of such an event lesbian clergywomen were once again rendered silent and invisible. Two actions were taken in response to this pain and exclusion. A group of women invited Rosemary Denman (a United Methodist clergywoman who was facing a church trial later that fall because she had revealed her lesbianism to her bishop) to join the consultation in order to share her experiences and receive support.

Also, a group of lesbian clergywomen decided to caucus. This was a very prophetic and courageous act. Out of that caucus came twenty statements that were read at the closing worship service of the consultation. The caucus requested that the anonymous statements be read by five clergywomen from various parts of the country. The statements were read by two district superintendents, one bishop, a seminary professor, and Rosemary Denman. I was the seminary professor. I will always remember the silence, the pain, the hope, and the awe of those moments of worship. These are the five statements I read:

1. Being thirty, lesbian, and single and serving in a rural area have left me feeling alone and abandoned. I am choosing to leave to experience the support and care I need to feel whole again.

2. My congregation treats me like a princess. How kind I am. How sweet. How approachable. How pretty. Kids like me. Parents like me. Grandparents adopt me. But nobody knows me. And when they do?...

3. I am a lesbian with a beautiful, strong lover. When her mother found out about us, she confronted me and threatened my job and career. I celebrate the courage and strength and love that I claim in myself, for keeping on with my work and my relationship in the face of such threats. And I still have a sense of humor!

4. I am a young woman, beginning in ministry; my future is uncertain because I am not accepted and affirmed for who I am.

5. I am an elder in full connection serving an upper-middle-class congregation. I am mostly who I am; I am partly defined by my culture and my congregation. I am female and feminine; strong and capable. I function in a largely straight and mainstream community, but I am lesbian. When my lover died of cancer, there was no one to tell: no one to grieve with me. When a subsequent relationship ended, there was no one to give support. Now I am growing older and I often wonder where and even if I will meet someone again. The closet is silent, dark, and lonely.

These were passionate, difficult statements for me to read, and for all of us to hear. The silence was momentarily broken, but tender, intimate expressions were forced to remain anonymous. In attempting to make the voices and lives of our lesbian sisters more visible, the power of their invisibility was shockingly apparent.[5]

Lesbians and gay men will not be forever silenced. At every major conference I have attended since that consultation the related issues of heterosexism, homophobia, heterosexual privilege, and the silencing of gay and lesbian people have surfaced. In feminist and womanist theological conferences in particular, the silence and invisibility are clearly evident. Women are challenging each other to claim and articulate the particularities of their lives, and yet lesbianism cannot be named. As a part of our deepening theological agenda in the church, women and men are urged to speak about their social location, yet truth about sexual identity cannot be revealed. This silence and invisibility exist in national church conferences, but they also dominate much of the life and ministry of our local churches. The silence and invisibility of lesbians and gay men and the oppression rendered by heterosexual privilege and denial are the responsibilities of the whole church and each individual member of it.

NAMING AND UNDERSTANDING THE VIOLENCE

To understand the condemnation of lesbians and gay men, religious people will need the courage to look at some of the fundamental assumptions of our culture and our society. Gay or lesbian sexual identity is not just a matter of individual nature; each is an alternative way of living and being in the world. Gary Comstock, in an address to the 1986 national gathering of the United Church of Christ's Coalition for Lesbian/Gay Concerns, spoke about the transforming nature of the lives of gay men and lesbians:

> While it may not have been our intention, I think we have to face squarely that our very lives, when lived openly and fully, fundamentally threaten the social order. When we begin to make decisions for ourselves instead of letting others tell us how we should live, we challenge those who have power at the expense of the disempowered and marginalized.[6]

The structures of the social order need to be challenged and changed, although this will involve a fundamental transformation of church and society. This transformation is what persons fear the most, and what many persons of privilege desperately want to avoid. "For centuries sexual attitudes, sexual taboos, and sexual practices have been used by dominant groups in society to keep others subordinate. Those who possess power define those who are powerless and then impose their own definition on the ones defined."[7] Those in power are being asked to give up exclusive privilege in search of a different kind of faith community in which power is shared among all God's people.

If preachers and religious communities commit themselves to responding sensitively to the lives of lesbians and gay men, as well as to the oppressive nature of heterosexism and homophobia, they must be attentive and vigilant toward attitudes, language, oppressive silences, and power. I want to suggest four areas of thought and ministry that might shape a contemporary preacher's personal and pastoral agenda: (1) naming, addressing, and understanding the present social problem as heterosexism and homophobia; (2) clarifying the connections between heterosexism, homophobia, sexism, and male domination; (3) discerning and understanding heterosexual privilege; and (4) attending to the repercussions of condemnation by our responses to the actual pain, terror, rage, and oppression of gay and lesbian persons.

Heterosexism and Homophobia

The realities of heterosexism and homophobia reflect the root cause of the condemnation experienced by gay men and lesbians.

Heterosexism is one of the fundamental structures of our social reality. "A 'structure' is a pattern of relational transactions that gives a society its particular shape."[8] In our society the structure of relations that is considered normative and dominant is heterosexual. The church has been one of the primary institutions that has articulated and reinforced this standard. This posture is so basic to much of what Christianity has stood for that it seems heresy to question its assumptions. But here is where I think pastors and preachers might begin their analysis.

In *No Turning Back: Lesbian and Gay Liberation for the '80s,* a very helpful distinction is made between "gay oppression" and the broader root cause of heterosexism:

> The term "gay oppression" is often used to refer only to the fact that some people are looked down upon and discriminated against because of our sexual preference. The term "heterosexism," on the other hand, refers to the *cause* of the oppression — the socialization of all people to fear their own and each other's homosexuality, and the reinforcement of traditional dominant male/passive female social/sexual relationships. Heterosexism makes an institution out of heterosexuality and enforces it through ideology and social structure.[9]

Heterosexism is built upon the assumption that relationships between men and women have primary relational meaning, exclusive social sanction, and superior moral and ethical value. This relational structuring of our social, political, and religious life is so foundational that primary relations between persons of the same gender are deemed immature at best, and immoral, unnatural, and sinful at worst. What are the origins of these condemnatory judgments, and why do they persist? Condemnatory judgment is not at the heart of New Testament

Christianity, and the reality of homosexuality is not addressed directly by Jesus in his ministry. Preachers need to ask themselves why this judgment persists and whose interests it serves.

Janice Raymond expands and deepens our understanding of heterosexism when she says, "*Hetero-relations* expresses the wide range of affective, social, political, and economic relations that are ordained between men and women by men. *Hetero-reality* describes the situation created by hetero-relations."[10] Hetero-relations are normative, and hetero-reality is the constant milieu in which all of us live. We are all taught to fear and to condemn persons who vary from this normative standard. *Homophobia* is a descriptive term for that fear. Homophobia is the irrational fear and hatred of those persons who choose others of their own gender as primary persons to bond with, love, and desire. It is a fear that manifests itself in the lives and actions of individuals and in the foundations of social structures. "Heterosexism is the systemic display of homophobia in the institutions of society."[11] This fear has fueled the condemnation of gay men and lesbians. In the reality of homophobia, fear is so linked with hatred that the two cannot be separated. Homophobia serves to keep heterosexism and hetero-reality in place.

Homophobia is a powerful force that is operative in all of our lives, a force frequently assumed and unexamined. Mary Hunt says, "Homophobia is powerful in church and society where some people are too frightened to talk about and listen to the variety of ways people can love. Homophobia keeps many of us from learning about the unknown, from facing the unacceptable."[12] The church is challenged to become a voice against this kind of violence, and individuals are being summoned to a deeper courage within themselves to face the unknown and utterly mysterious aspects of the ways people love and share life.

In reflecting on her own lesbian life and the effects of homophobia, Suzanne Pharr says, "In my life I have experienced the effects of homophobia through rejection by friends, threats of loss of employment, and threats upon my life: and I have witnessed far worse things happening to other lesbian and gay people: loss of children, beatings, rape, death."[13] This violence is not isolated and private, but is quite public and of a very frightening magnitude. The National Gay and Lesbian Task Force has researched growing incidents of homophobic violence in the United States. Some of their statistics reveal that differing kinds of violence against lesbians and gay men are increasing:

> The task force documented 2,042 incidents in 1985, including 445 physical assaults and 184 bomb threats, arson incidents and attempted bombings. Reports of such violence doubled in 1986, to 4,946. While 3,473 of the incidents were verbal harassment or threats, 732 were physical assaults, 10 were arsons or bombings,

and 80 were homicides.... In 1987, over 7,000 such anti-gay incidents were reported. The task force reported that in 1988, 7,248 incidents occurred. These statistics represent an increasing efficiency in documentation of homophobic violence, but they also represent an escalating problem.[14]

Many people who do not tolerate this kind of tyranny when expressed as white supremacy or North American imperialism fail to confront it when expressed as heterosexism and homophobia. "Heterosexism is to homophobia what sexism is to misogyny and what racism is to racial bigotry and hatred."[15] Heterosexism, sexism, and racism are all forms of supremacy and domination. Homophobia, misogyny, and racial bigotry are the feelings that undergird, reinforce, and perpetuate those structures of domination. One must fear and hate lesbians and gay men in order to justify annihilating their entire worldview and way of being human. The structures of hetero-reality and heterosexism would dissipate and change without the constant undergirding of this hate and fear. Heterosexism and homophobia are fundamentally and inseparably linked.

Our fear and hatred of gay and lesbian people are so irrational and so vehement that it is only possible to understand them when we look at them within the larger framework of our social relations. "Understanding heterosexism, as well as homophobia, involves analyzing, not just women's victimization, but also how women are defined in terms of men or not at all, how lesbians and gay men are treated — indeed scapegoated — as deviants, how choices of intimate partners for both women and men are restricted or denied through taboos to maintain a certain social order."[16] That certain social order has to do with sexism and male domination.

Sexism and Male Domination

Hetero-relations and heterosexism cannot be understood apart from sexism and male domination. I am in agreement with the many scholars and writers who believe that heterosexism is a tool of sexism and cannot be discussed apart from the larger analysis of patriarchy and male domination. "*Heterosexism* is a logical and necessary extension of sexism."[17]

In a world of male domination it is totally unacceptable for a woman to choose a woman. Domination must be maintained. In a heterosexist world women are destined to respond to male needs and desires. In a world of male domination, it is equally unacceptable for a man to choose a man. Domination is maintained only if men fulfill the dominating roles they are assigned. When men step out of these dominating roles there is often a violent response. "Visible gay men are the objects of extreme hatred and fear by heterosexual men because their breaking ranks with male heterosexual solidarity is seen as a damaging rent in the very fabric of sexism."[18] The system can maintain itself only if gender relations are rigidly and clearly structured and controlled. These gender relations are structured in a multitude of ways: through strict gender roles, through the institutions of traditional marriage and the nuclear family, and through compulsory heterosexuality. All of these systems support dominance and submission as the natural order of relations, and have an important role to play in the maintenance of patriarchy. Sexism, male domination, and heterosexism are completely dependent on men having total and unrestricted access to women, and women relating exclusively to men.

Adrienne Rich's classic work, *Compulsory Heterosexuality and Lesbian Existence*, makes very clear the connections between heterosexism and sexism, between compulsory heterosexuality and male dominance:

> But whatever its origins, when we look hard and clearly at the extent and elaboration of measures designed to keep women within a male sexual purlieu, it becomes an inescapable question whether the issue we have to address as feminists is, not simple "gender inequality," nor the domination of culture by males, nor mere "taboos against homosexuality," but the enforcement of heterosexuality for women as a means of assuring male right of physical, economical, and emotional access.[19]

As I come to understand the interconnections between sexism and heterosexism, male domination and homophobia, misogyny and hetero-reality, I more clearly understand the condemnation of lesbians and gay men. Male domination and patriarchy are at stake in any discussion of heterosexism and homophobia. When one understands the depths of the connections and the depths of the transformation that is needed, then the depth of condemnation and hatred directed at lesbians and gay men becomes at least more understandable, but certainly no more justified.

Discerning Power: A Critique of Heterosexual Privilege

If a society and world acknowledge and value only heterosexual relationships, then that society and world will grant to heterosexual persons certain rights, privileges, and protections that lesbians and gay men will not have. The magnitude of heterosexual privilege is significant:

> No institutions, other than those created by lesbians and gays — such as the Metropolitan Community Church, some counseling

centers, political organizations such as the National Gay and Lesbian Task Force, the National Coalition of Black Lesbians and Gays, the Lambda Legal Defense and Education Fund, etc. — affirm homosexuality and offer protection. Affirmation and protection cannot be gained from the criminal justice system, mainline churches, educational institutions, the government.[20]

A part of the work of preachers responding to the injustice of heterosexism and homophobia involves inviting heterosexual persons honestly to discern and take responsibility for their privilege while seeking to critique the ideology and social fabric that produce such inequality. Discerning and taking responsibility for heterosexual privilege are processes similar to acknowledging and claiming one's white racism or one's class privilege. In a white, racist society, white persons have a responsibility to acknowledge and change their own white, racist attitudes and behaviors. In a heterosexist society, heterosexual persons have a particular kind of responsibility to discern and change their own homophobic and heterosexist attitudes and behaviors.

Heterosexual privilege is a new term for many people. It is a term that can be illusive and unclear, and certainly threatening:

> Consciousness must be forged about the ways one's heterosexuality is asserted and the ways one assumes others are heterosexual. We must take a look at the limits it places on our lives. And especially we must examine the fear we have about losing its privileges, the sacrifices we must make to keep those privileges, and the ways we are threatened by those who choose to resist.[21]

Whenever one is a part of the dominant, normative culture, it is easy to become conditioned to one's privileges and rights.

Heterosexual persons who desire to be sensitive and compassionate in their relationships with gay and lesbian people will constantly be trying to discern what privileges they enjoy simply because of their sexual orientation. In a very sensitive pamphlet called *And God Loves Each One: A Resource for Dialogue about the Church and Homosexuality,* Ann Thompson Cook relates a series of poignant real-people experiences and asks readers to reflect on how they might feel in such situations. Some of the experiences she describes clarify and concretize heterosexual privilege and protection:

- The person you have loved and lived with for forty years is in intensive care and you are not allowed to visit because you are not "family."

- During coffee breaks, your co-workers often mention their spouses or people they are dating, but you feel you must remain silent about yours.

- Your partner has just died of AIDS. His parents, ignoring the fact that you have been living together for ten years, are coming to sell the house you and your partner shared.

- You are a single, gay man in seminary, and your married classmates in seminary are looking forward to moving into a parsonage after ordination. You wonder what will happen when you find someone *you* want to settle down with.[22]

Just as white privilege is difficult to discern in a white, racist society, heterosexual privilege is so thoroughgoing and normative that it takes constant vigilance to discern it and take responsibility for it. It has to do with every aspect of our lives, from holding hands with persons we love to assumptions we make about our privileged place in all the social and political systems of government and church. This privilege is not assumed or experienced by lesbians and gay men. Gay and lesbian oppression is the daily experience of being silenced when heterosexual persons may speak, being made invisible when heterosexual reality is the only reality assumed and affirmed, and being terrorized by the constant awareness that an inappropriate comment, look, reaction, or expression could change one's entire life. The church will be able to understand this reality only when it listens attentively to the everyday experiences of lesbians and gay men. This listening to the voice of otherness will tune our hearts and spirits to their oppression and our complicity.

Attending to the Repercussions of Condemnation

The destructive power of homophobia and heterosexism is severe. Sensitive rabbis, pastors, and religious communities are being called to attend to the repercussions of this violence in the individual lives of lesbians and gay men, and in whole communities. "Its power is great enough to keep ten to twenty percent of the population living lives of fear (if their sexual identity is hidden) or lives of danger (if their sexual identity is visible) or both. And its power is great enough to keep the remaining eighty to ninety percent of the population trapped in their own fears."[23]

For Christian communities that profess God's love and grace, this kind of fear and hatred is a shameful reality. How are we to understand a world that intimidates millions of people into silence about the primary relational bonds and commitments of their lives? How are we to respond to a world where people must live in constant terror simply because of their sexual identity?

The everyday violence of heterosexism and homophobia takes more active forms as well. John E. Fortunato, a gay man himself, recalls a story about a young gay man named Tim. Tim is twenty years old when his family discovers that he is gay. On his first visit home after his parents learn of this news, his mother makes a shocking statement. She says, "I've made only one mistake in my life." Tim asks her what she means. "Twenty-two years ago," she says, "I should have had an abortion."[24]

This is devastating abuse. Oftentimes the church has either denied homophobic violence or condoned it as the natural, punitive repercussion of unnatural and immoral life choices and acts. In the name of the gospel and its reconciling love, this kind of condemnation is wrong, and its impact is lethal. This kind of rejection and violence produces hopelessness and despair. When one's basic personhood is rejected, there is nothing to be done or said that can change the situation. It is not surprising that many gay and lesbian people describe their human and spiritual journey as that of being in exile.[25] This kind of rejection appears to be a very common experience in the lives of lesbians and gay men. What particular care does the church have to offer persons who suffer this kind of rejection, condemnation, and judgment?

In addition to daily silencing and frequent aggressive violence, lesbians and gay men live with daily decisions about self-revelation that most heterosexual persons never face. They must constantly assess with whom they can be honest, when it is appropriate and safe to reflect the truth about their lives, and what prices must be paid for hiddenness and disclosure. Gay and lesbian writers reveal the constancy of this struggle:

> Gay people are repeatedly faced with a dilemma — to come out and risk experiencing the pain of being rejected or stereotyped, or to stay in the closet and thus be essentially dishonest about who we are. This is not a choice that can be made once and then forgotten; it has to be made in every new situation in which we find ourselves, with every new person.[26]

This ongoing tension is a very distinctive dimension to the oppression of gay and lesbian people. Families, religious communities, and the society at large actually *require* persons to lie about the truth of their lives for protection and safety. That this situation continues is a powerful indictment of heterosexist culture and the disturbing complicity of religious communities. The pressure and necessity to lie are not abstract or impersonal; sometimes they permeate the very nature of a person's entire family relationships. These same writers go on to say:

We must be prepared to tell lies to people we love and to have ready (false) answers to questions about what we've been doing, where we've been, with whom, why, and what our future plans are. Then, in painful irony, we can expect to be accused of being silent and reserved, and of not sharing ourselves and our lives with our families.[27]

The repercussions of condemnation are many. Lesbians and gay men are violated not only by silence, invisibility, and lies, but also by inadequate health care, lack of access to housing, job discrimination, and a multitude of other oppressive realities. What distinctive words and actions will preachers speak and take on behalf of those who suffer a multitude of effects from this kind of condemnation?

As preachers and religious communities struggle to respond to the complex and painful agenda of dismantling heterosexism and homophobia, we need to be clear that our work is not simply about the acceptance and empowerment of gay men and lesbians, but is ultimately about social transformation. The most basic understandings of power in our social, political, and ecclesiastical structures must be changed. Dominance and submission at every level of human existence are called into question. Carter Heyward names alienated power as the illness of our age and describes the distorted notions of human reality it creates:

> In this situation, no action is, in and of itself, evil — except that which challenges the established order of alienated power relations: So, for instance, while hunger may be a problem, communism, which threatens the individual white male's autonomy and his rights to private ownership, is evil. While wife-battering may be too bad, gay sex, which threatens the established order of male control of female sexuality, is evil. While incest may be a shame, lesbian mothers embody the forces of evil that threaten to bring down the entire sacred canopy of alienated power.[28]

What might be the theological agenda for preachers who want to share in the work of bringing down this sacred canopy? What will be our homiletical and theological responses as we seek to address and dismantle the condemning violence of heterosexism and homophobia?

PREACHING GRACE

When I contemplate what transforming message of hope might be spoken and embodied in the face of heterosexist condemnation, I always return to grace. The grace of God becomes one of the most powerful messages preachers and religious communities might proclaim in faithful response to the violence of heterosexism and homophobia. The grace of God and the grace-filled love of human beings are powerful forces in human history. This power can shatter prisons of gender domination and submission, expose illusions of moral and ethical superiority, transform judgments into moments of profound acceptance, and empower us to dwell in the realm of mystery rather then condemnation.

The essence of this grace is God, but human beings within Christian communities are called also to become agents of grace-filled action and speech in the world. Susan Brooks Thistlethwaite and Mary Potter Engel clearly acknowledge the importance and power of grace in North American black, feminist, Native American, and gay and lesbian liberation theologies. They say, "Grace as the divine empowering of human beings (and of all creaturely and natural life) to live and work for a just and loving world has traditionally been spoken of as sanctification, the process of being made and making holy/whole."[29] God's distinctive love and grace are central to the task, but human agency in the work of reconciliation, community building, and justice making is central to a liberationist perspective on grace. In liberation theology, grace has less to do with the forgiveness of individual sins, and more to do with confronting and transforming social and systemic forces and structures that produce evil. In describing the voices of many liberation theologians, Engel and Thistlethwaite say, "They speak of grace as the divine empowering that heals the external and internal wounds inflicted on individuals and peoples by structures of oppression and as the divine empowering that liberates peoples from the bondage of systemic evil."[30]

Grace empowers human beings to participate in the redemptive processes of transformation and justice. The work of sanctifying grace accepts, empowers, indicts, exposes, and embraces. A grace that renders creation holy and participates in the liberation of all people is a grace that does not know or understand the boundaries of human acceptance. It is a love that empowers those whom society would strip of power. It is a grace that indicts and exposes all those human realities that destroy sacred community and embodied justice. And it is a love that eternally lifts, embraces, and calls people home. This grace and the work that it inspires are terrifying and exhilarating. This grace makes an enormous and total claim upon each of us and our religious communities.

How might a liberationist perspective on grace enable us to do the kind of sanctifying work that needs to be done in response to heterosexist condemnation? What claims will it make upon us? What truths will it reveal to us? What hope does it engender? In response to these questions and others, I want to look first at the *home* of grace; then I will examine two dimensions of human agency — dwelling in mystery and salvific deliverance from fear — that give us a picture of what sanctifying grace might look like in our day.

The Home of Grace

Liberation theology begins its task by looking at the concrete experience and reality of oppression. Out of their particular experiences of condemnation and oppression, lesbians and gay men know a great deal about exiled existence and being exiled from home. If the Christian church and other religious communities will see these men and women as our teachers, we might understand more fully the nature of grace.

John Fortunato, reflecting on the spiritual journey of gay Christians, describes a profound existential truth about many of their lives when he says, "When you put all of the particulars together, the gestalt is oppression. The experience is not of moving from one particular to another; it is a constant, chronic feeling of not belonging, of being threatened and rejected."[31] Perhaps all human beings can identify with the personal experience of feeling that one does not belong, or that one is threatened or rejected. The major difference is that our society *intends* and *structures* this reality for lesbians and gay men. If grace is a divine empowering toward human wholeness, toward shalom, and toward the just structuring of human relations, then this aggressive condemnation is the antithesis of grace. In deepest contrast to experiences of rejection and threat, the work of grace creates acceptance and an environment of safety. It is impossible to be engaged simultaneously in the work of condemnation and the work of grace.

In a provocative article about the way God ushers in a new economy, or a new household for the human community, Douglas Meeks uses the metaphor of home to describe justice. He believes that the experience of home is a basic individual and collective human need. He says:

> We have all had, at least fleetingly, an experience of home. Home is where no one ever forgets your name. Home is where no matter what you have done, you will be confronted, forgiven, and accepted. Home is where there is always a place for you at the table and where you can be certain that what is on the table will be shared. To be a part of a home or a household is to have access to life. The heart of justice is participation in God's economy or God's household. Unless the power of God's love creates a household, justice will disintegrate into meaninglessness.[32]

Heterosexism and homophobia keep the Christian community from creating a household in which every created person has a name, shares in the abundance of creation, and is held accountable for the resources and actions of her or his life. The violent fear and condemnation at the center of a heterosexist society and church are attempts to deny all gay men and lesbians access to life. The condemnation and privileges of heterosexism suggest that there is only room at the table for those who are heterosexual. This is the antithesis of sanctifying grace; through sanctifying grace, the sacred nature of all humanity is recognized and named, and resources are distributed in such a way that all might have life.

Christian persons need to understand the power and limitations of our attitudes and actions. Our condemnation may keep many of our religious communities from being *home* for gay and lesbian people, but it will never prevent the essence of God from being the home of grace for all. And let us be clear that when a home is divided by the condemnation of some, it ceases to be a true home for any.

The home of grace has to do with naming and blessing, knowing and embracing. In the last few lines of Marsie Silvestro's "Blessing Song," there is a challenge to the church:

> And we'll bless you our sister
> Bless you in our way
> And we'll welcome home ... all the life you've known
> And softly speak your name
> Oh we'll welcome home all the self you own
> And softly speak your name.[33]

The home of grace welcomes *all* the life people have known, all the self people own, and speaks the name of each created one. It is not a blessing free of confrontation or accountability, but it is an embrace of gracious acceptance. It is not a blessing that is free from expectation and work, but it is the assurance of sustaining love.

Chris Glaser speaks about the work of the church as consisting of a people opening up the household of God to others and to all creation. He believes that when the church discerns its true vocation as a kind of threshold for God's love, it will understand that it is the body of Christ standing in a doorway beckoning others to come home.[34] This is the vision of the home of grace. What is the human work that needs to be done in order to create and sustain it?

Dwelling in Mystery

The grace of God is awesome. As we seek to live it, the claim of that grace becomes more mysterious in its power, more transforming in its breadth, and more compelling in its depth. Preaching is a part of the ministry of the church that can forever challenge people to embrace the mysterious power and work of God's grace among and within us. If our preaching is honest it will acknowledge that we both covet and loathe the frightening mystery of God and the mystery of grace-filled human agency.

A part of what is most painful and challenging about grace is that it is by nature mysterious. This does not mean that it is not manifested in human action and ethical activity. However, divine empowerment in the work of grace forever remains partially mysterious. It is difficult for us to bear the mystery of God's grace, and it is difficult and often painful to bear the mystery of our created sisters and brothers. Mystery is life-sustaining, but it also engenders fear. A part of the responsibility of preaching is to help religious communities dwell in mystery and know that our capacity to accept and receive mystery has profound implications for our social and political life together.

In describing the work of the Presbyterian Task Force to Study Homosexuality, Chris Glaser suggests that the fundamental beginning point of their work together was a willingness to dwell in mystery. He says, "At heart, we of the task force found ourselves faced with two mysteries: the nature of sexuality, of homosexuality in particular, and the nature of God's grace."[35] Until religious communities are willing to accept the mysterious aspects of human life with wonder and reverence rather than condemnation, we will never be agents of God's redemptive grace. No amount of research on sexuality, sexual orientation, or sexual preference will ever completely explain the tremendous variance in human relationships and acts of loving. Sanctifying grace involves the work of dwelling in mystery — our own, each other's, and God's. This dwelling, with a desire to understand and embrace, renders life holy and moves the human community closer to wholeness.

Dwelling in mystery is not an abstract or illusive dimension of human agency; it is concrete and particular. It means accepting a person whose sexual orientation or preference is different from your own without judgment or condemnation. It means accepting the mysterious nature of human sexuality instead of attempting to reduce its power and passion with narrow biblical literalisms or archaic ecclesiastical traditions. It means building Christian and religious communities with persons of all sexual orientations, and it involves naming and celebrating the particularities of sexuality. To embrace the work of dwelling in mystery, we ask of ourselves and each other to cease the condemnation of that which we do not understand, and begin the process of allowing those differences to make a claim upon the work we do for justice. Leonardo Boff describes this aspect of grace as "love" when he says, "Love is this pristine capacity to freely communicate oneself to another who is different, to accept that other inside oneself, and to involve oneself in some definitive way with that other."[36] The healing and liberating work of grace invites us into the mystery of otherness and changes us forever.

Preachers need to be concrete in our invitations to congregations to dwell in mystery. The content and words of our sermons need the mystery of paradox, the mystery of the unknown, and the mystery of otherness. Stories about gay and lesbian long-term relationships become an occasion to teach our congregations about fidelity and commitment. Stories about gay and lesbian parenting open the hearts of communities to new ways of defining family. The political insights and critical thoughts of lesbians and gay men about domination and submission extend and deepen our understandings of mutuality and gender equity.

Dwelling in mystery is a part of sanctifying grace. It is a part of the honoring of creation. It is a part of creating and sustaining the home of grace.

Salvific Deliverance from Fear

The work of grace is healing and liberating. The power of grace speaks to and addresses human fear. Heterosexism and homophobia are forms of distorted and fearful social relations. Not only are heterosexism and homophobia alienating influences in our personal and social relations, but they also produce a profound self-alienation. No one in our society escapes the fearful grip of these distortions. An important part of the work of liberating grace is its ability to release persons from this kind of immobilizing and condemnatory fear. All persons stand in need of salvific deliverance from oppressing and oppressive fear.

For many heterosexual persons, experiencing the concrete lives of gay men and lesbians raises complex and frightening questions about sexuality, intimacy, and gender identity. In a culture that encourages disembodiment, perpetuates the denial of vital and passionate sexuality, and regulates and restricts any fluidity in gender identity, one of the expected responses to the presence of lesbians and gay men will be fear. The effects of this fear are enormous.

If we loathe and condemn the relational lives of lesbians and gay men, then any semblance of that reality is to be avoided. Homophobia leaves women justifying and trivializing the deep and satisfying friendships they have with other women, and leaves many men so fearful of emotionally intimate male bonding that their lives are void of meaningful male friendship. The fear that flows from homophobia leaves both men and women profoundly diminished.

The structures of heterosexism also produce and fuel human fear. How are we to understand our world, and ourselves, in the face of a mutual and intimate partnership between two men? How are we to understand our world, and ourselves, in the face of two women building a home together and raising a family? The possibility and fullness of these choices are terrifying. Heterosexism imprisons women and men in constricted gender roles and expectations that distort the fullness of human personhood. These rigid gender expectations rest on a foundation of control instead of mutuality, on a bedrock of gender complementarity instead of gender fullness.

As preachers, surely a part of our message of liberating grace is that deliverance from fear ultimately demands that we plunge our lives directly into those things we fear the most. Facing our own fears is not the same as dwelling in the mystery of otherness. Claiming one's own fear is an inward look into the deepest vulnerabilities and limitations of one's created self. In facing our fears, we may be able to be liberated and saved from them. And as we acknowledge those fears, we transform the need to condemn that which we fear.

Participating in the salvific deliverance of grace requires a courageous preaching ministry. It means that we might preach about all those things that we have been taught to deny and silence. It means that we find saving ways to speak about human erotic passion, embodied sexuality, and the risks of human intimacy. Until religious communities deal more directly with these dimensions of our human experience, we will continue to be victimized by homophobia and heterosexism.

Our preaching ministries need to acknowledge honestly the truths and ambiguities about human intimacy, the inconsistencies of sexuality, and the centrality of our concrete, embodied human existence. Until religious communities are released from their fears of these realities, lesbians and gay men will continue to receive the projected hatred, fear, and condemnation of unresolved human struggles. We might proclaim a profound understanding of grace as the agent and means of release and deliverance from these deepest fears of our own humanness. James Nelson speaks about this releasing, liberating grace as acceptance and describes its power with these words:

> You are accepted, the total you. Your body, which you often reject, is accepted by that which is greater than you. Your sexual feelings and unfulfilled yearnings are accepted. You are accepted in your ascetic attempts at self-justification or in your hedonistic alienation from the true meaning of your sexuality. You are accepted in those moments of sexual fantasy which come unbidden and which both delight and disturb you. You are accepted in your femininity and in your masculinity, for you have elements of both. You are accepted in your heterosexuality and in your homosexuality, and you have elements of both. Simply accept the fact that you are accepted as a sexual person! If that happens to you, you experience grace.[37]

This is a forceful description of the power of grace to deliver us from fear and to empower us toward the acceptance of self and other. If our preaching ministries are to be vehicles of this kind of liberating and salvific grace, then the content and presence of our preaching will need to be shaped by sacred acceptance. This sacred acceptance challenges the core of our preaching. Preaching will be challenged to affirm that the spiritual nature of one's human reality cannot be separated from one's embodied self. Preachers will need to be brave enough to declare that our sexuality is not to be willfully controlled but rather is to be embraced, celebrated, and ethically lived to its fullest. The images and language of our preaching can paint vivid pictures of mutuality and intimacy rather than dominance and submission. This kind of preaching is salvific and participates in the work of deliverance. When heterosexual persons believe and accept their own sacred sexual personhood, condemnation and fear are often transformed.

Heterosexual people are not the only ones who need salvific deliverance from fear. For gay men and lesbians, the concrete realities of heterosexism and homophobia produce immense anger and fear. That fear distorts and poisons individual relationships, erodes self-confidence and self-worth, and renders invisible the full relational matrix of gay and lesbian life. For some, this fear leads to anonymous sexual encounters, blatant denial of loved ones, compulsive and addictive behaviors that might numb the persistent pain, and family estrangement. Gay men and lesbians are also in need of salvific deliverance from fear. Not only do lesbians and gay men need to hear a liberating word about sexuality, embodiment, and intimacy, as do heterosexual persons, but the magnitude of heterosexist condemnation produces distinctive dimensions of self-hatred and fear.

The reality of AIDS has compounded fear in the lives of gay men and lesbians. Misinformation and homophobic propaganda about the nature of AIDS demonstrate the demonic magnitude of heterosexist fear and power. Carter Heyward talks about the social character of AIDS and challenges religious communities to be more responsible in their analysis and understanding:

> AIDS is a socially constructed disease with a number of interstructured foundations: the enigmatic biological character of the virus itself; the politics and economics of the disease (who gets it? what is being done to stop it? what is its cost, and to whom?); and public ignorance of, and misinformation about, the virus (what are its symptoms? how does it spread? who is most likely to get it?).[38]

AIDS has had a devastating impact on gay men and lesbians, a community already diseased with heterosexist oppression. What delivering word of grace will we preach in response?

God's grace is basic to the faith experience of deliverance for gay and lesbian Christians. "Their freedom to love and give in a hostile world hinges upon their coming to believe in their wholeness and in their having a rightful place in God's universe."[39] Grace is the affirmation that all people have a rightful place in God's universe. When lesbians and gay men know they have a rightful place, fear is transformed.

For many gay men and lesbians, the mediators of God's grace are other lesbians and gay men, and seldom the church. Salvific deliverance comes most often from an exiled religious community existing on the borders of, or completely outside, an oppressive institutional church. For Christian preachers, perhaps the greatest challenge regarding salvific deliverance is to look outside the bounds of the traditional church at the places that mediate liberating grace in the lives of gay men and lesbians.

Perhaps our preaching might change if we experienced the grace and vitality of gay men as they courageously struggle against AIDS. Perhaps our preaching might change if we experienced the strength and bonding of lesbian women as they struggle against their children being taken away through legal action. Perhaps our preaching might change if we experienced the concrete ways gay men and lesbian women build community from the pains of invisibility, silence, and condemnation. Our preaching needs to reach into these places and experiences of exiled community in order to understand more fully the face, context, and essence of deliverance and saving grace for lesbians and gay men.

✧ 5 ✧

Conversion Uproots Supremacy—
WHITE RACISM

OKASAN/MOTHER

twenty-five years she's been here
and still
> *a-me-ri-ka makes her mouth sour tight*
> *sticks in her mind like spit-wet thread*
> *caught in the eye of a needle.*

twenty-five years of doing christmas
and still
> *she saves generation-old*
> *bamboo mats for wrapping new year osushi/rice cakes*
> *hums songs of japan*
> *in the quiet dark of christmas mornings.*

every year
for twenty-five years she plans new year
and still
> *one more dress to sew, one more bill to pay.*
> *one more year passes.*
> *she celebrates*
> *sewing silk gowns for rich ladies.*

twenty-five years
and still
> *she tells no stories of war to a daughter*
> *she saves marriage lace and*
> *satin baby kimonos in a cedar chest for*
> *a daughter who denies her conversation*
> *watches her sew her life designs*
> *into someone else's wedding day*

twenty-five years of city living
people calling her oriental or chinese
sometimes jap

and still
  her eyes, like teardrops turned sideways,
  say nothing.
  with pride, she writes from right to left
  of the greatness of a-me-ri-ka to her people.

twenty-five years
alone.
still
she cries in japanese

—Sakae S. Roberson[1]

Supremacy is both an ideology and a concrete reality. As ideology, supremacy is the philosophy and belief that certain persons are superior. As a concrete reality, supremacy is the state of human existence where a select group of persons possess ultimate or supreme power and authority. White supremacy is a form of violence in which white human beings believe they are superior and create and maintain the kind of structures in human society that will give them ultimate power. White racism is an integral dimension of white supremacy. "Racism originates in domination and provides the social rationale and philosophical justification for debasing, degrading, and doing violence to people on the basis of color."[2] White racism becomes a primary ideology and structure of oppression that keep white supremacy secure.

White racism is the systematic denial, oppression, and domination of persons on the basis of race. To focus on *white* racism is to locate the problem and responsibility of racist domination and exploitation with white people. Morris Bratton in "What Can Christians Do?" says, "Nothing will change in US churches and society until we are clear about what racism is and that racism in the United States is a white problem — not because whites are the only people with prejudices, but because whites control the power structures of church and society."[3]

My primary agenda here is not to attempt a thorough explanation of white racism; nor do I intend to chart its roots and history in this nation in any systematic way. Rather I *assume* white racism as a real, concrete reality in the life of this nation and in the lives of religious institutions and communities. There are preachers and congregations committed to resist white racism and white supremacy. The pictures of white racism I describe and the concerns and issues that I raise about our theological agenda are an attempt to confront myself and the white Christian communities of which I am a part with the ever-present violence of white racism and white supremacy. Part of my aim, then, is to encourage and aid preachers and working theologians to develop a collective response to white supremacy and racism.

RADICALIZING MOMENTS

My assumption that white racism and white supremacy exist is based on my experience of them in my own life and in the lives of many people I know. I have also come to realize that the struggle to resist both my own white racism and the larger reality of white supremacy is a life-long process of very difficult work. I remain forever hopeful that white religious communities will help each other persist in this struggle.

I have experienced the pain and oppression of white supremacy, and I have experienced myself as one who perpetuates white supremacy. Both realities are violating and diminishing. White supremacy is *primarily* the violence white people inflict on people of color. It is important to remember, however, that white supremacy and white racism distort and deform the lives of white people in some very fundamental ways.

Three incidents have been influential and radicalizing in my own journey. They are moments of awareness that continue to be sources of deep reflection and new insight. These events moved me to new levels of understanding about the evil of white racism.

I grew up in Wheelersburg, Ohio, a small town in the southern part of the state. The area was politically conservative. During the time I lived there, from 1953 to 1971, Wheelersburg itself was exclusively white. In the neighboring town of Portsmouth there was a distinguishable African-American community. In 1970 my sister Pam began to date an African-American man from Portsmouth. This was a serious relationship and over time our two families socialized occasionally. This experience in the life of our family became a formative one for us all. The social life of our entire family changed. Friendships disappeared, particularly for my sister, and relationships became alienated and strained. Each of us was the recipient of white racist remarks, and there was a quiet isolation that settled in around our family life. As our family has reflected on this experience over the years, we continue to be shocked at our own white racism. It was a very long time into the process before any of us even considered the repercussions in the lives of this young man and the rest of his family. Somewhere in the honesty of our conversations with them we began to understand the potential and threatened violence to all their lives. In the midst of a growing relationship, we also became aware that these parents had their own distinctive fears, anxieties, and reservations. In the beginning, my own family was somewhat oblivious to everything that did not affect us directly. Throughout it all there were ugly moments; there were painful moments; there were joyful and transforming moments. White racism and white supremacy are not just personal family issues. They are issues at the heart of all our social relations.

A second event was confrontational and transformative in a completely different way. In the spring of 1983 I was working on the staff of the Center for Women and Religion in Berkeley, California. I was one of three coordinators for a women's conference we were holding. We felt we had carefully attended to racial diversity in the leadership of the conference, in the rituals and worship moments, and in the plenary sessions. Toward the end of the conference an African-American woman stood and confronted both the planners and the participants with the reality that while we had attended to token racial diversity in the leadership slots of the conference, the basic theme and agenda of the conference were irrelevant to the lives of women of color, and deeply racist. The theme of the conference was "Birthing Our Unity." I felt incredibly defensive and hurt and wanted to deny the indictment. It took a long time before I could allow the truth of her words to change me. Simple assimilation is not enough; it will never be enough, or even appropriate, in the midst of white supremacy.

I painfully recall the two weeks we spent on racism in the Princeton "Theological Interpretation for Contemporary Preaching" class. There was so much silence and denial in the room it was shocking. It took me months even to begin to understand why these two class sessions were significantly different from the other sessions on classism, sexism, handicappism, ageism, and heterosexism. The first major insight came while taking a course entitled "Class as a Critical Theological and Ethical Category" from Beverly Harrison in the fall of 1989. In a session about the relationship between class and race, Harrison spoke about the ideological manifestations of racism. One of those was color symbolism. She made the point that when white people study and discuss such ideological manifestations of race, they are not actually dealing with the thing itself. One must confront the harsh realities of racist domination.[4]

In our class at Princeton, Mark Taylor and I had chosen color symbolism as the starting place for discussion. I now understand that we should have begun our discussion about white racism with the concrete historical realities of slavery in the United States, or the internment of Japanese Americans during World War II, or the perpetual exploitation of Hispanic farm workers, or the present genocide of Native Americans in this country. These discussions would have dealt with the material realities of white racism, not an ideology that undergirds and flows from it. White racism and white supremacy thrive on abstractions and the mystification of concrete historical and contemporary reality. White people must begin to perceive their own complicity in this abstraction and mystification.

As you move through these pages, I invite you to remember the radicalizing moments and events in your own journey with white racism. Our honest individual and collective remembering will guide us in facing and resisting white supremacy. It is a journey filled with pain and hope, and one that is absolutely necessary for the transformation of white people and the ultimate eradication of white supremacy.

UNDERSTANDING AND NAMING THE VIOLENCE

In the United States white racism has continued to be manifest in the structures and attitudes of our everyday lives. However, it has become increasingly difficult to speak openly about it and take direct action against it. There are many reasons for this. Many white people believe that the civil rights movement of the 1960s addressed the fundamental problem of racism. This simplistic analysis serves as one of the many indicators of our denial. High levels of pain and guilt keep many white people from seeing the blatant realities around them. Work on white racism today must take a distinctive and different form from some of the work that has been done in the past. For many white people it has become clear that work on racism means work on *white racism* and work with white people. Many people of color refuse to be exploited as the educators of white people and are demanding that white people do the work that is theirs to do in the eradication of this violence.

Another reason that white racism is so difficult for the society in general to understand and resist is that it has become increasingly hidden and mystified. This mystification confuses and immobilizes white people and people of color, although whites are more easily seduced by the power and benefits that still accrue to them within a system of white domination. Joel Kovel speaks about the development of white racism and the stages through which he believes it has moved. He names the contemporary manifestation of racism when he says, "We have *metaracism*, the racism of technocracy, i.e. one without psychological mediation as such, in which racist oppression is carried out directly through economic and technocratic means."[5]

In Kovel's analysis white racism is so fundamentally intermeshed with economics and technology in late-capitalist society that it becomes increasingly removed from our personal and social encounters and more difficult to discern or resist. We certainly can see much of its resultant impact, but it is perpetuated and maintained by structures of power and force that are technologically sophisticated and removed from daily observation.

At the present time, the main force of racist oppression is being administered impersonally, through the cold savagery of the economy. I do not mean to imply, to be sure, that this works without human hands. Quite the contrary, it is a very human process, even to the degree of mystification which is applied to make the economy seem a natural force instead of the expression of class conflict.[6]

This is not to suggest that white racism is not also expressed in this country in direct physical violence, abhorrent acts of discrimination, and attitudes of aversion. The rise of racist violence can easily be seen in the white supremacist movement of our day and the continual blatant hate of the Ku Klux Klan.[7] Kovel is suggesting, however, that the structures and mechanisms that keep white racism intact, and demand it as ideology and concrete reality, are central to the economy of this country and to its role in the international economy.

Understanding white racism and the structures of its manifestation is an extremely illusive and complex process. While Kovel and others try to examine the roots of white racism among white people, writers like Cornel West chart some of its evolution and manifestations from the perspective of African Americans in this country. So convinced is West of the inseparability of economics and racism that he charts the genealogy of modern racism and then proposes the wedding of African-American Christian thought with Progressive Marxism. His genealogical approach to racism can neither be reduced to individual psychological insights about white people nor reduced to exclusively economic analyses. West says, "Therefore I do not believe that the emergence of the idea of white supremacy in the modern West can be fully accounted for in terms of the psychological needs of white individuals and groups or the political and economic interests of a ruling class."[8] He then proceeds to look at developments in history that have shaped human understandings of race and the cultural exploitation and violence of white racism. He analyzes two of these historical developments in some detail. The first is the scientific revolution of the seventeenth century, in which science became associated with ultimate truth, and scientific investigation became increasingly aligned with racist pronouncements about people of color. The second is the classical revival that began in the Early Renaissance (1300–1500) and continued well into the eighteenth century; within that revival classical aesthetics and cultural ideals led to an entrenched system of valuing and ordering human persons.[9]

West's theoretical inquiry into the variables related to the evolution of modern racism expands our understanding of its complexities and its impact. West takes economics seriously, but he also attempts to develop a framework out of which African Americans and others might come to comprehend fully the multilayered impact of racism upon the lives of people of color. Speaking about why he draws attention to the force of the scientific revolution and the classical revival, he writes:

This variable is significant because it not only precludes reductionist treatments of modern racism; it also highlights the cultural and aesthetic impact of the idea of white supremacy on black people. This inquiry accents the fact that the everyday life of black people is shaped not simply by the exploitative (oligopolistic) capitalist system of production but also by cultural attitudes and sensibilities, including alienating ideals of beauty.[10]

The origins of white supremacy and white racism are complex and multilayered, and understanding their contemporary forms and manifestations demands a rigorous analysis of historical developments and human psychological tendencies.

White Racism in Our Religious Communities

White racism does exist in the Christian church. It has many forms and is expressed in a complex array of institutional policies, ecclesiastical structures, and personal prejudices. Even though the violence of white racism has become more subtle and masked in many of our churches and denominations, it is very present and alive. Even so, there are some religious communities that are trying to move toward the honoring of racial and cultural difference. In a number of our church communities there continue to be frequent conversations about ethnic diversity and cultural pluralism, and in many places there is a genuine desire to move toward the profound respect of difference.[11] In seminaries across this country the globalization of theological education is not only discussed, but recently there have also been concrete strategies adopted in an effort to transform the fundamental learning environment and curricula of academic and religious institutions.[12] Some of these movements are an indication that our religious communities recognize white supremacy and white racism and desire to break the violence of cultural imperialism. In the midst of these positive changes, it is essential that we not be deceived. White supremacy is not easily dismantled. Many of the predominantly white local churches of mainline Protestantism continue to have limited or no connection to black, Asian, Native American, or Hispanic congregations. The everyday ministries of white pastors and lay people reflect a deep ethnocentrism, and there is a frightening silence among white Christians about the escalation of racist violence.

It is difficult to keep white racism at the top of our theological and religious agenda. As white people honestly try to address the issue of white racism and faithfully respond to its many manifestations of domination and violence, there will be moments of intense confusion, painful awareness of our own complicity, a sense of indictment, and a degree of disorientation. These moments in our own lives, and in the lives of our religious communities, are painful and frightening. When the Christian church deals with white racism, the depth of shock and disorientation persons experience and the depth of people's denial and hostility only confirm the dire need for confrontation and transformation within our religious lives. There are powerful forces of denial and resistance among us. Audre Lorde in *Sister Outsider* says:

> Mainstream communication does not want women, particularly white women, responding to racism. It wants racism to be accepted as an immutable given in the fabric of your existence, like evening time or the common cold. So we are working in a context of opposition and threat, the cause of which is certainly not the angers which lie between us, but rather that virulent hatred leveled against all women, people of Color, lesbians and gay men, poor people — against all of us who are seeking to examine the particulars of our lives as we resist our oppressions, moving toward coalition and effective action.[13]

In the midst of the violence and evil of white supremacy and white racism, how will we as preachers speak? How might our voices enable our communities to acknowledge complicity? How might our listening empower the voices of people of color in our predominantly white congregations? In what ways can our preaching ministries break through the silence that surrounds racist domination and help communities discern the ways in which they can resist?

Definitions and Assumptions

I name the strand of evil discussed in this chapter as *white racism* and *white supremacy* because I firmly believe that this is the most accurate description and labeling of the problem in the United States. I have come to understand racism as the distinct combination of prejudice and power that leads to systematic domination and oppression of entire communities of people. In the United States and in many other places around the world, this domination and oppression are primarily perpetrated by white people. The general term *racism* implies that any and all people are capable of this expression of violence and domination. Perhaps as a universal human reality this has truth. However, in our national context I believe that, while all people are capable of prejudicial behavior, white people have the power to structure their prejudices into the very fabric of social reality. Racism is such a systematic form of domination and exploitation that it requires the power of enforcement, and this is a power white people possess, maintain, and control.

This is a difficult definition for many white people to accept. They have been conditioned to believe that racism is a personal and private attitude toward persons who are racially different from themselves. They are taught that this attitude or prejudice is something that all people are capable of possessing and acting upon. This conditioning leads white people into the illusion that they can somehow be just as violated and oppressed by racism as people of color. This is simply not true. In the United States, people of color do not possess the power to enforce, systematize, and institutionalize their prejudices. If we are to understand white racism fully and take action to resist it, we must learn to identify it and take responsibility for it with accuracy and honesty.

A first step for white preachers and for predominantly white congregations would be to understand more fully the many faces and expressions of violence that white racism perpetrates. I am confronted by my own ignorance about the root causes and manifestations of white supremacy and white racism, and perceive that this ignorance is shared by many of my colleagues and many of our church communities. White supremacy and white racism show themselves in many ways. Economic violence and cultural imperialism are two manifestations I want to highlight.

Economic Violence

In this country it has become impossible to isolate racism from other structures of oppression. Gender and class are paramount to the discussion of white racism and its resulting violence.

To understand white racism as it exists throughout our world, one must look at economics. We cannot understand white racism without also analyzing the imperialistic economic policies of the United States and its international politics. In the final words of an article entitled "Racism and Economics: The Perspective of Oliver C. Cox," Katie Cannon highlights Cox's understanding of racism and international imperialism. She writes: "The myth of racial inferiority enables capitalist governments, economic organizations, and financial structures to penetrate the world. The hatred and fear of people of color now has developed into a global system of ideological subjugation, justifying the legitimacy of control of Third World countries through massive debt, monopoly industry, and direct military imperialism."[14]

In addition to a serious analysis of international economic imperialism and its connection to white racism, one cannot understand white racism without at least acknowledging the atrocities that have been committed in the name of economic progress and development within our own borders. A part of the legacy of white racism is the extermination of Native Americans in this land:

> The most virulent form of the disease of racism has been used against Native America. Like other oppressed people, we have known slavery, poverty, and political conquest. We have also

known something else — genocide. The greatest mass extermination of any race, any culture, any people happened here. It happened to us.[15]

There is a clear and obvious link between the white racism of Western colonialism and its economic and cultural exploitation of Native Americans.

Historically, there is a horrifyingly clear connection between the concrete reality of chattel slavery in the United States and the exclusive economic gain for white people that resulted from such exploitation. "Chattel slavery was an extreme institutional expression of capitalist exploitation. The frightful principle of capitalism — private ownership of the means of production, including labor — dictated that the greater the need for black labor, the greater would be black subjugation."[16]

All we need do is look around us to see the clear connections between white racism and U.S. capitalist economics. White racism clearly produces economic exploitation and injustice, and capitalism demands racist domination and exploitation. We see the connection in the present annihilation of black men in this country and the domestic labor of black women.[17] We see the connection in the massive numbers of Asian women who are exploited in the garment industry in many of our major cities.[18] We see the connection in the exploited and unrecognized labor of immigrants from Mexico and other countries of Latin America.[19] Everywhere one looks white racism creates and thrives upon economic violence.

Many women of color certainly know and experience that their gender deepens the economic exploitation that they suffer due to their race. In any adequate discussion of white supremacy and white racism, some attention must be given to the additional violence that women of color experience. "Black women are the most vulnerable and the most exploited members of the American society. The structure of the capitalist political economy in which Black people are commodities combined with patriarchal contempt for women has caused the Black woman to experience oppression that knows no ethical or physical bounds."[20]

Black women not only face the economic exploitation and violence that accompany white supremacy and white racism, but they also face the violence of misogyny that accompanies sexism. This is the historical and contemporary reality of black women's lives. Katie Cannon describes an early stage of black women's triple oppression in this way: "As a slave, the Black woman was subjected to the threefold penalization of legal servitude, sexual exploitation and racial discrimination."[21] The overwhelming assertion in Cannon's book *Black Womanist Ethics* is that black women are not only victimized by the triple oppression of their lives, but they have lived, and continue to live, manifesting a distinct moral agency and strength. The qualities of this life are best described as invisible dignity, quiet grace, and unshouted courage.[22]

Physical violence and death are a part of the ultimate repercussions of economic violence. There were distinctive dimensions to white male violence in the lives of black slave women, but white women inflicted violence as well. "The white woman's frustration at her own property-status, which reduced her to a non-human existence, was often vented in violent behavior against black women."[23]

In this country it is not just black women who experience the triple oppression of racism, classism, and sexism. All women of color live within this violent reality. While there is a distinctive quality to black women's oppression in this country that is rooted in the historical reality of slavery, all women of color are in jeopardy in the United States.

Making Waves: An Anthology of Writings by and about Asian American Women is a book that charts immigration patterns from the middle of the nineteenth century until our day. It also looks at war, work, identity, injustice, and activism in the lives of thousands of Asian-American women. In it Deborah Woo describes some of the exploitative economic realities within these women's lives and exposes the myth of the "model minority" Asian woman.[24] She believes that Asian-American women continue to be victimized by the kind of economic violence that flows from white supremacy and white racism. She says, "When we consider the large immigrant Asian population and the language barriers that restrict women to menial or entry-level jobs, we are talking about a group that not only earns minimum wage or less, but one whose purchasing power is substantially undermined by living in metropolitan areas of states where the cost of living is unusually high."[25]

A part of the dominating strategy of white capitalists is to highlight a picture of the economically successful Asian-American woman or man. This picture suggests that the link between white supremacy and economic domination and exploitation has been broken within Asian-American communities. This is another strategy that serves to mystify and mask the underlying realities of white racism and economic injustice. "In 1980 foreign-born Asian women with four or more years of college were most likely to find jobs in administrative support or clerical occupations."[26] The full reality of Asian-American women's lives is not revealed to the American populace, and the statistics that are revealed are often distorted:

> For example, after adjustments are made for occupational prestige, age, education, weeks worked, hours worked each week, and state of residence in 1975, Chinese American women could be expected to earn only 70 percent of the majority male income. Even among the college educated, Chinese American women fared least

well, making only 42 percent of what majority males earned. As we noted earlier, the mean income of all women, Anglo and Asian, was far below that of Anglo males in 1970 and 1980. This was true for both native-born and foreign-born Asians.... In 1980, this inequity persisted.[27]

These examples of economic exploitation and violence from the lives of black women and Asian-American women are only two of the many ways one could highlight the impact of racism, classism, and sexism. In political, social, and economic systems that are interstructured by racism, classism, and sexism, women will be the objects of more economic violence than white men, and the lives of women of color will be affected most severely.

Cultural Imperialism

To describe more fully the complex violations of white supremacy and white racism, the reality of cultural imperialism must be addressed. White supremacy seeks to repress, control, and annihilate the cultural values, symbols, languages, and social mores of persons and communities that are not white. Cultural imperialism and ethnocentrism can be viciously blatant, and they can also be insidiously quiet.

White Western culture, flowing from Western European roots, dominates the human landscape of our country. White cultural symbols and values, even as diverse as they are, have become the structure and climate of our social reality. English is the official language, and in recent years there has been a tremendous reactionary force in this country to establish English as the exclusive language of our social and legal life. In the midst of extensive racial and ethnic diversity in this country, this kind of domination needs to be named honestly as cultural imperialism. Karen Lebacqz gives us one perspective from which we might view cultural injustice: "Cultural injustice takes many forms. Primary is the destruction of culture itself — the removal of people from their homelands and imposition of a different way of life."[28]

This destruction of culture is a necessary part of white supremacy and power. Sometimes cultural imperialism involves the removal of people from their homelands — as was, and is, the case with Native Americans in this country; as was the case with the removal of Japanese Americans from the West Coast during World War II; as is the case with the systematic removal of black farmers from farmlands across this nation.[29] Sometimes cultural imperialism involves the daily imposition of a different way of life on individuals and whole communities. This imposition takes place through the subtle violence of assimilation and integration.

White people in the United States find it exceedingly difficult to comprehend the depth and breadth of cultural imperialism. We have not known its isolation or its humiliation. White people are often so far removed from an awareness of what it means to be white that many have difficulty understanding the power and importance of cultural identity and the tenuousness of cultural survival. "White people do not have to see themselves as White. They have the luxury of seeing themselves as individuals, whereas people who are oppressed by the system can never forget who they are racially."[30] I believe this is an important truth about white existence and the privileges that flow from white domination. White domination is so pervasive that white people often do not understand their own whiteness and, thus, their own white supremacy.

Judith Katz raises a series of questions that are designed to help white people become more acutely aware of the deeply ingrained cultural imperialism that resides within them:

1. Which colors have positive connotations and which have negative connotations?

2. How do values become translated and reflected onto people of a given color — that is, of a given race?

3. What are the norms — characteristics — of beauty? Who decides them?

4. What are the standards for intelligence? Who developed them?

5. What is the difference between the expressions "culturally deprived" and "culturally exploited"?

6. What traditions are celebrated? What religion is most often practiced? What norms and values are generally accepted?[31]

In many ways, these questions touch only the surface of cultural imperialism. But for many white people, questions like these are the beginning of an essential process of consciousness raising. Another beginning step in addressing cultural imperialism is to listen to the voices of those oppressed and violated by this form of domination and to let those voices and truths confront us and change us.

Gloria Anzaldúa speaks about the daily humiliation of growing up as a child trying to live between two cultures. Having been born near the Texas-Mexican border, she found herself living between Mexican culture, with a heavy Amerindian influence, and Anglo culture, the culture of colonization. What follows is the description of the violence of cultural imperialism:

I remember being caught speaking Spanish at recess — that was good for three licks on the knuckles with a sharp ruler. I remember being sent to the corner of the classroom for "talking back" to the Anglo teacher when all I was trying to do was tell her how to pronounce my name. "If you want to be American, speak 'American.' If you don't like it, go back to Mexico where you belong." . . . At Pan American University, I, and all Chicano students were required to take two speech classes. Their purpose: to get rid of our accents.

Attacks on one's form of expression with the intent to censor are a violation of the First Amendment. . . . Wild tongues can't be tamed, they can only be cut out.[32]

Cultural imperialism sometimes seeks to change people, or "tame" them; sometimes it seeks to silence them altogether. It is maintained by power, the power of individual threats, the power of intimidation and abuse, the power of massive force. It is difficult for individuals and communities to remain culturally strong in the midst of such constant attack. Gloria Anzaldúa's courageous and persistent claiming of her own cultural roots and identity blatantly exposes the subtle and clear impact of white supremacy.

From the different perspective of a Cuban woman living in the United States, Ada María Isasi-Díaz speaks about the violence done to Hispanic culture. "It is sacked and raped every time we are told that our children cannot learn in Spanish in school, when our customs are ridiculed, when our cultural artifacts — typical dress, music, etc. — are commercialized."[33] Cultural imperialism also happens through the trivialization of a people's culture, and the treatment of it as a commodity.

Samuel Wong offers a final perspective about the invisibility of Asian Americans and the myths that a white racist society perpetuates about the "model minority": "Thanks to institutional racism, Asians in America are not only invisible, we are also inaudible. We learn an inapt foreign language in order to communicate among ourselves and with white America, and our linguistic efforts are often received with critical condescension. . . . As long as Asian Americans remain acquiescent, we are the 'model minority.' "[34] This statement clearly reveals the violence of assimilation and integration. Assimilation means the loss of one's culture and the public denial of one's distinctive identity. Assimilation is the quiet silencing of a people. Assimilation requires people to turn away from their cultural roots and heritage and take on the imposed dominant culture. Bell Hooks speaks about assimilation as a clear strategy in the larger system of white supremacy: "It is a strategy deeply rooted in the ideology of white supremacy and its advocates urge black people to negate blackness, to imitate racist white people so as to better absorb their values, their way of life."[35] Assimilation and integration become closely aligned, and serve as tools in the maintenance of domination.

It is important for white people in the society and in the church to look critically at assimilation and integration. Often integration is offered as the liberal answer to racial injustice. However, integration in a society that is ruled by white people often means political, social, and cultural suicide: "Liberation from racism does not automatically mean integration. Blacks, Asians, Hispanics, and Native Americans have discovered with sadness that integration has meant the subjection of ethnic minority people to white-dominated churches and nation. Integration meant mixing, but it did not mean a change in racism."[36] Cultural imperialism flows from white supremacy, and white supremacy is not altered or transformed by assimilation or integration. White supremacy is dethroned by a radical shifting of power, a transformed understanding of what is humanly valuable and important, a total reconstruction of social and culture reality, and a commitment to reparation.

PREACHING CONVERSION

There are many important pastoral, theological, and ethical issues to be considered in an agenda for addressing white racism and white supremacy in our preaching ministries. However, my reflections here will be focused within the framework of one theological concept and category, that of conversion.

Even though conversion as a traditional theological category has a complex and debated history in the Christian church, it best represents a very essential dimension of our spiritual and theological agenda. In traditional terms, conversion involves turning *from* one reality and turning *toward* another. Conversion involves the whole person and transforms the intellectual, spiritual, emotional, and physical dimensions of our personhood and our society. Only change that is this profound is worthy to be called conversion.

Conversion is so thorough in its transforming implications that it cannot be separated from justice and reparation. Justice is the goal we hope to reach, and reparation gives us concrete clues about the necessary human actions that might move us closer to that reality. Reparation points to dimensions of the agenda that are very difficult for us to embrace: making amends, atonement, repairing. Before racial justice will ever be a reality there are actions that must be taken, amends that must be made, repairs that must be done. Conversion must involve all these things, and more.

Dimensions of Conversion

Conversion means fundamental and radical change. In relation to white racism and white supremacy, conversion for white people means several things:

1. It means changing one's basic worldview, as one struggles for an equal valuing of all, not a selective valuing of some.

2. It means repentance and relinquishment — repenting for one's own white racism and relinquishing power.

3. It means reparation. It means listening more than speaking, hearing more than being heard, learning more than instructing. It means healing and repair.

4. It means accepting the rage of people of color as important and necessary, even when one is the recipient.

5. It means living through transforming deaths and giving up all the unquestioned assumptions one makes about natural birthright.

6. It means being out of control, disoriented, and lost as one strives to turn from a known world in which one dominates to an unknown world in which one shares.

7. It means justice. Conversion involves actively struggling against powers, structures, attitudes, and institutions that provide the foundation and justification for white supremacy.

Confession of Complicity and Sinfulness

For white Christians and preachers, the necessary starting point of their pastoral, theological, and ethical agenda might be the profound confession that their social structures are sinful to the root. "Sin, like its companion mystery, grace, cannot finally be understood; it can only be stood under, contemplated, and *confessed*."[37] Many things lead to human transformation and conversion. Knowing that something in our human relations is radically amiss or experiencing the social structuring of our world as fundamentally wrong might be preludes to conversion.

It is painful and overwhelming for white people to discern and acknowledge that the very foundations upon which this country rests are sinful. In "We, the White People," Calvin Morris says:

> The founders of this nation faced a dilemma posed by the conflict between freedom and slavery. A people proclaiming as the bedrock of their political existence the concept of human liberty as a natural endowment given by God nonetheless held others in

chains. Thus, the United Stated was founded upon political and moral ambiguities so profound that its characterization of itself as a land of freedom and human liberty has to it the sound of hypocrisy.[38]

To label this reality as a kind of sinfulness that thoroughly permeates our social fabric seems one important way of naming the depth of the violence. This is a kind of sinfulness that goes beyond the confines of individual morality. The embodied and systematized sinfulness of white supremacy suggests that there is fundamental alienation and violence at the very core of our human existence. The Christian church has unfortunately often given more attention to individual and personal understandings of sin than to the collective dimensions of this reality of our human situation. Douglas Hall speaks to the collective nature of sin in his book *God and Human Suffering*.[39] In an effort to clarify some of the original intentions behind a traditional concept like original sin, Hall says: "In the classical traditions of Christian theology, this sense of the tragic used to be named *original sin*. The dogma of original sin, one of the dogmas that theological liberalism discarded (perhaps it had to), was meant in its better expressions to symbolize precisely this sense of sin and of the suffering caused by collective human sin."[40]

Original sin unfortunately has been reduced to an individualistic notion of the fall so that it has lost much of its clarity and power as an understanding of the collective human condition. Hall also points out that in an effort to understand and name the mystery of collective sinfulness the Christian tradition has used such language as "principalities and powers," and such concepts as the demonic. "There are 'principalities and powers' which transcend the individual thoughts, words, and deeds through which they come to be enacted and are perpetuated."[41] He calls us back to the mystery of human sinfulness. This in no way relieves one from the concrete human responsibility one has for one's actions in the world or from complicity with evil. However, understanding the mystery of sinfulness and accepting that it can never be fully understood allow us to move on to the more important tasks of repentance, conversion, and reparation. Confessing the radical sinfulness of one's own individual white racism and one's participation in the radical sinfulness of white supremacy is a necessary step in the process of conversion.

Naming and Understanding Whiteness

For white people in the larger society and in the Christian church, a part of the work of conversion involves naming and understanding their own whiteness. This is particularly crucial in understanding and resisting cultural imperialism.

In 1990 I participated in a Women and the Word event sponsored by the Anna Howard Shaw Center at Boston School of Theology. Its theme was "Honoring Difference: Women's Cross-cultural Realities and Preaching." Sungmin Haesun Kim (formerly Haesun Kim), who is Korean, Joan Martin, who is an African American, and I were the three women who composed the primary leadership team, although there were many women who gave additional leadership through preaching, liturgical celebrations, reflection groups, and administrative work.

From the moment the theme of "honoring difference" was established until the culmination of the conference, this event became a powerful source of confrontation, growth, and transformation for my life. Preparations for this event and my close work with Joan and Sungmin became a constant process of dealing with my own white racism. This conference challenged me to discern and acknowledge the powers and privileges of my own white supremacy and to reflect on the implications of my whiteness. I have heard many women of color say that white women must "do their work" before there can be any authentic dialogue, and certainly any "honoring." In many ways I did not know what that meant. I assumed it meant doing one's work to expose and resist white racism. I did not fully understand that it also meant doing one's work to delve into and understand the terrain of one's whiteness. I have also heard women and men of color speak about social location. I understand that the specificity and particularity of one's social location are critical in the shaping of a person's theology, ministry, and preaching. But I did not understand how to name my particularity beyond such general labels as woman, or feminist, or middle-class person. I still have much to learn about this kind of naming.

In the opening plenary of the conference I spoke the words that follow. (I include them in their entirety, and unchanged from how I spoke them publicly.) This kind of confessional statement is a part of the work of understanding one's whiteness and acknowledging what social location actually means.

I am aware that the evolution of my social and theological consciousness has been fundamentally shaped by the realities of my social location. My roots are in southern Ohio. I grew up in the small town of Wheelersburg, in many ways in the heart of Appalachian reality and culture. My mother, Betty Smith, was an elementary school teacher for twenty-five years, and my father, Raymond Smith, worked as a conductor on freight trains for the Norfolk and Western Railroad for thirty-eight years. My maternal grandmother, Estella Brooks, worked in the home, and my maternal grandfather, Jesse Brooks, ran a small, self-owned business in Portsmouth, Ohio. My paternal grandfather, Stanley Smith, painted houses, and my paternal grandmother, Lucina Bolton, worked most of her life at a shoe factory in Portsmouth.

My parents were strong union people. They articulated very strong, supportive commitments about racial equality, the civil rights movement, the inhumanity of capital punishment, the shame of Kent State, and the tragedy of Vietnam. As a family we were a strong, cohesive unit. My mother was highly involved in the local community, and we had plenty of friends, but there was an enormous and painful isolation because of the way we thought, and the way we lived. These realities are the roots of my present social location.

Several other realities shape my present social location. I am white; I am a woman; I am a feminist; I am a middle-stratum, North American person; I am able-bodied; and I am a person who continues to choose the Christian church as my primary religious community. Sometimes for me to comprehend the privileges connected to most of these realities, I need to say these affirmations in a negative way. My evolution has been just as fundamentally shaped by my *not* being a person of color, by my *not* being a man, by my *not* being a person with any discernible disability, by my *not* being a person who is poor in this country, by my *not* being a person from the Two-Thirds World, and by my *not* being a person who is Jewish or Muslim or Hindu. I find that it is very hard work to get clear, and stay clear, about who I am, what I am, and what that means, and to get clear, and stay clear, about who I am not, what I am not, and what that means. This clarity is essential in the *honoring of difference*, and these distinctive particularities have everything to do with the quality and meaning of my own theological, social, and political evolution.

Let me then say a word about some of what I feel it means that I am white, a woman, a feminist, a middle-stratum North American, an able-bodied person, and a religious person within the Christian church.

Being white means that I know the experience of being dominant. When this dominance protects me from exploitation, suffering, and oppression, I feel grateful. When this dominance separates me from much of the human community, I feel guilty, immobilized, enraged, and enlivened to act. I experience the shame and the power of my whiteness being considered normative by systems, values, structures, and persons that uphold white supremacy. I experience the illusion, and the truth, that I have a choice as to whether I speak against racism and work to resist it, or remain comfortably silent.

Being a woman means that I know the experience of being dominated. Being a woman means that I continually feel afraid of male violence and power. Being a woman means there are times that I feel invisible, devalued, and despised. Being a woman means that I am economically and politically disenfranchised because of my gender. Being a woman means that I know and experience relational power more than political and institutional power.

Being a feminist means I experience and know the strength of white woman's bonding, participate in and create women's coalitions across lines of difference, and share in women's diverse work for transformation. Being a feminist means I unapologetically commit primary time, energy, and resources to the empowerment of women. Being a feminist means that I am committed to a worldview and praxis that seek to address the systematic injustices of classism, racism, heterosexism, ageism, handicappism, imperialism, and sexism, from the perspective of women and their lived experiences of oppression.

Being a middle-stratum North American means that I experience economic abundance in relation to most of the people of the globe. It means that I understand that the economic abundance in which I share directly results in economic poverty in vast places in the world. It means that I do not experience my life as one of survival, for I do not actively struggle for enough to eat, a place of shelter, or adequate health care. It means I am isolated and separated from daily poverty, and I must continually work to raise my consciousness about, and my level of involvement in, the concrete, material realities of the poor.

Being an able-bodied person means that I presently live my life relatively free of anxiety or concern about mobility and access. It means I grew up thinking about myself as normal, and either thinking about people with disabilities very little, or thinking people with disabilities were something other than normal. It means I will spend a lifetime trying to unlearn this assumption. It means that I do not have to spend my own economic resources for hearing aids, wheelchairs, attendant care, special learning materials, and large quantities of prescription medicine. It means that I spend a lot of my energy reacting against my own physical dependence and being painfully quiet about my own physical limitations and frustrations.

Being a religious person within the Christian church means that I live in constant theological and spiritual struggle. It means I embrace and participate in God's ongoing revelation in the community of Christian persons who work for just structures, who participate in the healing of creation, and who speak and act on behalf of life. It also means that I find myself a part of a church community that does violence with sacrificial theology, judges with simplistic moralisms, and oppresses with endless justifications for present social reality. It means that as a person ordained to word and sacrament I actively participate in clericalism. As a member of the United Methodist Church, I keep my membership in a denomination that silences lesbian and gay people, and as a teacher within a Christian seminary, I participate in the training of religious leaders for work in a religious institution that I am outraged by, and yet respect.

This is only some of who I am; this is only some of who I am not; this is only some of what it means for me to be the person I am today.

I do indeed find it very hard work to get clear, and stay clear, about who I am, what I am, who I am not, and what I am not, and about the meaning and significance of all this for my work in the world. But honoring human difference, my own and others, is what this clarity is all about, and the honoring of women's cross-cultural differences is what this event is all about.

There is a vastness in the differences among us as human persons. There are so many human realities I have not touched, have not known, and have not understood. This is not an excuse for ignorance, for unquestioned privilege, or for a release from accountability and responsibility. This is a descriptive fact, and it becomes an occasion for profound caution about my own limitations, continual confrontation about my own denial of difference, and empowered acceptance of my own particularity.

I believe this statement has everything to do with naming and resisting white supremacy, and understanding whiteness. I believe it has everything to do with theology, and with preaching. A part of our conversion process as white preachers is the naming and claiming of our whiteness and what that reality truly means.

Acknowledging and Transforming Our Language

Language is a central part of all cultures. Language reflects the worldview of individuals and communities. In many ways, preachers understand the power of language. Language can empower or diminish; it can hurt or it can heal; it can stereotype or it can free; it can imprison or it can liberate.

It should be no surprise to white people that in a world where white supremacy is the reality language will be racist. "If one accepts that our dominant white culture is racist, then one would expect our language — an indispensable transmitter of culture — to be racist as well."[42] A part of the conversion process for white preachers and congregations involves an honest examination of their language.

The Racism and Sexism Resource Center for Educators has published a helpful book entitled *Racism in the English Language*. The book examines eight ways our language reflects white racism:

1. Obvious bigotry — blatant words like "Jap," "chink," or "spic"; or referring to African-American persons as colored, etc.

2. Color symbolism — the symbolism of white as positive and dark as negative, white as purity and black as evil.

3. Ethnocentrism — words or phrases that represent particular perspectives, like "slaves" versus "African people held in captivity," or "the master raped his slave" versus "the white captor raped an African woman held in captivity."

4. Passive tense — omissions in our descriptions, such as saying "the continental railroad was built," without speaking about the fact that Chinese laborers built much of it, and were terribly oppressed in the process.

5. Politics and terminology — phrases that have political implications, such as "culturally deprived" versus "culturally dispossessed," and "economically disadvantaged" versus "economically exploited."

6. Loaded words — words that have a particularly negative impact on certain racial or ethnic communities — words like "victory" in the description of battles won by white people, and "massacres" as the indiscriminate killing done by Native Americans, or words and phrases like "darkest Africa," "primitive," or "uncivilized" used in reference to the location and social reality of Africa.

7. Qualifying adjectives — words that reflect racist qualifiers, the "well-dressed" black man and his wife, the "passive and quiet" Asian.

8. Speaking English — the depiction of people of color speaking English in ways that make them appear ignorant and incapable.[43]

Our language is critically important, and every aspect of our language conveys a message. There are the countless negative associations in our language with the color black and the quality of blackness. There are the predominantly positive associations with the color white and the quality of whiteness. It is naive to underestimate the power of these associations fundamentally to shape our experience of color in human relationships and in the social fabric in which we live. Color symbolism abounds in the Christian faith. It is found in the sacred scriptures of our faith, the hymns and doctrines we have inherited, and the theological assumptions we do not question. The issue of color symbolism is critical, and the issue of language is not trivial.

There are many examples from the Gospel of John that demonstrate the association of light with purity, darkness with sinfulness. This association flows into the association of white with goodness and black with evil. I would invite white preachers to reflect on what these unquestioned lines and affirmations from scripture might really imply: "The light shines in the darkness, and the darkness did not overcome it" (John 1:5); "And this is the judgment, that the light has come into the world, and people loved darkness rather than light, because their deeds were evil" (John 3:19). Those who worked on the *Inclusive-Language Lectionary* clearly comment on the racism of color symbolism:

> The New Testament imagery of light versus darkness is often used to contrast good with evil. The equation of darkness with evil, or that which is done in secret and out of the light, has unfortunately led some persons and groups to condemn and reject anything that is black or any dark-hued person as evil or somehow condemned by God.... While the biblical context may be free from racist intent, the too-easy misconception that dark people are also condemned and to be avoided has led to the use in this lectionary of terminology other than "darkness and white" as metaphors for what is either condemned or loved by God.[44]

Preachers should not be deceived into believing that color symbolism is unimportant. In a recent newspaper of a mainline Protestant denomination, there were letters to the editor in response to the editor's comments on color symbolism and language. One woman said, "The main issue here has nothing to do with a person's skin color. The color white is understood throughout the world as being clean, pure and wholesome no matter what color we are."[45]

In this woman's attempt to claim the objectivity of language, she powerfully reveals the impact of its subjectivity and bias. White preachers must begin to demonstrate conversion in the use and content of their language.

Equally offensive are images of "free persons and slaves" that permeate the language of many sermons. Many white preachers use slave imagery without clearly thinking through its devastating implications for African Americans. If large numbers of white persons had had ancestors who were in slavery in this country, I believe this imagery would cease. Even though it is biblical imagery, we need to understand the social context in which we preach and choose alternative imagery for our expressions about the conditions of human life.

Transformation as Re-membering

The acts of remembering and re-membering are important in the lives of many contemporary women. We remember and honor the women who have gone before us, and we re-member, or make whole, our collective body, claiming and acknowledging the women who have helped make us a whole people.

I invite white preachers, women and men alike, to bring these acts of remembering and re-membering into the liturgical life of our congregations, and into the content of our preaching. These acts of remembering/ re-membering become a part of our ongoing conversion process away from white supremacy and white racism.

What might happen to our Christian communities if we were to remember/re-member Yom HaShoah — Holocaust Remembrance Day — in our worship life and in our sermons each spring?[46] What words of repentance and confession might we speak on Columbus Day for the millions of Native American people who were annihilated and removed from their land? It would be good if we could find the courage to speak words of mourning in addition to words of celebration for both the loss and the abundance represented by Thanksgiving. How might our communities see themselves differently if each year preachers and communities across this country remembered/re-membered the internment of thousands of Japanese Americans in concentration camps within our own borders?[47] And during the weeks of February when this nation celebrates the history and culture of African Americans, how might our understanding of the violence of white supremacy be altered if we remembered/re-membered the concrete human conditions and realities of slavery in the United States? And how might we learn to struggle against imperialism differently if February 2, 1848, was remembered/re-membered in our religious communities as the day when U.S. military forces divided the Mexican people, claiming what is now Texas, New Mexico, Arizona, Colorado, and California as U.S. territory?[48]

Conversion involves change and transformation. But the direction for that change might be powerfully informed by white preachers and communities honestly remembering/re-membering critical and indicting events in the saga of white supremacy.

Honoring Difference

I want to say a word about the violence and denial that are aspects of unity and reconciliation, and then a final word about the power of honoring difference. For much of white Christianity, the quest for unity and reconciliation too often becomes a religious naming for assimilation. Our religious communities are being called to dwell in the land of honoring difference, and to dwell there for a very long time. Unity and reconciliation can happen only when the just and powerful act of honoring difference breaks the power and structures of white supremacy. Unity and reconciliation are a part of the kind of religious and theological agenda that keeps white racism and white supremacy distant, mystified, and intact.

Susan Thistlethwaite has deepened my understanding of honoring difference and confronted me with my own quest for unity. She says:

> As a member of the white women's movement, I have not confronted the terror of difference. Instead, I have sought to obliterate it in "connections." The point I have tried to convey ... is that white women's selves have been forged by the dominant culture to provide the connections: This learning has its strengths, but in relation to cultural and racial difference, it should be defined as sin for white women.[49]

White preachers and congregations are now called to linger in the terror of difference. White people are being called to turn from our need to unify, to reconcile, to connect, toward the work of confessing, resisting, and honoring. A part of our conversion will be found in that lingering. Honoring difference is about people calling each other's lives into question. It is about confusion and disorientation, and it is about new clarity and reorientation. It is about the deepest and most profound respect we know. Honoring difference is about respecting the truth and the reality of another, and allowing one's self to be challenged and changed. To honor is to speak our differences, to live them, to be them. It is to sometimes be silent in the face of their mysteries, and to allow them to make powerful claims upon our lives.

Conversion is an important part of the theological and ethical agenda for white preachers and congregations struggling against white supremacy. Conversion is the changing of people and the transformation of social reality. It is a turning, it is a rebirth, it is a metamorphosis, as religious individuals and communities move from supremacy to parity, from domination to honoring.

✧ 6 ✧

Crosses Reveal Privilege—
CLASSISM

THE DIAMONDS ON LIZ'S BOSOM

The diamonds on Liz's bosom
are not as bright
as his eyes
the morning they took him
to work in the mines
The rubies in Nancy's
jewel box (Oh, how he
loves red!)
not as vivid
as the despair
in his children's
frowns.

Oh, those Africans!

Everywhere you look
they're bleeding
and crying
Crying and bleeding
on some of the whitest necks
in your town.

—Alice Walker[1]

Classism involves the systematic denial, domination, and oppression of people because of their economic conditions and status. Classism exists where there is an unequal structuring of economic realities and power. Classism depends upon, and reinforces, differential treatment, economic stratification, and social distinctions. The violence of classism cannot fundamentally be separated from all the other forms of oppression. The particularities of race, gender, age, disability, and sexuality all form a constellation of factors that complicate and contribute to class distinctions and economic oppression.

Economic conditions are foundational realities in human existence. Class distinctions have direct and immediate ramifications in people's lives. There are people in this world who experience the abundance of creation while others do not have enough to sustain life. There are people who live in comfortable homes while millions of people are homeless. There are people who have enough food, adequate health care, and constant employment. There are others who are hungry, without health care of any kind, and unemployed. Classism has to do with unequal economic distribution, intentionally created poverty and exploitation, and the concentrated power of elites. In a world where there is an unequal distribution of resources and wealth, there are worlds of privilege and worlds of survival. These worlds are in direct relationship to one another.

Jon Sobrino poignantly confronts us with a truth we would like to deny:

> At present human kind is not simply differentiated but deeply divided. The basic difference is between being close to life or close to death, between affluent societies where life and the most basic rights of the human person are safeguarded, and societies where misery, blatant violation of human rights, and death prevail. What makes this division especially critical is that these differences do not simply coexist; they stand in a mutual cause-and-effect relationship.[2]

For worlds of privilege to continue for some parts of the human family and in some corners of the globe, class distinctions must be rigidly maintained, and extreme measures must be taken in order to secure the status quo. This is how I have come to understand better the role of global economic imperialism and the necessity of militarism. Global imperialism has to do with the specific measures world powers will elect and carry out in order to enforce systematic economic exploitation. Militarism is often the alignment of military strength and terrorism with the economically elite and powerful. Imperialism and militarism are the global repercussions of classism.

When I originally envisioned the chapters in this book, I imagined a chapter on classism and a chapter on imperialism. I now believe that they must be understood and analyzed together as different dimensions of basic economic disparity. Violence in the inner cities of the United States, rural Appalachian poverty, and the exploitation of women workers all along the border between Mexico and the United States are intricately related to the foreign debt of Bolivia, international trade agreements, systems of apartheid, and military dictatorships worldwide.

The connections and complexities of global economic realities appear difficult and overwhelming, and in the face of these challenges, preachers and religious communities have often been painfully silent. I understand the silence well. It is not happenstance that it has taken me months to write this particular chapter. Economic realities leave many of us feeling inadequate in our analysis, complacent in our privilege, and despairing about systemic change. J. Philip Wogaman expresses what many people feel when he says, "Most people care about what happens to society, and some care passionately. But the relationship between our dreams and visions for the common life and the hard realities of economics often remains obscure."[3]

The words that follow are an attempt to make aspects of our collective economic life less obscure. In the face of such an enormous challenge, I have organized my reflections and analysis in this chapter around some of the specific repercussions of class stratification and economic disparity, holding in tension and dialogue both the national and international manifestations of the violence.

RADICALIZING MOMENTS

Understanding classism has been a slow and painful process in my social and theological evolution. Three experiences are worth noting in terms of my growing understanding of how class influences the personal, national, and international dimensions of our lives.

My life has been shaped in a significant way by my parents' understandings of labor, their commitments to the rights of the working class, and their positive attitudes about union organizing. My father was a strong union man on the Norfolk and Western Railroad, and my mother was a bold spokeswoman for her local teacher's association. I grew up with a very clear understanding that working people had to struggle for just wages and benefits whether they were elementary school teachers or conductors on freight trains. I soon came to realize that this struggle involved power, bargaining, and danger. As an adult, I more fully appreciate the dramatic way my parents' convictions and worldviews have shaped my own views of work, economics, and class.

But it was not just what was *spoken* about work and class that influenced my life; what was not spoken was critical as well. I now understand that *classism* is what elevated the role and education of a school teacher and devalued the manual labor of a railroad worker. As an adult I continue to reflect upon the enormous gap between the world of my paternal grandmother, who worked in a shoe factory most of her life, and the education and enculturation of her two granddaughters. This gap pertains to the pain and alienation of classism within a family. I am still trying to comprehend the differing worlds of my mother's and father's childhoods. My mother grew up in a well-to-do home; my father grew up in a home where they could eat meat only on Sundays. These vastly different worlds had to do with classism, and both of these worlds continue to influence and shape my commitments and ideas about economic injustice and class.

In the spring of 1989 I represented Princeton Theological Seminary at a gathering of theological educators who were invited to the University of Dubuque Theological Seminary to examine its Rural Ministry Program Center for Theology and Land. One of the Dubuque professors made a profound impact upon my analysis and thinking. He contrasted his work among the indigenous Mayan Indians in Guatemala with his work among rural Iowa farmers. He noted that Guatemalan Indians displaced from the land understand the situation of their lives to be one of economic exploitation and oppression while Iowa farmers understand farm foreclosures as indications of personal failure.[4] This insight plunged me into a great deal of reflection about the levels of denial of economic realities operative within the American populace and the inability of many individuals in our country to make national and international connections.

How is it that people in this country still believe that personal laziness accounts for the thousands of homeless people on the streets of all our cities? What keeps hundreds of family farmers from seeing that their farms are being intentionally and systematically closed down by a new economic order? What will it take for people to acknowledge that we live in a time when many people who are fully employed still cannot pay their monthly bills and have no hope of ever owning a home? Preachers and religious communities have a crucial role to play in helping people begin to make connections between the economic realities of their daily lives and the global economic realities that are powerfully shaping our world.

Even though I will speak more fully about Guatemala later in this chapter, I want here to lift up my time there as one of the most radicalizing experiences in my life regarding economic imperialism and militarism. U.S. imperialism, as it relates to the economic exploitation of other countries, no longer is distant and removed from particular countries and particular people. Guatemala has become the place and the reality that help me confront the tyranny and violence of U.S. economic imperialism. The truth of the cause-and-effect relationship of privilege and poverty became real to me during a trip to one of the largest barrios in Guatemala City. Barrio Esperanza (that is, Barrio Hope) was filled with thousands of people who had been displaced from their homes due to the military terror and violence rampant throughout the countryside. This violence is directly funded and supported with U.S. dollars. Two women workers led us through the streets of Esperanza speaking clearly and directly about the struggles and the suffering of the people there. When we were ready to leave, one of them walked us to our van, looked each of us in the eyes, and said, "Work for change in the United States."⁵ This was a powerful moment. The lives of the people in Esperanza depend on political change in the United States. The work preachers and religious communities do on their behalf changes the cause-and-effect relationship of privilege and poverty.

NAMING AND UNDERSTANDING THE VIOLENCE

In previous chapters some of the repercussions of classism have been described: economic violence in relation to people of color, growing numbers of older adults who live in poverty, and perpetual devaluation and exploitation of women's work in the global market economy. It is impossible to understand fully white racism, sexism, and ageism without a clear recognition of the places where these experiences of oppression intersect with class and economic exploitation. I want to continue this descriptive process by naming some additional repercussions of classism in the United States, followed by a description of the more global dimensions of economic imperialism as it relates to the particular country of Guatemala. What follows is largely intended as a descriptive naming of some of the realities that preachers and religious communities must seriously consider in preaching and education; it is not intended as a thorough analysis of any particular dimension of the violence of classism.

Class: Silence, Denial, and Alienation

One of the indications of just how basic class is as a foundational dimension of our individual and collective lives is the degree to which it is surrounded by silence and denial. Class distinctions create separate cultures, different value systems, and diverse worldviews. "Class is a crucial factor in defining how people see the world, their place in it, and their response to it."⁶ But in the United States, a country deeply divided economically, these cultures, value systems, and worldviews do not coexist; they are in direct competition with each other.

This competition has to do with the valuing of people's labor and the monetary benefits and rewards that come from that labor. This competition has to do with people's time and bodies and with the control of production. This competition has to do with people's identity and freedom and the extreme differentials between people in terms of self-determination and geographic mobility. This disparity and competition are foundational to capitalism, yet there is a strange, pervasive silence about their devastating repercussions. Richard Sennett and Jonathan Cobb in *The Hidden Injuries of Class* boldly name the violence when they say, "The terrible thing about class in our society is that it sets up a contest for dignity."[7]

A contest for dignity would be violating enough, but in a class-stratified society, all the criteria that determine degrees of worth and dignity are controlled by those who are economically at the top. Management and professional jobs possess greater status and social rewards than the jobs of manual laborers. Mental work is valued more than manual work. Independent, self-sufficient workers are envied and admired more than workers whose work depends on the collective efforts of an assembly line. This unequal valuing of human beings based on education, kind of labor, degree of autonomy, and level of monetary compensation produces deep levels of anxiety and alienation.

The specific faces of this alienation among us are complex and inextricably related to our class position. Barbara Ehrenreich writes about the "fear of falling" in her book about the tenuous life of the middle class:

> For the American middle class is not, of course, a ruling class. Even its most privileged members find themselves blocked by higher powers. The magazine editor must bow, occasionally, to the financial power of the publisher or the advertisers. Industrial scientists and engineers see cherished innovations dropped because they will not realize quick profits. The tenured faculty finds its autonomy checked by the aggregated wealth of the board of trustees. Whatever power can be won through skill, ambition, and strength of will can ultimately be outweighed by the force of capital.[8]

These are difficult words for many middle-class people in the United States who continue to believe that professional status, higher education, or individual initiative will ultimately protect them from the harsh realities of class hierarchy.

The church has often been a place where illusions of economic security are reinforced for the middle class as preachers encourage and perpetuate myths of rugged individualism and the American dream of autonomy and success. The discrepancy between what middle-class people *want* to believe is economically possible in their lives and what concrete *limits* actually exist is often the cause of great denial and alienation. Understanding "the force of capital" as well as the limits of middle-class power is a part of the pastoral and political responsibilities of contemporary preachers.

Another face of this alienation shows itself in the lives of those who have been traditionally understood as the working class. Working hard is highly valued, and one of the primary beliefs held by the working class is that America is a land of endless opportunity and economic possibility. How then will working-class people understand their lives when hard work, perseverance, long hours, and job loyalty still send them spiraling downward economically, or leave them unemployed? Karen Bloomquist, in a chapter about the struggles and dilemmas of working people, suggests that they compensate in four distinctive ways:

1. blaming the disparity on an impeding situation over which one has little control, for example, the economy or job market;

2. lowering one's personal aspirations so that they are more in line with one's actual achievements . . . ;

3. inflating or counterfeiting one's achievements to convince oneself and others that one really has not fallen short . . . ;

4. contrasting one's relative "success" with the situation of those who are more visible "failures," in order to feel superior to "them."[9]

All people must have ways of making sense of reality when their hopes are in such dramatic contrast to the actual possibilities. It is a powerful source of alienation for working-class people to continue to believe in the myth of the American dream while simultaneously experiencing this myth as a lie in their own lives. This alienation takes the form of self-blame and individual shame, even though the violence is systemic and structural. "The real self is confined to the private realm of [people's] family and friends, feeling powerless to change the wider realities that impact their lives."[10]

As this country faces a growing number of people who are literally the working poor, it is increasingly critical that preachers and religious communities understand this alienation. "In 1990 approximately 40.3 percent of poor persons 15 years and over worked, and 9.4 percent worked year around, full time."[11] These figures are shocking as they confront us with the reality that millions of people actually work year round and still cannot move out of poverty. What will the church and its preachers say in the face of what Bloomquist calls "the dream betrayed"?[12]

There are specific dimensions of the denial and alienation of classism that pertain directly to privilege and affluence. In *The Poverty of Affluence*, Paul L. Wachtel says:

I believe it is time for a fundamental reexamination of our assumptions about the relation between economic productivity and personal well-being. Much of what we produce we neither need nor really enjoy. In many instances, the adverse effects upon both the physical and the social environment have far outweighed the benefits of the goods produced. Indeed, it may not be too farfetched to suggest that as we now pay farmers not to grow certain

crops, we might derive a certain societal benefit by paying workers — at least over a transition period — not to produce certain
goods we have been paying them to produce.[13]

These words may seem absurd, but they quickly immerse us into some
of the destructive and alienating repercussions of affluence, consumer-
ism, and ever-increasing production. Not only do possessions often
leave the affluent empty and disconnected, but many people who experience some of the privileges of the middle class are caught up as well
in wasteful consumption that is threatening our very survival on the
planet. Pollution, minimally regulated technology, and decline of community are manifestations of deep alienation in relation to the earth and
to the larger human community in the lives of the affluent.[14]

In the face of unemployment, subsistence living, work that has no in-
trinsic meaning, and limited health care, these dimensions of alienation
may not seem as important. In reality, the alienated and exploitative
relations of the affluent do indeed threaten the well-being of all. The
contrast between worlds of privilege and worlds of survival does not
simply exist between the First World and the Two-Thirds World; the
same contrast exists in this country and is created by some of the repercussions of affluence. Just as preachers are challenged to speak to a
fearful middle class and also to working-class people who feel betrayed
by the illusions of the American dream, the lives of the affluent in this
country stand in need of a discerning and confrontational word.

There is one additional aspect of denial and alienation that is important to acknowledge here — the obvious alienation and conflict
that exist across class lines. There is conflict because power is unequal.
Clearly there will be class conflict in a classist society. It is not difficult
to discern and name some of the obvious expressions of that conflict.
There is struggle between assembly-line workers and factory owners.
There is conflict between union organizers and management. Small-
town businesses struggle to survive in relation to conglomerates. These
struggles and conflicts are not benign; they are oftentimes economically
and socially devastating.

> For working-class people, relations with the middle class are usu-
> ally a one-way dialogue. Ideas seldom flow "upward" to the mid-
> dle class, because there are simply no structures to channel the up-
> ward flow of thought from class to class. Graduate-school courses
> do not invite "ordinary" people to speak to classes of professionals-
> in-training. Managers (outside of experiments in improving the
> "quality of work life") do not solicit new approaches from their
> subordinates. Members of the helping professions seldom invite
> suggestions or criticism from their clients, especially clients per-
> ceived as lower class.[15]

Who speaks and who listens, who is consulted and who is ignored, who possesses valuable knowledge and who is expendable — these are all a part of the power and control of class distinctions.

Some of the conflict is more subtle, mystified, and concealed but is no less a part of the oppressive web of classism's alienating impact in people's lives. Some of the conflict, such as the profound class alienation within American families, is so close that we cannot always perceive it. Working-class parents make sacrifices throughout their lives in hopes that their children will rise above them economically, educationally, and socially. This is a kind of alienation that professional, middle-class parents never face. Sennett and Cobb in *The Hidden Injuries of Class* describe this disparity between different classes of working fathers in Boston:

> A middle-class father may pass off the tensions of his work by thinking he is doing it for the kids, but in the process he needn't desire that they rise to a higher class — i.e., that they become unlike him. Working-class fathers . . . see the whole point of sacrificing for their children to be that the children will become unlike themselves.[16]

What will preachers say about the kind of class alienation within families that enculturates some children to rise above their parents' identity and reality, and some children to emulate and model their mothers and fathers? This alienation is difficult to name and discuss, perhaps because for many working people in some fundamental way to do so is such an ultimate betrayal.

In addition to this profound alienation, class creates other discrepancies between working-class families and more affluent families. In *Worlds of Pain*, a landmark study about white, working-class families, Lillian B. Rubin confronted contemporary America with some of those differences. Children in struggling families have a difficult time imagining the future while children born into professional, middle-class homes have dreams of great possibilities. Upward mobility has been a very real possibility in the lives of the professional middle class, a distant dream for most working-class families. Work life is not planned and careers are not charted in the lives of many working-class people; work simply happens. The quality and possibility of leisure time are vastly different for more privileged families than for families struggling for survival.[17] Some of these realities have changed and shifted, but the quality and quantity of differences between families of differing classes are enormous.

This truth challenges the contemporary preacher to deepen her or his analysis and comprehension of some of the more subtle and silenced forms of alienation structured into the very fabric of family life. Until preachers and religious communities are willing to break the silence and denial of class conflict and alienation that exist among us, we will never have a clear picture of the devastating forms of alienation that flow from that disparity. And if we are unable even to acknowledge these "worlds of pain," these "hidden injuries," then we will never be in a position of envisioning a world that might be free of them.

Classism: Worlds of Poverty in the United States

Classism produces hidden pain and injury, alienation within families and communities, conflict in the work place, and wasteful consumption. But classism also produces abject poverty, unemployment, malnutrition and hunger, a ghetto underclass, homelessness, and death. These are some of the harshest faces of classism, and the most denied. These are the daily repercussions of economic disparity in the United States.

Poverty   Michael Harrington in *The New American Poverty* describes what the United States faces today when he says, "Two decades after the President of the United States declared an 'unconditional' war on poverty, poverty does not simply continue to exist; worse, we must deal with structures of misery, with a new poverty much more tenacious than the old."[18] Harrington has been confronting contemporary America with the stark realities of poverty for thirty years. His classic, *The Other America: Poverty in the United States*, describes in shocking detail pockets of poverty nationwide that form "the other America." He is clear that there is no one form of poverty that characterizes the other America, but rather poverties, and structures of misery that support them.[19] Although his research is now dated, his shocking revelations are still true. He has been urging people in the United States to attend to the specific contexts and concrete realities of the many faces of poverty among us.

Highlights from *Poverty in the United States: 1990*, published by the United States Bureau of the Census, give us an updated look at some of that specificity:

Persons living below the official government poverty level numbered 33.6 million, representing 13.5 percent of the nation. (This is based on a poverty threshold ranging from $6,652 for a person living alone, $13,359 for a family of four, and $26,848 for a family of nine or more members.)

Approximately half of the nation's poor in 1990 were children under 18 years (40.0 percent) or were elderly (10.91 percent). In addition, another 18.2 percent of the nation's 11.3 million people who are "near poor" are persons who are elderly.

The poverty rate for Blacks (African Americans) was 31.99 percent.

The poverty rate for persons who are of Hispanic origin was 28.1 percent.

About 28.4 percent of the poor receive no assistance of any type, cash or noncash benefits.

The poverty rate for families was 10.7 percent, slightly higher than the 1989 rate of 10.3. And families with a female householder represented 53.1 percent of all poor families.[20]

In recent years growing attention has been given to the poverty of the African-American urban underclass,[21] to poverty and female-headed families,[22] and to poverty and women.[23] Each world of poverty is distinctive, but children, women, African Americans, Hispanics, and Native Americans experience the violence of American poverty in the most severe ways.[24]

There are many people who refuse to acknowledge the reality and causes of poverty in the United States, including many of the religious people in churches and synagogues. Preachers have a moral and ethical responsibility to break the silence of this denial, to educate, and to encourage responses of compassion and justice. In *Economic Justice for All: Pastoral Letter on Catholic Social Teaching and the U.S. Economy*, the U.S. Catholic bishops lift up the concept of social solidarity in addressing the issue of poverty. "The principle of social solidarity suggests that alleviating poverty will require fundamental changes in social and economic structures that perpetuate glaring inequalities and cut off millions of citizens from full participation in the economic and social life of the nation."[25] Preachers need to ask themselves if they are prepared and willing first to explore faithfully the nature and shape of those fundamental changes and then to proclaim what they discover.

Homelessness   It is difficult to determine just how many people are homeless in America. Estimates have varied from over 2 million to less than 250,000.[26] What is true, however, is that the plight and reality of the homeless have become topics of public discourse and debate. The homeless have become some of the most visible signs of economic disparity in this country.

> Huddled over steam vents, in doorways, on the benches of subway and train stations, they remind us daily that economic recovery has not lessened poverty or tempered inequality. They bear the most visible cost of the transformation of American cities by urban renewal, gentrification, and downtown revitalization; of the dismantling of the old industrial economy; and of the government's war on welfare. They show that the richest and most powerful nation in the world cannot provide all its citizens with a decent and secure place in which to live.[27]

Just as the homeless are not easily counted, they are not easily categorized or stereotyped. Homelessness spans all categories of gender, race, age, and social and economic backgrounds. Although people are homeless for varying lengths of time, families with children are the fastest growing category.[28] There are many social and political reasons for the growing numbers of homeless persons in the United States. The job market has changed dramatically in most of our cities, and urban renewal has removed much of the low-income housing that once provided shelter for those that are now homeless. "In only a little more than one decade, between 1970 and 1982, nearly half of all single-room units in America, some 1,116,000, vanished."[29] During this same period of time social welfare programs have been cut or abolished. In a report entitled *The States and the Poor: How Budget Decisions in 1991 Affected Low Income People*, there are up-to-date statistics about the impact of budgetary decisions on the lives of the poor in relation to housing, health care, income assistance, and supplements for elderly individuals living alone. In terms of housing and homeless assistance, the impact was enormous. Ten out of twenty-nine states that had emergency housing assistance programs for the homeless significantly cut their programs. Almost half of twenty-six states appropriating funds for low-income housing programs reduced these appropriations. And even though a few states increased funding for these programs, total state funding for low-income housing programs of various kinds was reduced by $246 million nationwide.[30] All these factors, and many others, give us a clearer picture about our nation's homelessness.

Religious people need to ask many questions about the causes of homelessness and the simplistic judgments that continue to be made. Perhaps our judgments might be tempered by another shocking statistic related to housing. "Publication of the tax expenditure budget can, however, be an embarrassment, since it documents enormous handouts for the middle class and rich; 84 percent of the $19.6 billion in annual lost revenue from the deductibility of mortgage interest goes to people earning more than $30,000 a year."[31] What will preachers say about the homeless in light of this welfare benefit for the more affluent? If we allow this gross inequity to transform our thinking, our words and attitudes about homelessness might not ever be the same.

Unemployment   During 1991 an average of 8.4 million civilian workers were unemployed in the United States. This was a significant increase over 1990, during which the annual average was estimated to be 6.9 million. This figure does not include the estimated 1 million people who have looked for employment, not found it, and given up the search; nor does it include an additional 6 million who desire work full time and can only find part-time employment. In the past four years, unemployment has steadily risen.[32]

Work is necessary for basic survival and for full and active participation in the larger social systems of which people are a part. "To be deprived of the opportunity to work is therefore something worse than the simple loss of income, bad as that usually is. For without meaningful work opportunity we are dehumanized."[33] One of the most alienating and oppressive dimensions of unemployment is the rampant assumption held by countless people that all people can find a job if they really desire one. This simplistic judgment shows no awareness of the complex factors that contribute to unemployment. In 1991 African-American teenagers were unemployed at a rate of 36.3 percent; the unemployment rate of African Americans in general was 12.4 percent; Hispanic unemployment was 9.9 percent; and the unemployment rate of African-American women and men over twenty years of age was almost double this same category of white women and men.[34] These statistics reveal some of the complexity of unemployment. Jobs have disappeared from urban areas; there are great financial difficulties in relocating an entire family; and technological changes have dramatically changed the nature of jobs that are available. People who are looking for jobs simply do not have the skills needed for many of the available employment opportunities. Another critical factor in understanding unemployment is the world market. Jobs have disappeared in this country as plants have closed, moving their capital and work into countries where cheap labor is readily available. Even this simple analysis makes it obvious that unemployment is a highly complex problem with many causes and resultant injuries.

Preachers have a serious challenge to speak a relevant word in a nation that seems to tolerate more than 8 million of its own people being unemployed at any given time. We must not be seduced into thinking that this rate of unemployment is acceptable or necessary in our common life. Preachers might once again be challenged by the words of the U.S. Catholic bishops: "We must first establish a consensus that everyone has a right to employment. Then the burden of securing full employment falls on all of us — policy makers, business, labor, and the general public — to create and implement the mechanisms to protect that right."[35] What role will American preachers play in shaping that public consensus, and what concrete words and visions will we speak calling religious communities to create strategies and structures that secure the right of employment for all people?

Hunger In 1984, the Physician Task Force on Hunger in America, composed of physicians, health experts, and academic and religious leaders from across the nation, was established. Its primary goals were to document the nature and scope of hunger, analyze its regional variations, assess the health effects of hunger, determine why it is a problem, and make recommendations for public response. There were several major findings and conclusions from the task force's study:

- Hunger is a problem of epidemic proportions across the nation.

- Hunger in America is getting worse, not better.

- Malnutrition and ill-health are associated with hunger.

- Hunger is the result of federal government policies.

- Present policies are not alleviating hunger in America.[36]

The task force estimated that some twenty million citizens are hungry for a portion of each month; emergency food programs have increased in every region of the country; health problems and chronic diseases accompany hunger; poverty is at the highest rate it has been in twenty years; and the poorest 40 percent of the American population have significantly less buying power than they did in 1980.[37]

It is difficult to fathom the magnitude of the problem in a country that pays farmers not to grow food and exports some 40 percent of what our national cropland produces.[38] It should be shocking and unacceptable to all of us that social, political, and economic policies create and maintain hunger as a justified repercussion of class inequity. "Hunger occurs because policies either produce it or fail to prevent it.... As a result, America has become a 'soup kitchen society,' a specter unmatched since the bread lines of the Great Depression."[39] During these same years that hunger has been increasing, government decisions and policies have decreased assistance to many of the individuals and families in greatest need. Aid to Families with Dependent Children has become increasingly limited and restricted; the purchasing power of food stamps has decreased; there have been very high rates of inflation; and national budget and tax policies continue to hurt those who are the poorest among us.[40] Public assistance simply does not reach many hungry people in America.

The physicians end their report with a clear challenge not only to political leaders and politicians, but also to religious communities with moral and ethical responsibilities. They certainly offer a challenge to preachers:

> We would not tell sick patients that they might improve without medical treatment if we have the means to treat them and limit their present pain and discomfort. Neither should our political leaders hope that hungry Americans will one day be less hungry when our nation now has the means to respond to their suffering and its underlying cause.[41]

Classism and Global Imperialism

People suffer immensely from homelessness, unemployment, hunger, and poverty within the borders of this nation and around the world. The repercussions of classism and economic injustice are devastating. Many Americans still hold tenaciously to the belief that individuals are primarily at fault rather than social, political, and economic structures. Blaming the individual rather than holding public policies and systems accountable is a part of the attitudinal milieu that creates and sustains the violence of classism.

The same kind of denial, fear, and individualistic thinking that perpetuates a passive tolerance for human oppression in this country spills over into many U.S. citizens' views of and responses to countries of the Two-Thirds World. Economic injustice dominates our national life and flows directly from this country into other nations. Maintaining class inequity demands global economic imperialism and, ultimately, militarism and terror.

In most places in the world economic imperialism is so fundamentally linked with racism that it becomes impossible to distinguish between economic exploitation and genocide. Imperialism leads to a level of tyranny and terror and a breadth of violence that threatens the very existence of communities and nations. Whether those who undergird imperialism in this country and around the globe admit it or not, this kind of tyranny is ultimately about annihilation of some and the preservation of privilege of others.

> Under the cover of rhetoric about "freedom," "democracy," and fighting the "communist menace," the United States is waging a war against the poor and in defense of privilege and empire. Low-intensity conflict is a term that refers to any challenge to U.S. privileges throughout the third world short of conventional or nuclear war. Low-intensity conflict is also the strategy of warfare through which the United States seeks to maintain a system in which death through international finance is the norm, and poor people — not poverty — is the enemy.[42]

My time in Guatemala expanded my understanding of the tyranny and violence of economic imperialism and deepened my awareness of the silence of pulpits and preachers in the United States. The tyranny of economic imperialism and militarism is of such great magnitude globally that it can seem to become an abstraction. Choosing to focus exclusively on the impact of imperialism on Guatemala helps us gain a clearer picture of the specificity and breadth of the violence.

Guatemala is Central America's third largest country, though it is no larger than Tennessee, and has a population of 8.5 million people.

Fifty-five percent of Guatemala's people are Mayan Indians, making up twenty-two language and ethnic groups. Even though the indigenous Mayan population is diverse in language and culture, the major and pronounced division in Guatemala is between the indigenous Indian people and the ladinos. Ladinos are people of mixed Indian and European (largely Spanish) ancestry. Since the Spanish Conquest in 1524 the Indian peoples have been systematically removed from their land and have been terrorized and dominated first by Spanish landowners and then, for at least the past several decades, by the Guatemalan army.[43]

The distribution and use of land are the paramount human and economic issues in Guatemala, as land is the paramount issue in most of Central America. The indigenous population has less and less access to land that is rightfully theirs, and, thus, less means of survival:

> The poor throughout the third world are generally victims of dual injustices. Neither the international economy nor their internal economies are structured to meet their needs. Land and other productive resources remain concentrated in the hands of relatively small minorities. Credit is controlled by and targeted to the rich, and foreign-exchange earnings are squandered in luxury consumption. Land-use is geared to the production of coffee, bananas, beef, fruits, vegetables, and other export crops for foreign markets. The upper and middle classes ensure adequate nutrition by relying on imported foods, but the emphasis on export agriculture, together with a lack of access to productive land, makes hunger a daily companion to the poor.[44]

Over the past few decades communities of the Indian population have been removed from their land and placed in what the military refers to as "model villages." These are only another name for a kind of containment camp where life is directly and indirectly controlled by military force.

Throughout the country, the labor of the indigenous population is exploited on large *fincas* (farms or plantations) owned by a few elite families and in the homes of the economically privileged in Guatemala City. A very small percentage of the population dominates the resources and wealth of the entire country.

In addition to the systematic economic exploitation of the indigenous population by those of Spanish descent within the country itself, there has been economic exploitation from outside. In 1954 the United States invaded Guatemala to protest land reform proposals being inaugurated by President Jacobo Arbenz:

> The profound crisis in Guatemala today began in 1954 with a brutal violation of human rights and of the norms that govern relations

between neighboring countries. At that time, the democratic government of Jacobo Arbenz was destabilized by the covert hand of the U.S. government, backed by the Honduran government and a group of high Guatemalan military officers. This was one of the first victories for "the Company" — the CIA.[45]

The United States invaded Guatemala to defend the economic interests of large U.S.-owned companies and corporations that had operations in that country. United Fruit Company was centrally involved in the covert destabilization of the country's government. Exports by this company had been tax-exempt, and it controlled one-tenth of the Guatemalan economy through exclusive rights related to railroad and telegraph systems.[46] This invasion in 1954 was the beginning of what has now been three and a half decades of escalating violence and terrorism. The United States continues to invade Guatemala politically, culturally, and economically.

Militarism, the systematic control of people by armed terror and violence, serves as the perpetual force and tyranny that ultimately perpetuate the overwhelming suffering of the indigenous people. The military assures cheap sources of labor and protects land use for export crops instead of food staples that will feed hungry Guatemalans. This kind of repression has forced thousands of Guatemalans into Mexico and the United States, and into the hillsides and forests of Guatemala itself:

> Guatemala has long been infamous as the hemisphere's worst violator of human rights. . . . Some sources place the total number of deaths at 50,000 to 75,000 for the periods 1978 to 1984. Guatemalan government sources estimate that 100,000 children lost one or both parents to political violence in the early 1980's. And approximately 35,000 people have disappeared at the hands of government security forces over the past two decades.[47]

This indeed is political and economic imperialism, and for Guatemala the forces of that tyranny and violence come from within as well as outside its borders.

The story of Guatemala is overwhelming enough, but many of us in the United States know that this is just one very small part of our country's imperialism within Latin America and around the world. How is a religious person to respond to such violence and tyranny? How do we preach a word of relevance and meaning when entire populations of people are being annihilated inside our country and outside? Why are so many preachers and churches so perversely silent about suffering of this magnitude? This horrible silence and complicity must be broken, and an important part of that process involves a serious look at aspects of our North American theologies that directly and indirectly justify and condone economic violence.

PREACHING: CROSSES AND SACRIFICIAL THEOLOGY

As I have struggled to understand the denial, the oppression, and the violence of classism and economic injustice nationally and internationally, I have been most confronted and encouraged by the work of liberation theologians of Latin America. The clarity of their work in relation to Christology, crosses, and contemporary crucifixions has been powerfully illuminating. Some theologies of the cross serve to justify human suffering and oppression, while other theologies of the cross work in the service of liberation. I want to turn now primarily to the voices and work of those liberation theologians, for I believe that they are challenging the world to do essential deconstructive and constructive theological thinking in relation to economic injustice.

The Theology and Agenda of the Poor

When we attempt to find a way to preach and act in response to classism and its repercussions, we are first and foremost confronted by the poor; and it is the poor who are the central and obvious starting place of Latin American theologians' work. When Leonardo Boff is asked about how to view reality today, he answers: "In Latin America reality must be regarded from where the poor live — from the place of the poor. By 'place of the poor,' I mean the cause of the poor, their sacrificed existence, their struggle, their yearnings for life, labor, dignity, and pleasure."[48]

For persons who have never experienced this kind of poverty and who have lived their entire existence comfortably distanced from this reality, this imperative seems impossible to understand. The only way it becomes truly meaningful is when we take seriously the title of one of Boff's books: *When Theology Listens to the Poor*. It is the poor who must speak their own truths to the world. It is the poor who must do their own theological naming. It is the poor who are organizing collectively to become agents of their own liberation. This is the *ideal* toward which Boff points us, even though we know the empowerment of the poor is far from being realized. Building solidarity with those who are poor and doing what we can to add to that empowerment become our work. Jon Sobrino says:

> This response to the suffering of the poor is an ethical demand, but it is also a practice that is salvific for those who enter into solidarity with the poor. Those who do so often recover in their own life

the deep meaning they thought they had lost; they recover their human dignity by becoming integrated into the pain and suffering of the poor. From the poor they receive, in a way they hardly expected, new eyes for seeing the ultimate truth of things and new energies for exploring unknown and dangerous paths.[49]

Those who would build solidarity with the poor of every nation must be willing to do the difficult and far less romantic work with theologies, structures, and systems that create and maintain the violence of poverty that dominates their world. Solidarity begins with an acknowledgment of complicity and the discernment of one's own direct participation in the oppression one sees in the lives of others.

The Violence of Sacrificial Theology

There is a cause-and-effect relationship between the concrete reality of the First World and that of the Two-Thirds World, and there is also a deep connection and relationship between the theological foundations of economic imperialism and its subsequent tyranny. Sacrificial theology is at the heart of the Christian church. Central to the Christian faith and its traditional theology are symbols, doctrines, and faith statements that extol crucifixion, suffering, crosses, and self-sacrifice. For many in the Christian church there are unquestioned theological assumptions and affirmations that proclaim that sacrifice has saving power, that suffering is redemptive, and that crosses are something we are to bear. In the face of the poor of Guatemala, and in the face of millions of Americans who are unemployed, hungry, and homeless, this foundational Christian theology has never seemed more obscene. It not only masks the violence and horror of human suffering, but serves also to justify its existence and continuation. It is naive and irresponsible for theologians and preachers to think that this kind of proclaimed theology does not substantially encourage thousands of people in the United States to fail to respond to suffering within their own country and around the world.

Latin American theologians also help us understand more clearly how such theology functions to undergird and condone incessant violence in Latin America. Two of these theologians have already been mentioned. The liberationist work of Leonardo Boff, a Brazilian theologian, and Jon Sobrino, a theologian and philosopher from El Salvador, continues to challenge and change my theology and my assumptions about the content and act of preaching. The theological affirmations and insights of these two scholars and activists are both instructive and corrective in a theological quest that seeks to begin with the cause and agenda of the poor. Their theologies of the cross, understandings of redemption and salvation, and affirmations of resurrection are radically different from the dominant theology still espoused in most of our churches.

A crucial step in building solidarity with people suffering under the tyranny of imperialism and the oppression of poverty is to stop articulating and proclaiming sacrificial theology. Boff will not let us deny the atrocity of the cross:

> The presence of sin as a destructive historical force is manifest in the thousands of crosses human beings prepare for one another. The crucified are legion. Nearly every human being on the face of the Earth hangs on some cross. This cross is wicked, and an abomination to God. A horrible, persistent cross hunches the shoulders of Latin America's subjugated black and Amerindian cultures.[50]

There must be a fundamental reworking of this theology at every level of the church's life. Not only does sacrificial theology suggest that sacrifice, suffering, and crucifixions are saving, but it also suggests that these experiences are a necessary requirement of human existence and a prerequisite for the Christian moral and ethical life. Thus we must go even further in our critique and reworking of this theology.

In our preaching and in our theology, these Latin American theologians challenge us to stop suggesting that crucifixions are necessary and that suffering is virtuous, and they compel us to declare that all types of inflicted suffering, all intentional crucifixions, and all exploitative sacrifices of life are unjust and fundamentally wrong. There is no confusion in Boff's words, "The *inflicted* death and cross are criminal."[51] As preachers we have a particular responsibility to help our religious communities to begin to name crucifixions as demonic expressions of evil, and we also have the responsibility of helping to enable those same communities to harness their power, their rage, and their ethical activity in an effort to stop the crucifixions. Unemployment, hunger, homelessness, and poverty that can be alleviated *are* inflicted crucifixions.

Crosses and Redemptive Possibilities

As clear as Boff is about the devastating and destructive nature of sacrificial theology, he continues to struggle with what might be redemptive about crosses and, more specifically, how we might preach the cross in this day and age. He poses seven approaches to preaching about death and the cross in a chapter entitled "How Ought We to Preach the Cross in a Crucified Society Today?"[52] His intent is both to expose crosses as evil and to suggest that particular attitudes and approaches to the cross might hold redemptive possibilities for our lives of faith. Three of his approaches seem particularly important to consider:

1. Death and the cross suffered as sacrifice on behalf of those who produce them;

2. Death and the cross accepted as an expression of solidarity with the crucified of history;

3. Death and the cross as locus and moment of their own defeat: resurrection as victory over death and the cross.

Boff examines the idea that crosses suffered as sacrifices can be ultimately embraced as means of transforming those who produce and inflict them. When human beings understand that they are choosing the cross out of freedom and faithfulness, they often are given a clear understanding that the very love and life they embrace and model in their own sacrifice participate in the transformation of a world where crosses prevail, and in the transformation of those who inflict crosses. He believes, "This attitude of acceptance springs from the profound, trusting conviction that only love and forgiveness will ever reestablish the harmony of a broken creation."[53]

Boff is clear that crosses continue to be crimes and that we ought never think they can be legitimated or justified, but ultimately he is suggesting that a part of their possible redemptive power resides in the sheer fidelity to life they may often represent. Boff seeks to confront us with the radicality of this particular approach to the cross: "The Christian way to preach death and the cross is to invite men and women to exercise the capacity residing within them never to leave off loving, cost what it may."[54] This affirmation resonates deeply with my own journey of faith in understanding the life and work of Jesus. However problematic the cross has been for me, I have found the notion of Jesus' fidelity to life at all costs central throughout my life of faith. In our preaching and in the ministry of the Christian faith, we must work diligently to keep this fidelity to life ever present and foundational.

Another equally challenging and transformative approach to the cross might be that persons would see this as an act of solidarity with those who have been crucified throughout history. This approach suggests that to "take up one's cross" is perhaps the ultimate act of solidarity. Our preaching must not suggest that crosses are an end in themselves, but rather that they are the natural repercussion of transforming work in the world. This work is so crucial and so necessary that the church is called into an ultimate investment of its life and ministry. In contrast to crosses being ways of saving those who inflict them, in this approach we are urged to see and name crucifixions as experiences of solidarity with those who are suffering and oppressed. Here we urge the church to take its stand beside the work of the poor and to accept the consequences. "To preach death and the cross in a genuinely Christian manner is to invite our fellow Christians to embrace this powerful, revolutionary love, which is an identification with sufferers such that we actually join them in their struggle with the mechanisms that produce crosses."[55]

Finally, Boff suggests that crosses become the moment and the locus of resurrection. When we witness the crucifixion of one who has been completely faithful to life, even unto death, we in that moment are already standing in the presence of resurrection. When individuals and communities are absolutely committed to life, even in the face of death, there is resurrection power. He offers poignant insights about resurrection:

> Theologically considered, Resurrection is not the sudden appearance of a new life in place of the old one after we die on the cross. No, the option whereby we accept life's mortality with equanimity as we share the lot of the sufferers, as we embrace the consequences of their struggle against their crosses, as we sacrifice ourselves on behalf of those who torture and kill so that we may be able to maintain with them at least that minimal communion called forgiveness, already possesses within itself a degree of vital intensity that death is helpless to overwhelm.[56]

The very moment and act of embracing the consequences of solidarity with the poor and oppressed become a moment and act of resurrection. In this understanding of the cross, sacrifices on behalf of life, struggles with those who oppose their own and others' crosses, and the forgiveness of those who inflict death on others are all possible moments of resurrection and loci for new life.

Boff's approaches to the cross are filled with possibility and with hope. However, there are places in his theology that are troubling, and attitudes and affirmations from which I depart. Even though throughout his work he is very clear about the violence and evil of inflicted suffering, at moments in his work it is as if redemptive meaning and possibility become too concretely identified with the actual crosses and crucifixions of our day. Participating in the transformation of those who inflict crosses still does not make a crucifixion experience in and of itself redemptive. Believing that one's death is in solidarity with the crucified of history still does not transform that concrete experience of suffering into a triumphal moment. Transformation and solidarity can be expressions of redemptive activity in the world, but it is that activity that is saving, not the crosses that call it forth. In *Passion of Christ, Passion of the World*, Boff says, "The cross is to be understood as God's solidarity with men and women in the condition of human suffering — not to eternalize it, but to suppress it. And the manner in which God seeks to suppress it is not by domination, but by love."[57] There are times when I wish Boff's distinctions between redemptive activity and the actual experiences of death and suffering were even more clearly delineated.

Language of Redemption

There are some fundamental questions that must be asked by Christian theologians, preachers, and communities as any theology of the cross is constructed or critiqued. What in fact do we mean when we use the word *redemption?* What does the word *salvific* mean, and what in life and death has "saving" power? What are we suggesting and affirming when we say that an act, a person, or an experience has redemptive power? These questions ought to haunt Christian communities and preachers, for in some ways we must be able to answer them in order to understand the implications and consequences of any theology of the cross.

One of the ways the Christian community uses redemptive language clusters around the questions we raise about the *meaning* of events, actions, or moments. In a profound way, Boff is asking about the meaning of suffering in Latin America and throughout the world. As a theologian, and as a faithful Christian person, he is trying to infuse some meaning into actions, events, and situations that are human atrocities. In the face of radical evil, which often appears so utterly senseless, and confronted with human conditions that seem to be meaningless, to ask questions of meaning is not only appropriate, but essential. Perhaps meaning in the face of meaninglessness is redemptive.

Another way the Christian community uses salvific language centers around questions we raise about the *impact* of events, actions, or moments. Our affirmations and reflections often suggest that the Christian community believes that something is redemptive if it instructs and inspires. An event is redemptive if it instructs individuals and communities how to live the Christian faith more faithfully, or people or moments are redemptive if they instill in us the courage to move toward life. Perhaps impact in the face of indifference is redemptive.

Other times the Christian community uses language of salvation and redemption to suggest that actual events of suffering are *transformed* into events of hope, experiences of death into moments of life, situations of despair into unknown possibilities. This is the language that I find most objectionable. In some fundamental way, in these affirmations of transformation, what we come to mean by the use of the words *redemptive* and *salvific* is that our human situation is overcome or transcended. I think this is a horrible illusion at best, and a kind of lie at worst. No cross is changed into a moment of glory; no experience of suffering is transformed into an experience of joy or hope. Human beings do not transcend crosses and crucifixions; they experience them in all their horror and degradation. When we suggest that an experience of human suffering, an event where persons are tortured or violated, or a situation of destruction and death can be transformed, we immediately mask the horrors of that real, concrete human reality and distance ourselves from the actual devastation that occurs. This is the same language that permeates our hymns, our affirmations of faith, and our traditional Christian doctrines; it is a language that suggests that sin has been conquered, death has no sting, and suffering is swallowed up in victory. This is the traditional language of Christian salvation and atonement.

If we take a very honest look at the world in which we live, we know that sin has not been conquered. Sinfulness as an expression of human limitation and violence is astonishingly real and powerful. The violence of classism is a living testimony to that fact. How can we make sense of this traditional language of atonement in a world such as ours?

If atonement means that human beings are not solely bound by the sinfulness of their own condition; if it means that in the face of Jesus' ministry, life, and death, human beings have seen new possibilities for their lives and their ministries in the world — then I can believe that Jesus' death on the cross was redemptive. If atonement means that human beings are saved from a fatalistic power of evil in their lives by embracing and being convicted by the power of God we see incarnate in Jesus the Christ, then I can believe that the repercussions of Jesus' death on the cross had saving dimensions. If the radical love that Jesus lived and died for is so compelling that human persons seek to find their own at-one-ment with God, with the human family, and with the earth, then I can believe the impact of Jesus' death on the cross had purpose, meaning, and power.

But I will never understand or embrace language that suggests that Jesus' death on a cross, or any death on a cross, breaks the power of sin, transforms human conditions, or shatters evil. Not only is this a perverse denial of truth, but to suggest that the power of transformation *resides* in crosses, conditions, and human sin obscures the mandate of the gospel. *We* are to be the agents of redemption and the loci of emerging new possibility, radical justice, and global economic transformation. In the ministry and life of Jesus, we have seen the possibility, the power, and the witness of redemptive, saving activity in the world. How we respond to this life of Jesus as well as to his cross and to all the crosses that have happened throughout history will determine whether we have been saved, redeemed, or transformed. There is no inherent goodness in crucifixions, even though they may become the occasion for individual and collective transformation and the inspiration for present and future redemptive activity.

The critique of sacrificial theology I am proposing goes to the heart of our Christian faith. Any suggestion that we stop preaching sacrificial theology from the pulpits of this nation also goes to the heart of

Christian preaching. As a theologian and preacher, I am compelled to move in the direction of making that suggestion; what compels me are my understandings about class inequity and economic injustice and the crosses and crucifixions they produce. My critique does not emerge in isolation. Conversations with feminist and womanist theologians and preachers, reflections on the theologies that are being forged by our Latin American sisters and brothers, and my own growing awareness of the magnitude and obscenity of human suffering have converged to fuel and deepen my critique. It will take much courage and conviction for individuals and communities in the United States to look seriously at this treasured and often unquestioned theology of sacrifice, atonement, and redemption that undergirds our Christian churches.

For many of us who are white, North American people of privilege, the cross has become sanitized, romanticized, and abstracted from concrete human suffering. When this happens, our reflections upon its meaning and impact often become just as romanticized, sanitized, and abstract. Perhaps in preaching classrooms we would hear very different sermons and experience very different theology if first we shared together an experience in inner-city Trenton, New Jersey, or made a trip to Nicaragua, or spent a semester in South Africa. Christian preachers desperately need to connect the cross, the central symbol of our faith, with the everyday anguish and terror of modern-day crucifixions. In the day-to-day ministry of Christian churches, in the religious training and theological education of seminaries, in the daily reflection and praxis of our own individual lives, Christian people who are committed to justice and to the eradication of economic violence and class inequity must undertake the task of waging a major critique against traditional sacrificial theology, and enter into the constructive task of "re-imaging redemption."[58]

The Poor as Moral and Ethical Agents

As long as our theology justifies and romanticizes crosses and crucifixions, we will never be able to see clearly and name the abhorrent human acts and systems that inflict them. Equally important to us as religious people is the knowledge that if we do not see economic crosses and crucifixions for the expressions of evil they are, we will never be able to see and experience the full humanity and human agency of those who experience them. Sobrino and Boff not only construct new theologies that are shaped from within the world and agenda of the poor for the transformation of the Christian church, but they also shatter our prejudices, our stereotypes, and our illusions about who the poor are.

In *Spirituality of Liberation: Toward Political Holiness,* Sobrino explores what an adequate spirituality might look like in the context of Latin

America. He does not look elsewhere for spiritual truths and disciplines that might be imposed on the people of this context; rather he works to name the spiritual truth and wisdom that already exist among the people. He asserts that the poor in Latin America are a people filled with hope:

> Because the poverty...is real, it is scandalously tragic. It calls us to account. It unsettles us. And yet these poor have hope. This is scandalous too, and we are simply taken aback. Despite all these years of oppression and repression, and despite the fact that a macrostructural view only threatens the Third World with greater poverty still, the poor of Latin America today are peoples filled with hope. Indeed, hope is one of the essential characteristics of their poverty, so that there is no understanding them apart from it.[59]

Never would Sobrino suggest that poverty is good or redemptive because it instills hope, but rather he would suggest that the hope of the poor is rooted in a radical identification with the possibilities of life and a concrete resistance to death. For me, the hope of the poor is a profound witness to redemptive activity in the world.

Hope means many things in many different contexts. In Latin America it means that in the midst of escalating poverty and suffering, there is hope for changed conditions. It means that in the midst of the terror of disappearances and executions, there is hope for organized action and protest. It means that in the midst of death, there is the hope for meaningful existence. Sobrino proclaims, "The hope of the poor is a hope that struggles to tear out poverty and death by their very roots, against everything the guardians of the status quo can do to prevent it."[60]

From the pulpits and churches of North America far too often we hear only of the victimization of the poor. To suggest that the poor, the homeless, the unemployed, or the hungry are only victims and not agents of life is to perpetuate another kind of violence on a people. If we can remove ourselves from those victimized by economic injustice with the patronizing act of labeling them victims, then we can remove ourselves from the confronting power of their agency in the world. This is ultimately another form of social and political imperialism. It is a far more difficult theological and religious task to name the worldwide victimization of the poor as demonic reality and then remain committed to a view of the poor that enables them to confront our lives and break open our worldviews.

While in Guatemala, our seminary group visited with members of G.A.M. (*Grupo de Apoyo Mutuo* [Mutual Support Group]), an organization for the families of the "disappeared." This group was formed in Guatemala on June 5, 1984, by a group of women in Guatemala

City.[61] The work of G.A.M. is stunning. The members write letters to the government; they organize marches and demonstrations in Guatemala City; they unearth corpses in clandestine graves; they respond to the government's murderous acts and to the needs of those who suffer. The group is political and courageous, demanding that the government respond to the enormous numbers of human rights violations that have taken place in Guatemala for decades and that it account specifically for the disappearances of hundreds and thousands of people who are beloved family members and friends. Each day members of G.A.M. are threatened and terrorized. They know very well they may be the next to disappear, yet they work on with strength, persistence, and urgency. During our visit, a woman spoke of her son's disappearance several years before, and a man spoke of his brother's disappearance.

Five days after we visited their office, it was bombed late one night. No one was injured, but the building was almost totally destroyed. This experience made the ethical agency, courage, and hope of the Guatemalan people more real for me and others from the seminary, frighteningly real. There is a strength here, in the face of repression, that is difficult to understand. This kind of mobilization of people in the face of such a terrorist state is difficult to comprehend. This is the kind of hope the poor proclaim.

There are organizations like G.A.M. throughout Latin America. They are a witness to us in more ways than we can articulate. Sobrino says:

> The most important thing is that the practice of the poor includes a focus on the "other" — that great "other" constituted by the poor majorities and by the totality of the society for whose construction the struggle is waged. It is this reference to the other that renders their toil, their struggles, formally love.... The hope that God has aroused in them has been transformed into active love for others.[62]

Preaching as an Act of Solidarity

From the perspective of Latin American theologians, solidarity is the act of living one's life involved in and committed to the cause and agenda of the poor. If preachers, as working theologians of the Christian church, desire solidarity, then confronting the violence and tyranny of classism and economic imperialism becomes paramount work in their proclamations. Preachers and communities will be challenged to discern the most effective ways to shape their preaching ministries in response to such a commitment.

For preachers who desire to be in solidarity with the poor, a part of our commitment will involve the sharing of explicit information, illustrations, and stories from the lives and struggles of the people who are indeed suffering from the oppression of poverty, unemployment, homelessness, hunger, and physical violence around our globe. I also am convinced that a part of our commitment to solidarity involves a careful and critical examination of the impact of traditional sacrificial theology on the actual lives of those who suffer from inflicted economic crosses and crucifixions worldwide. Preachers who make such a responsible critique of traditional Christian theology might, in turn, find a richness awaiting them if they would then focus their attention on the distinctive political, cultural, and social perspectives of the poor, the unemployed, the working class, the hungry, and the homeless. Their theological wisdom and their social and political insights might be lessons of indictment and transformation for the churches of America.

✧ 7 ✧

SERMONS AS WEEPING, CONFESSION, AND RESISTANCE

In this final chapter, I want to return in a very explicit way to the metaphors of weeping, confession, and resistance. These metaphors have taken on profound meaning in my own life of faith and continue to inform my basic understandings of existence and my justice work. In many ways, all of the chapters of this book are fundamentally shaped by my understanding of these dimensions of the faithful life.

Weeping, confession, and resistance are indeed metaphors that describe the faithful life. They are also metaphors that reflect what redemptive preaching might look like, and they suggest a method of sermon crafting. When I say that they suggest a methodology for sermon crafting, I envision this broadly and creatively. From the inception of this book until this moment, my intent has always been multidimensional. I do not conceptualize preaching in response to the violences of our day as "preaching on social issues." Rather I am inviting preachers to ground their entire preaching ministries in the kind of deep and passionate social analysis that will change the shape and nature of all their sermons. I do not conceptualize preaching in response to massive human suffering as "preaching prophetically." Rather I am pleading with preachers to embrace a kind of preaching ministry that makes little distinction between pastoral and prophetic, individual and social. When we enable people to understand the powers and forces in this world that close family farms, bring genocide into Native American communities nationwide, lock women into homes of violence, and force gay and lesbian persons to deny the lovers in their lives, we are preaching pastorally and prophetically, and we are addressing individual and collective human need.

The sermons that follow are my own examples of preaching as weeping, confession, and resistance. In each sermon I wanted the community to *experience* some of the pain and challenge described in various illustrations and stories rather than simply hearing "about" it. To weep passionately, we must experience and feel. I also wanted the sermons to be truthful and bold, even though some of the vivid description continues to make me wonder and question. To confess, we must be frighteningly honest. And finally, I wanted the sermons to point to concrete expressions of resistance and action. To resist, we must place our resources and our bodies in concrete places where suffering is addressed.

It is with some reservation that I share these sermons. I only hope they will add some clarity to the intent of the entire book and challenge preachers to craft their own distinctive sermons of weeping, confession, and resistance.

✧ UNSPEAKABLE LOSS ✧

A Sermon on Judges 11:29–40

This sermon was prepared for Women in Ministry Week at Perkins School of Theology, February 1991. The intent of the sermon was twofold. I wanted to address explicitly the issue of violence against women, and I wanted to struggle with the problematic and violent biblical text.

There are losses in this world of ours — losses that are unbelievable, losses that are unbearable, losses that are unspeakable. I ask myself and I ask us together this day why so many of them have to do with women's lives.

I want to deny the violence in our streets, in our churches, in our homes, and in our families. I want to be silent in some desperate belief that the magnitude of this violence is not true. Violence against women is so widespread, so deeply ingrained in us, so commonplace, and so trivialized that the *losses seem unbelievable.*

And I want to cry, to scream out, to fight back, to hurt those who would hurt. I want to shout with mind and heart and body in some desperate sorrow that the constancy of this violence is such an indelible mark across all our human history that the *losses feel unbearable.*

And I want to mourn, to re-member, to bring to memory, to give voice to. I want to graft to my human heart the senseless pain, the violent deaths, the cruel invisibility of all these girls and women throughout time; and I want to do this in some desperate hope that in lamenting the suffering, remembering the forgotten, and speaking the unspeakable, something redemptive, something saving might happen among us.

I have felt for so long that this passage from Judges 11 is a story of unbelievable, unbearable, unspeakable loss. A daughter becomes the sacrifice for a senseless, unfaithful act of trying to control, trying to bargain with, trying to win favor with God. How strange it is that still to this day religious persons speak of the faithful obedience of Jephthah.

Is human life so cheap that we sacrifice one another on the altar of power and pride and control and then call it the altar of faithfulness? I cannot understand why Jephthah's words have not shocked and angered people throughout the ages: "If you will give the Ammonites into my hand, then *whoever* comes out of the doors of my house to meet me, when I return victorious from the Ammonites, shall be the Lord's to be offered up by me as a burnt offering" (11:30–31; emphasis added). These are perverse and chilling words.

Who is this man who makes bargains with God? Who is this man who makes such a reckless vow involving human life? Who is this man who assumes the ownership of his daughter without question or pause? He is Jephthah — a man like men of every decade, every era, every generation.

He is not a man in isolation. He is the product of a culture that values men more than women, a culture that leaves women nameless and without power, a culture that encourages male ownership and control at any cost. He is Jephthah — a man like men of every neighborhood, every country, every culture.

His words sound hauntingly familiar: "Alas, my daughter! You have brought me very low; you have become the cause of great trouble to me. For I have opened my mouth to the Lord, and I cannot take back my vow" (11:35).

Alas, my daughter, my mother, my wife, my lover — you have brought me very low. You have become the cause of great trouble to me, for you have not learned to let boys win and to hide your real strength . . . ; for you have brought forth five beautiful daughters, but no sons . . . ; for your independence, your strength, and your beauty have provoked me to violence . . . ; for you were not the kind of mother I needed . . . ; for you want to be a partner, not just a wife. . . .

It is painful and true that we know this man well; we know his actions; and we know his words.

We know him — he is Jephthah; he is the oppressor, the victimizer, the ruthless father who sacrificed his daughter by making a senseless bargain with God.

We know him, but do we?

The text must be put in context; the story must be made whole. At the beginning of chapter 11 the writer of Judges says:

Now Jephthah the Gileadite, the son of a prostitute, was a mighty
warrior. Gilead was the father of Jephthah. Gilead's wife also bore
him sons; and when his wife's sons grew up, they drove Jephthah
away, saying to him, "You shall not inherit anything in our father's
house; for you are the son of another woman." Then Jephthah fled
from his brothers, and dwelt in the land of Tob. (11:1–3)

Jephthah is not dismissed as easily as my human mind and heart
would like him to be.

He is not just the oppressor — he has been oppressed. He is not just
the victimizer — he has been and is a victim.

He was the son of a prostitute, and when his stepbrothers grew up,
they drove Jephthah away — away from an inheritance, away from
family, away from the land of his birth.

The text confronts me with another Jephthah — one who might be
desperate for acceptance and approval, one who would rather bargain
with God than be exiled again into a strange and foreign land. His bargaining now sounds hauntingly familiar; his fear creeps in a little too
close; his humanness is much too real for my liking. Our contemporary
understanding ("Those who are victimized by violence will turn one day
to victimize another") is stretched to its outermost limits.

Who is this man? He is Jephthah. We know him — the *male product
of male violence, the alienated man with other men*, the one who is a mighty
warrior . . . and a terrified man.

Who is this man? He is Jephthah — a man of every time and every
place; and before we move so comfortably to the daughters of Israel and
their remembering, the redemptive power and presence of God call his
brothers and his sisters to feel and lament his victimization and to hold
him *accountable* for his victimizing. What an incredibly angering challenge — for those of us who would judge his actions and condemn his
life.

Perhaps we know him, know him well, for he is Jephthah.

It is also true that we know the movements, the actions, the wordless
rituals of the daughters of Israel: "So there arose an Israelite custom that
for four days every year the daughters of Israel would go out to lament
the daughter of Jephthah the Gileadite" (11:39–40).

In *Just a Sister Away*, Renita Weems speaks about the women in this
way:

So, the women cried inconsolable tears that day. They wept for
Jephthah's daughter. They wept for themselves. And they wept for
their daughters. They knew that the worst lie of all was that, in the
end, this would not be the daughter's story, but the father's. So,
they wept for a name never known and a whole story that would

never be told. And the silent horror of it all would drive them back out to those mountains year after year to cry all over again.[1]

We know the actions of these women well — the weeping, the bonding, the holding sacred, the eternal remembering in the face of a world that rendered them invisible and powerless. They became visible and powerful for each other. In the midst of a culture that encouraged their denial and their silence, they wailed forth the loss; and in the midst of a way of life that would have them forget, they returned and remembered, and returned again and remembered again..., and the redemptive courage and hope of their lives pour into ours across centuries of history and across miles of difference. It is their weeping, their bonding, their holding sacred, their eternal remembering that guide us as we struggle to know the shape and expression of redemptive activity in our day. Across the miles and differences they teach us how to break silence, how to mourn loss, how to empower each other, and how to move toward life in the face of death.

When a woman decides to leave her home and seek the safety of a women's shelter, the silence of her oppression is broken. In that same act, the silence and denial of male violence are shattered, if only for a moment. This impulse to reach out for help is a movement toward life. When a girl child decides to tell a family friend that her father is sexually abusing her, the silence of her abuse is broken. In that same act, the silence and denial of destructive family privacy and distorted male sexuality are shattered, if only for a moment. This impulse to tell is a movement toward life. When a woman decides to press charges against an acquaintance who has raped her, the silence of her domination is broken. And in that same act, the silence and denial of male ownership and supremacy are shattered, if only for a moment. This impulse to hold accountable is a movement toward life. These are the movements and the impulses of the daughters of Israel.

These impulses toward healing, accountability, and transformation are movements toward a healthy sense of self, relationality, and community. These impulses come from a desire for survival itself and for an end to violent abuse. These are faithful, saving acts.

> So there arose a custom...
> and every year,
> for four days of every year,
> the daughters of Israel would go out,
> and they would lament,
> they would lament the daughter of Jephthah.

Our world has much to learn from these daughters of Israel about lamenting, about resistance, about wailing the loss.

At Christmastime friends gave me a book written by a Cherokee/ Appalachian woman. When I opened the book the poem that lay before me was entitled "Women Die Like Trees":

> Women die like trees, limb by limb
> as strain of bearing shade and fruit
> drains sap from branch and stem
> and weight of ice with wrench of wind
> split the heart, loosen grip of roots
> until the tree falls with a sigh —
> unheard except by those nearby —
> to lie . . . mossing . . . mouldering . . .
> to a certain softness under foot,
> the matrix of new life and leaves.
> No flag is furled, no cadence beats,
> no bugle sounds for death like these,
> as limb by limb, women die like trees.[2]

The daughters of Israel are calling to us, shouting to us, wailing to us to act, but perhaps their actions remind us that even unfurling a flag or beating the cadence of a drum or blowing a brass bugle will not be enough. Women will die like trees, limb by limb, until silence is broken with confrontation, violence is resisted and stopped, and the women and men of our world know and believe that the breath, the souls, and the bodies of women everywhere are sacred.

The daughters of Israel are calling to us, shouting to us, wailing to us to act.

I recently returned from five weeks in Nigeria. I taught at a United Methodist seminary in a village named Banyam. A clinic exists in the adjoining village of Worum. Two German nurses live and work there. One who is an eye specialist, Uli, has been in Nigeria only about eight months. The other, a midwife, Ilse, has been there for eighteen years. These two women are joined with a team of Nigerian women in the operation of a small birthing facility. A woman is present there twenty-four hours a day. Thousands of women have come to this place. Women and children have died there, in a land where limited health care still puts women's lives in greatest jeopardy; but thousands of children have been safely born there, and thousands of women have been helped and comforted and strengthened in the task of bringing forth life. The clinic sits at the top of a hill where it is a place of continual refuge and life day and night. If you were to go there at night you would see something unspeakably powerful, unspeakably hopeful. Each night and every night in the stillness of the rich blackness of the night there burns at the top of that hill a small kerosene lantern beckoning women, welcoming women, proclaiming with its light that there is a place where women will be helped, will be comforted, and will be honored, where all that can be done will be done so that women will not die like trees.

These Nigerian and German nurses have heard the wailing of the daughters of Israel, and they have joined in the faithful movements, actions, and wordless rituals of their lamenting. In the face of endless violence in our day, somehow in the midst of men and women weeping, bonding, remembering, and holding sacred, there is a sacred presence stronger than violence, and there is a sacred power stronger than death.

✧ DISCERNING THE FULLNESS OF THE BODY ✧

A Sermon on 1 Corinthians 11:17–34

This communion sermon was preached at the United Theological Seminary, New Brighton, Minnesota, in December 1991. The intent of the sermon was to expand the pastoral and theological understandings of the Eucharist as not only a feast of individual comfort and inspiration, but also an inclusive feast of solidarity with the entire body of God's creation.

When I think about our journey to this table, a flood of images, smells, sights, and emotions surrounds me. I smell fresh bread baking, and remember the women at Epworth church who baked bread for our communion celebrations. I fondly remember many groups of restless teenagers who were transformed into weeping communities beside a lake at Camp Asbury in southern Ohio. I still remember being overwhelmed as a friend and I walked down the aisle of a church in Chichicastanango, Guatemala. It was late one night, and in a strange and different world, but it was a comfortable, familiar sacrament. I feel overwhelmed when I recall the times I have fed my own mother and my father this bread of life and offered them this cup of salvation. I hear the quiet awe in hospital rooms where words are meaningless compared to the substance and power of this bread and this cup. And I will never forget that first time I served communion after my ordination — looking people in the eye and offering the same gift of grace and redemption that has been offered for thousands of years and in thousands of places worldwide.

Our journey to this table becomes a metaphor for our ministry and vocation in the world. Journeying to this table, we commit ourselves to be the bearers of God's sacred mystery of grace and love. We say yes to a life that knows no separations from the totality of God's family. We claim and are claimed by an eschatological vision that compels us to move to the outer edges of risk and passion. We affirm that our lives are rooted in community, and as we eat this bread and drink this cup, we reaffirm and proclaim anew that life is indeed about pouring ourselves out for the sake of God's shalom and justice. These are the truths of our ministry in the world; these are the truths to be found at this table; these truths are comforting and confronting.

Over fifteen years ago, I saw a religious musical performed called *Celebrate Life.* Toward the end, the choir sang a song entitled "In Remembrance." These are not the identical words, but the meaning has remained with me to this day:

> In remembrance of me, eat this bread.
> In remembrance of me, drink this wine.
> In remembrance of me, pray for the time
> When God's own will is done.
>
> In remembrance of me, heal the sick.
> In remembrance of me, feed the poor.
> In remembrance of me, open the door,
> And let your (neighbor) in.

These words expand our understanding of this meal. The Eucharist cannot be separated from the concrete realities and conditions of people's lives and the Christian community's response to them. The Eucharist cannot be separated from the church's basic vision and hope that someday God's reign will come and that our work to bring that day into reality will be fulfilled. The Eucharist cannot be separated from letting our neighbors in — into our hearts and lives, into our church communities, into the blessings of life so fundamentally deserved.

The Christian church has forever struggled to weave these dimensions into our feasting. In the passage read from 1 Corinthians, we see and hear Paul pleading with the community to understand and to uphold the sacred dimensions of this meal of life and redemption. He believes that the divisions and separations among them profane the body; he believes the gap between those who fill themselves with an abundance of food and those who are hungry disgraces the gospel; he believes that the private and individualistic nature of their eating shames the church community.

We are not unlike the early Christian community. We also have to be reminded continually about the power and possibility of this meal. This is not just a meal that comforts us, but a meal that changes us. We believe that when we rise from this table, we are different and our responses to the world are different.

Each time I come to this table, I find abundant gifts of love and grace, but I also find haunting truths. When I prepare myself to *receive*, I am overwhelmed with thanksgiving for the abundance of blessings in my life. But, in the midst of thankfulness, I cannot escape the reality that many of God's people do not receive enough of creation's goodness to sustain life. This division of those who survive, and those who die, is as profane as human life can get.

When I *kneel at the altar* with the gathered community, I am profoundly grateful for people who have nurtured me with love, instructed me with care and clarity, and sustained all my many journeys. But, in the midst of gratitude, I cannot help but contemplate those who are not present with us, and those of our sisters and brothers whom the church refuses to welcome. This conspicuous absence and conscious exclusion disgrace the gospel.

When I *hold my hands* out to receive the "body of Christ broken for you," and I drink the "blood of Christ shed for you," I feel the mystery and awe of God's self-giving nature and companionship. But, in the midst of that inspiration, I am poignantly reminded of the places in life where we do not invest our bodies and pour out our life blood in a passionate response to the larger community of God's people. This failing does shame our church community. When I come to this table, I do find abundant gifts; I always have; but I also find haunting truths.

Family meal times are a lot like the Eucharist. We sit down together, hoping for quality time — a moment to reflect upon what is most meaningful in our lives, an experience of family intimacy — and in the midst of all these hopes, milk is spilled into the middle of a plate of chicken and mashed potatoes; mom or dad never quite stops cooking to join us at the table; family members look at each other and have nothing to say; children ask if they really have to eat those awful lima beans again; and people fight. Meals sometimes become feasts of celebration and vocation, but most often remain "eating on the run." For a meal to become a feast, people must be hungry enough, invested enough, present and attentive enough, and wanting enough to transform this moment of eating and drinking into a sacred, transforming banquet where ordinary food becomes celebrative food, and ordinary time becomes kairos moment; where people are willing to be changed by the feast itself; and where people transform a small family meal into a feast of solidarity with all creation.

The power of the Eucharist is that it is not just a commemoration of the death of Jesus, but it is a moment when we are challenged to become agents of redemptive grace ourselves; it is a moment when we are keenly conscious that we are called to stand beside, and commune with, every human person, every living thing. When we gather at this table, we are not asked simply to remember, but we are asked to mobilize our feet, hands, hearts, and resources in response to the needs of all God's creation. This feast breaks into our limitations, our fears, our silences, and moves us into the greater mysteries of life. This meal urges us to look beyond what we know, beyond what is familiar, into God's infinite possibilities.

A few weeks ago I watched again the movie *My Left Foot*. It is about the life of Christy Brown, a man with cerebral palsy. During the years of his childhood, Christy never speaks, and his family and friends assume he has no creative or intellectual capacities. Even though they clearly love him, he is treated like a kind of plaything one moment, isolated and ignored another. There is an unforgettable scene in the movie. One evening Christy is sitting in a corner on the floor, where he usually is placed away from the family; but this night, he picks up a piece of chalk with his toes, and slowly and painfully writes out "Mother," while looking at his mom, who has tenderly and persistently been by his side. This moment is overwhelming for each member of his family, but particularly for Christy's father, who has often treated him with cold, indifferent silence. The father grabs Christy, lifts him up, and takes him all the way to the local pub, where he announces to all his friends: "I have a son."

He had always had a son, but until this moment Christy had been such a profound mystery that no one understood what fullness resided in his being. All who had known him slowly began to realize how limited they had been in their capacity to discern the fuller mystery of this one they love. Life is more than what is known.

When we journey to this table we find the known mystery of God's grace and love, but there is always more, and so God urges us to look beyond the mysteries of this feast we know into the fuller mysteries of creation — mysteries that confront, mysteries that sometimes indict, mysteries that leave us weeping and in pain — for the community that gathers around this table in the countless places you and I will minister will only be a small part of the fuller body we are to care for and love.

When we bring our commitments to all creation to this feast — where divisions are healed, abundance is shared, and whole communities are transformed — we make sacred the body, the gospel, the church.

Sometimes when we come there will be the spilling of drink, there will be partial and distracted presence, and there may even be fights; but we come, and we keep coming with hunger and hope and urgency. Come: eat and drink in holy reverence; journey to the table and beyond.

✧ BEHOLD CRYING MESSENGERS ✧

A Sermon on Mark 1:1–8

This Advent sermon was prepared for my then home church, St. Paul
United Methodist Church, in Trenton, New Jersey, December 1990.
The intent of the sermon was to explore the radical claims of
conversion (baptism) and to encourage that local community
in the midst of the inner city of Trenton.

Advent is a time of quiet waiting and deepest longing, a time of holy anticipation and passionate searching. It is a season of preparation when our spirits need to be rekindled with awe, our lives need to find clarity and direction once more, and our world needs the promise of Advent hope. But are we, or is our world, ready for that which we await? It is not just the birth of the baby Jesus that we await; we await the coming of Christ, the incarnation of God — God coming to us, and dwelling with us, in human form.

In this Gospel text from Mark, John the Baptizer steps into our waiting and surprises us. He comes as one crying out, shouting out, in the wildernesses of our lives. He comes as one calling for our repentance. He comes as one offering us the transformation of baptism, and he points to one who will come after him. "The one who is more powerful than I is coming after me; I am not worthy to stoop down and untie the thong of his sandals. I have baptized you with water; but he will baptize you with the Holy Spirit" (1:7–8).

This John the Baptizer is not a likely character to be calling for the transformation of lives. He even seems a bit strange to the people of his day, as well as to us, in his camel's hair clothes, eating locusts and honey, and wandering in the wilderness. Nonetheless, this unexpected one is the *one* who becomes the crying messenger who turns the lives of people upside down. "And people from the whole Judean countryside and all the people of Jerusalem were going out to him, and were baptized by him in the river Jordan" (1:5).

We want to think of John the Baptizer as the one who long ago prepared the way for the Christ. It is harder for us to let his voice and message come alive in our hearts and spirits this day. He did not simply announce the coming of Christ; he participated in the conversion of hearts and lives, and those changed hearts and lives became a part of the path to the incarnation of God.

> Every valley shall be lifted up,
> and every mountain and hill be made low;
> the uneven ground shall become level,

and the rough places a plain.
Then the glory of the Lord shall be revealed,
and all people shall see it together
(Isa. 40:4–5)

Are we ready and is our world ready for such a revelation?

Repentance and confession — this crying messenger makes a claim upon the people's lives. He invites them to come into the waters of baptism, waters of truth and repentance, waters of acceptance and empowerment. John the Baptizer is the kind of crying messenger who changes lives, and the world is never the same again.

One writer said, "Advent pilgrims on the way to the manger must pass through the desert where John is preaching." And for those who encounter him, there is *no passing through.* They pause, as we must too, to be plunged into the waters of baptism, and to be birthed again into new life. Advent is no passive waiting, it is a time to plunge ourselves into the baptisms of faith and life.

In baptism we not only celebrate community, but we celebrate the common Christian vocation and ministry into which this sacrament initiates us. James White affirms that baptism is "the sacrament of equality"; it is a sacrament that breaks through all human barriers and critiques and judges all forms of human oppression and division. One is not only baptized into this community of equals, but one is baptized into the task of creating, shaping, and sustaining this church, this community of equals in the world. Baptism makes a claim upon our lives; it comforts, but it also compels; conversion of self and world is at the heart of this sacrament.

Two friends told me about a baptism that took place in their church a few weeks ago. There was a couple with an infant and a three-year-old. The infant was baptized, then the three-year-old boy. Even though the three-year-old son was held firmly in the arms of one of his parents, he kept reaching out for the water in the baptismal font. The minister reached in, took a handful of water, and, after swishing it around in the font, he handed some water playfully to the child. When the parent put the little boy down to walk with the pastor into the congregation, the small boy headed straight for the font, reached in, took water, and put it on his own head.

This is what plunging into the waters of baptism looks like — on the other side of feeling the water, reaching for the water, dipping into the water, we are changed and turned again toward the world in which we live.

John the Baptizer knew that if people were to discern and experience the Christ, there had to be an acting, a repentant shedding, a powerful turning.

There are crying, shouting messengers of our day; their voices turn us around and their lives call our own lives into repentance and transformation.

In the past six weeks there have been some powerful crying messengers in my own life. In some ways these weeks have been an unceasing Advent, a never-ending time of preparation, a profound opening up to the possibilities of Christ.

Just a few weeks ago a group from the Women's Division of the United Methodist Church sponsored a study trip to El Paso, Texas. I traveled with them as a kind of theological consultant. We went to look at the conditions of women workers in factories along the border. The crying messengers in that place were painful to hear — women paid three dollars a day, families living in single-room homes, Mexican families split by the breadth of the Rio Grande River. But one must hear these voices if one is to see and know the Christ. In the middle of our time we visited a place called Annunciation House, a safe home for those our government reduces to the status of illegals. We sat down to a simple meal of beans and rice and tortillas with this family. Most of these men and women had fled violence in Central America, and this home had become a life-saving refuge. As we sat around that table, I knew I was in the presence of the Christ. Here was a place where people were welcomed, protected, loved, honored. If God is incarnate in places where strangers are shown hospitality, where violated ones are sheltered and safe, where people who are despised and hated are loved, and where those who are foreigners are truly honored, then in this place was the Christ. Crying messengers of pain and hope open us up to new realities of the human family, and in the midst of our own transformations, we see the Christ more clearly. Here was the Christ, in and among these human beings we call illegals.

The next week I spent four days in Nashville talking with five persons with disabilities about a theology of enablement or a theology of access. Beside me at the table each day sat Kathy, an African-American, United Methodist clergywoman who is legally blind; across from me sat Raoul, an African-American, Pentecostal pastor who is severely limited by cerebral palsy. Next to him was Don, a layman with a history of mental illness; next to him Cindy, a laywoman with multiple sclerosis that has left her partially deaf and blind; and next to her Holly, a laywoman who became deaf in her adult years.

For days these crying messengers spoke honestly about the limitations and gifts of their lives and the oppressive attitudes and structures they face. These voices call the church into confession and repentance. They also help us look at our own embodied vulnerability, and they help us know that all people are interdependent and connected. These crying messengers prepare us for the Christ.

As Cindy walked confidently in and out of meetings with her See-ing Eye dog, Murphy; as Holly said, "It took me twenty-five years to say, 'I AM DEAF' "; as I wheeled Raoul into the dining room and we ab-sorbed together the painful stares; as Kathy wept over her own losses and struggles; and as Don talked about creating a ministry called Recla-mation for those who are mentally ill — as all that occurred I knew again that God was incarnate in this place, in this moment, in this community.

If Christ is where people are restored and empowered, where people find the grace to struggle against oppression and envision a different world; if Christ exists where people have the courage to change in the presence of each other, then here was the Christ gathered around the table with us; here was God dwelling with us, embodied in these we call disabled.

Who are the crying, shouting messengers around you making claims upon your life, calling you into repentance, and plunging you into the waters of transformation? These messengers are to be welcomed and feared, for they take seriously the coming of the Christ, the incarnation of God, and they will prepare the whole world for this coming.

I have been thinking so much about this church, St. Paul, in these days of Advent. I have been asking myself what crying messengers we need to listen to and what voices of transformation are needed within our church community to help us be more faithful. But I have also been thinking about St. Paul being a *crying, shouting messenger* of hope and promise in the Trenton area in particular, and the larger world in which we live. While I think there is much for our church to do to be increas-ingly responsive to the human needs around us, I think that what this community represents and embodies is a sign of God's presence in the world.

After looking for a church home for four years, I can still remember well the first Sunday I walked into this church in the early part of this year. I saw three pastors — an Anglo woman, a Liberian man, and an Anglo man — working together. I heard gender-inclusive language. I saw children, teenagers, middle-aged and older adults. I saw cultural diversity in people's faces, people's clothing, and heard it in people's speech. I saw economic diversity. I saw single people, married people, people with disabilities.

This congregation is a crying, shouting message of hope and prom-ise. It is rare, and it is incredibly important. It is a sign of the Christ among us. Radically inclusive communities are difficult to find, and even harder to sustain. They plunge people into human differences, grace-filled mo-ments of transformations, and family fights — and in the midst of all of this, we find God. They ask much from us, and they keep inviting us back to be immersed in the waters of baptism.

One of our great Advent hymns says, "Fling wide the portals of your heart...." In attending to crying messengers, in being crying messengers, we "fling wide the portals of our hearts" so that we might be ready for, so that we might partake of, so that we might usher in the coming of the Christ.

NOTES

Introduction / Preaching as a Theological Act

1. Beverly Wildung Harrison, *Making the Connections: Essays in Feminist Social Ethics* (Boston: Beacon Press, 1985), 18.
2. Fernando Bermúdez, *Death and Resurrection in Guatemala* (Maryknoll, N.Y.: Orbis Books, 1986), 62–64.

1 / Revelation Confronts Denial — HANDICAPPISM

1. Adrienne Rich, "Transit," in Marsha Saxton and Florence Howe, eds., *With Wings: An Anthology of Literature by and about Women with Disabilities* (New York: Feminist Press, 1987), 128.
2. I do not assume that every resource in those three libraries was explored. Even with this in mind, pictures were conspicuously absent.
3. I want to express my thanks to Rev. Kathy Black, who has continually raised my consciousness about disabilities. It was in a conversation with her in 1988 that *handicappism* became an important term for me in my understanding of the oppression and denial inflicted by the able-bodied community on the lives of persons with disabilities.
4. Christine M. Smith, *Weaving the Sermon: Preaching in a Feminist Perspective* (Louisville, Ky.: Westminster/John Knox Press, 1989).
5. *Funk & Wagnalls Standard College Dictionary* (New York: Harper & Row, 1977), s.v. "disability."
6. Ann Cupolo Carrillo, Katherine Corbett, and Victoria Lewis, *No More Stares* (Berkeley, Calif.: Disability Rights Education and Defense Fund, 1982), 11.
7. *Education Newsletter*, Office of Education, Programme Unit III, Education and Renewal, World Council of Churches, no. 1, 1988, 1.
8. Elana Dykewomon, "Notes for a Magazine," in *Sinister Wisdom 39: On Disability* (Berkeley, Calif.: Sinister Wisdom, 1989), 6.
9. Carrillo, Corbett, and Lewis, *No More Stares*, 8.
10. Jack R. Gannon, *The Week the World Heard Gallaudet* (Washington, D.C.: Gallaudet University Press, 1989), 20.
11. Ibid., 16.
12. Ibid., 175.
13. Ibid., 38.
14. Ibid., 81.
15. Oliver Sacks, *Seeing Voices: A Journey Into the World of the Deaf* (Berkeley, Calif.: University of California Press, 1989).
16. Holly Elliott reminded me of this truth about the dominant reading and writing language in our culture and thus about the complexity of the bilingual reality of many deaf persons' lives.

17. Sacks, *Seeing Voices,* 87.

18. Ibid., 116.

19. Carol Padden and Tom Humphries, *Deaf in America: Voices from a Culture* (Cambridge, Mass.: Harvard University Press, 1988), 2.

20. Ibid., 14.

21. Susan E. Browne, Debra Connors, and Nanci Stern, *With the Power of Each Breath: A Disabled Women's Anthology* (Pittsburgh and San Francisco: Cleis Press, 1985), 93.

22. Dykewomon, *Sinister Wisdom 39: On Disability,* 18.

23. Saxton and Howe, *With Wings,* 125.

24. Ibid., 110.

25. Ibid., 40.

26. Dykewomon, *Sinister Wisdom 39: On Disability,* 106.

27. Harilyn Rousso, *Disabled, Female, and Proud!: Stories of Ten Women with Disabilities* (Boston: Exceptional Parent Press, 1988), 26.

28. Ibid., 9.

29. Carrillo, Corbett, and Lewis, *No More Stares,* 88.

30. Yvonne Duffy, *All Things Are Possible* (Ann Arbor, Mich.: A. J. Garvin & Associates, 1981), 121.

31. Dai R. Thompson, "Anger," in Browne, Connors, and Stern, *With the Power of Each Breath,* 83.

32. Elisabeth Schüssler Fiorenza, *Bread Not Stone: The Challenge of Feminist Biblical Interpretation* (Boston: Beacon Press, 1984), xiii–xiv.

33. George Stroup, "Revelation," in Peter C. Hodgson and Robert H. King, eds., *Christian Theology: An Introduction to Its Traditions and Tasks* (Philadelphia: Fortress Press, 1985), 114.

34. Ibid., 115.

35. Mary Weir, "The Good News!" in *Education Newsletter,* Office of Education, Programme Unit III, Education and Renewal, World Council of Churches, no. 1, 1988, 14.

36. I was invited to be the guest editor of a journal called *Wellsprings,* for spring 1990. One of the articles that was submitted was by Rev. Kathy Black. In that article she asks, "IS GOD DEAF?" I am grateful to her for that provocative question.

37. Prudence Sutherland, "Backlash!" *Disability Rag* (Louisville, Ky.) (May/June, 1987): 5.

38. This insight was shared by Helen Betenbaugh, along with many other insights that have fundamentally informed this chapter.

39. This insight about what the disability community might know about the interdependence of God came from a conversation with a friend and colleague, Virginia Pharr.

40. Debra Connors, "Disability, Sexism and the Social Order," in Browne, Connors, and Stern, *With the Power of Each Breath,* 97.

41. Douglas John Hall, *God and Human Suffering: An Exercise in the Theology of the Cross* (Minneapolis: Augsburg Publishing House, 1986), 54–55.

2 / Embodiment Challenges Marginalization — AGEISM

1. Terri L. Jewell, "Investment of Worth," in Sandra Martz, ed., *When I Am an Old Woman I Shall Wear Purple* (Manhattan Beach, Calif.: Papier-Mache Press, 1987), 76.

2. Ken Dychtwald, *Agewave: How the Most Important Trend of Our Time Will Change Your Future* (New York: Bantam Books, 1990), 6–8.

3. Michael C. Hendrickson, "The Role of the Church in Aging: Implications for Policy and Action," *Journal of Religion and Aging* 2/1, 2 (1986): 11.

4. Richard A. Kalish, "The New Ageism and the Failure Models: A Polemic," in Carol LeFevre and Perry LeFevre, eds., *Aging and the Human Spirit: A Reader in Religion and Gerontology* (Chicago: Exploration Press, 1981), 124.

5. Ibid., 127.

6. Robyn I. Stone, "The Feminization of Poverty among the Elderly," *Women's Studies Quarterly* 17/1, 2 (Spring/Summer 1989): 22.

7. Ibid., 22.

8. Edward Paul Cohn, "Suicide among the Elderly: The Religious Response," *Journal of Religion and Aging* 3/1, 2 (1987): 167. The author is discussing Nancy Osgood, *Suicide in the Elderly* (Rockville, Md.: Aspen Systems Corporation, 1985). This figure may be high, but there still appears to be a positive correlation between age and suicide.

9. In Dieter Hessel, ed., *Maggie Kuhn on Aging* (Philadelphia: Westminster Press, 1977), 13.

10. Maggie Kuhn, "Aging — Challenge to the Whole Society," in Dieter Hessel, ed., *Empowering Ministry in an Ageist Society* (Salem, Oreg.: Eagle Web Press, 1981), 4.

11. Henri J. M. Nouwen, *Aging: The Fulfillment of Life* (Garden City, N.Y.: Image Books, 1976), 101.

12. David J. Maitland, *Aging: A Time for New Learning* (Atlanta: John Knox Press, 1987), 93.

13. Dychtwald, *Agewave*, 8.

14. Carol LeFevre, "A Demographic Profile of the Over-65 Population," in Carol LeFevre and Perry LeFevre, *Aging and the Human Spirit*, 89.

15. Louis Harris, "Who the Senior Citizens Really Are," in Carol LeFevre and Perry LeFevre, *Aging and the Human Spirit*, 120.

16. Jacob S. Siegel and Cynthia M. Taeuber, "Demographic Dimensions of an Aging Population," in Alan Pifer and Lydia Bronte, eds., *Our Aging Society: Paradox and Promise* (New York: W. W. Norton & Co., 1986), 101.

17. John N. Morris, "Issues in Publicly Subsidized Long Term Care Systems and Implications for the Religious Sector," *Journal of Religion and Aging* 2/1, 2 (1986): 155.

18. Sandra L. Boyd and Judith Treas, "Family Care of the Frail Elderly: A New Look at 'Women in the Middle,'" *Women's Studies Quarterly* 17/1, 2 (Spring/Summer 1989): 67.

19. Ibid., 69.

20. Gunhild O. Hagestad, "The Family: Women and Grandparents as Kin-Keepers," in Pifer and Bronte, *Our Aging Society*, 150.

21. Kerry M. Olitzky, "Old Age as the Sabbatical Transformation of Life: A

Model for All Faiths," in Kerry M. Olitzky, ed., *Interfaith Ministry to the Aged: A Survey of Models* (New York: Human Sciences Press, 1988), 213.

22. Blaine Taylor, *The Church's Ministry with Older Adults* (Nashville: Abingdon Press, 1984), 21.

23. John H. Lindquist, "Prognosis for the Future: Looking at the Past," *Journal of Religion and Aging* 3/1, 2 (1987): 111.

24. Kuhn, "Aging — Challenge," 13.

25. Stone, "Feminization of Poverty," 22.

26. Ibid., 24–25.

27. Robert N. Butler, *Why Survive? Being Old in America* (New York: Harper & Row, 1975), 31–32.

28. Ibid., 103–138. In this chapter, Butler has a very full discussion on the housing needs of older adults. He looks at where older adults live, home owner and renter issues, public housing, retirement communities, mobile homes, and homelessness.

29. Carl D. Chambers, Kathryn S. Pribble, Michael T. Harter, "Biomedical Ethics in the Year 2000," *Journal of Religion and Aging* 3/1, 2 (1987): 53.

30. Lindquist, "Prognosis," 115.

31. Rebecca Donovan, "We Care for the Most Important People in Your Life: Home Care Workers in New York City," *Women's Studies Quarterly* 17/1, 2 (Spring/ Summer 1989): 57.

32. Ibid., 61.

33. Ibid., 62.

34. David B. Oliver, "The Real Nursing Home Scandal: Will It Get Worse in the Future?," *Journal of Religion and Aging* 3/1, 2 (1987): 154.

35. James D. Anderson, *Building Bridges to Improve the Quality of Long Term Nursing Home Care: A Responsibility of the Whole Community* (Washington, D.C.: Cathedral College of the Laity, 1988), 11.

36. James B. Nelson, *Embodiment: An Approach to Sexuality and Christian Theology* (Minneapolis: Augsburg Publishing House, 1978), 45.

37. Carter Heyward, *Our Passion for Justice: Images of Power, Sexuality, and Liberation* (New York: Pilgrim Press, 1984), 139.

38. Nelson, *Embodiment*, 21.

39. Dorothee Soelle, *To Work and to Love: A Theology of Creation* (Philadelphia: Fortress Press, 1984), 30.

40. See the following sources for a fuller discussion about disengagement in the aging process: Urban T. Holmes, "Worship and Aging: Memory and Repentance," in William M. Clements, ed., *Ministry with the Aging: Designs, Challenges, Foundations* (San Francisco: Harper & Row, 1981), 91–106; Donald Sukosky, "Disengagement and Life Review: The Possible Relevance of Integrating Theological Perspectives," *Journal of Religion and Aging* 5/4 (1989): 1–12; Ann Belford Ulanov, "Aging: On the Way to One's End," in Clements, *Ministry with the Aging*, 114; Maitland, *Aging*, 51–63.

41. Soelle, *To Work and to Love*, 30.

42. W. Paul Jones, "Death as a Factor in Understanding Modern Attitudes Toward the Aging: A Symbolization-Avoidance Theory," *Journal of Religion and Aging* 3/1, 2 (1987): 85.

43. Ibid., 79.

44. Henri J. M. Nouwen, *In Memoriam* (Notre Dame, Ind.: Ave Maria Press, 1980), 56.

45. Jones, "Death as a Factor," 78.

46. Nouwen, *Aging*, 58.

47. Chambers, Pribble, Harter, "Biomedical Ethics," 58.

48. Joseph A. Sittler, "Epilogue: Exploring the Multiple Dimensions of Aging," *Journal of Religion and Aging* 2/1, 2 (1986): 169.

49. Ibid., 170.

50. Ibid.

51. Mem Fox, *Wilfrid Gordon McDonald Partridge* (Brooklyn, N.Y.: Kane/Miller Book Publishers, 1985).

52. Ibid., last page of the story.

3 / Breaking Silence Exposes Misogyny — SEXISM

1. Cherrie Moraga, "What Does It Take?" in *Loving in the War Years* (Boston: South End Press, 1983), 65–66.

2. Kathleen Barry, *Female Sexual Slavery: From Prostitution to Marriage, the Landmark Study of All the Ways Women Are Sexually Enslaved* (New York: Avon Books, 1979), 163.

3. Leonard Schein, "All Men Are Misogynists," in Jon Snodgrass, ed., *For Men Against Sexism* (Albion, Calif.: Times Change Press, 1977), 69–70.

4. Misogyny is named in various ways throughout the literature. Kathleen Barry in *Female Sexual Slavery* speaks about sex colonization (163); Diane H. Russell in *Rape in Marriage* (Bloomington, Ind.: Indiana University Press, 1982) speaks about femicide, the killing of wives (286); Andrea Dworkin in *Pornography: Men Possessing Women* (New York: E. P. Dutton, 1979) describes this reality as men possessing women. See also Marie Marshall Fortune, *Sexual Violence: The Unmentionable Sin* (New York: Pilgrim Press, 1983), and Diana E. H. Russell, *The Secret Trauma: Incest in the Lives of Girls and Women* (New York: Basic Books, 1986), as well as Russell's *The Politics of Rape: The Victim's Perspective* (New York: Stein & Day, 1974).

5. Dworkin, *Pornography*, 13–22. See Dworkin's larger discussion of male power and its many subtle and complex dimensions.

6. Schein, "All Men Are Misogynists," 70.

7. Barry, *Female Sexual Slavery*, 202–203.

8. Beverly Wildung Harrison, "Misogyny and Homophobia: The Unexplored Connections," in Carol Robb, ed., *Making the Connections: Essays in Feminist Social Ethics* (Boston: Beacon Press, 1985), 138.

9. Catharine A. MacKinnon, *Feminism Unmodified: Discourses on Life and Law* (Cambridge, Mass.: Harvard University Press, 1987), 15.

10. Joanne Carlson Brown and Carole R. Bohn, eds., *Christianity, Patriarchy, and Abuse: A Feminist Critique* (New York: Pilgrim Press, 1989), 112.

11. Joy M. K. Bussert, *Battered Women: From a Theology of Suffering to an Ethic of Empowerment* (New York: Division for Mission in North America — Lutheran Church in America, 1986), 3.

12. MacKinnon, *Feminism Unmodified*, 6.

13. Ibid., 7.

14. Barry, *Female Sexual Slavery*, 194.

15. Snodgrass, *Men Against Sexism*, 12–13.

16. Fortune, *Sexual Violence*, 16–19.

17. Ibid., 20.

18. Russell, *Politics of Rape*, 13.

19. Fortune, *Sexual Violence*, 7.

20. Robin Warshaw, *I Never Called It Rape* (New York: Harper & Row, 1988), 12.

21. Warshaw's entire book (*I Never Called It Rape*) details the results from this national survey.

22. Ibid., 13.

23. Russell, *Rape in Marriage*.

24. Russell, *Politics of Rape*, 71.

25. David Finkelhor and Kersti Yllo, *License to Rape: Sexual Abuse of Wives* (New York: Free Press, 1985), 138.

26. Ibid., 5.

27. Mary S. Winters, *Laws Against Sexual and Domestic Violence: A Concise Guide for Clergy and Laity* (New York: Pilgrim Press, 1988), 1–2.

28. Catharine A. MacKinnon, *Toward a Feminist Theory of the State* (Cambridge, Mass.: Harvard University Press, 1989), xiii.

29. Susan Schechter, *Women and Male Violence: The Visions and Struggles of the Battered Women's Movement* (Boston: South End Press, 1982), 16–17. Schechter's research suggests that battered women are frequently raped and subjected to verbal abuse as well.

30. Bussert, *Battered Women*, 43–46.

31. Lenore E. Walker, *The Battered Woman* (New York: Harper & Row, 1979), 37–38.

32. Ibid., 19–29, passim.

33. Ibid., 19.

34. Ibid., 42–54. In this chapter, entitled "Psychosocial Theory of Learned Helplessness," Walker discusses the roots of women's learned helplessness.

35. Schechter, *Women and Male Violence*, 24.

36. Del Martin, *Battered Wives* (San Francisco: Volcano Press, 1976), 17.

37. Winters, *Laws Against Sexual and Domestic Violence*, 2.

38. Barry, *Female Sexual Slavery*, 99.

39. Ibid., 111–112.

40. Winters, *Laws Against Sexual and Domestic Violence*, 36.

41. Fortune, *Sexual Violence*, 11.

42. From a lecture I heard Laura Davis give in New Mexico. She is the coauthor, with Ellen Bass, of a book entitled *The Courage to Heal: A Guide for Women Survivors of Child Sexual Abuse* (New York: Harper & Row, 1988).

43. Russell, *The Secret Trauma*, 81.

44. Ibid., 81–84. Throughout these pages Russell explores various explanations for the increase of sexual abuse of children.

45. Lenore E. Walker, *Terrifying Love: Why Battered Women Kill and How Society Responds* (New York: Harper Perennial, 1989), 152.

46. Susan Brooks Thistlethwaite and Mary Potter Engel, eds., *Lift Every Voice:*

Constructing Christian Theologies from the Underside (San Francisco: Harper & Row, 1990), 166.

47. Marie M. Fortune, "Forgiveness: The Last Step," in Anne L. Horton and Judith A. Williamson, eds., *Abuse and Religion: When Praying Isn't Enough* (Lexington, Mass.: Lexington Books, 1988), 217.

48. Mary Potter Engel, "Evil, Sin, and Violation of the Vulnerable," in Thistlethwaite and Engel, *Lift Every Voice*, 156–162. In these pages Engel is constructing a fundamentally new understanding of sin.

49. Ibid., 156.

50. Brown and Bohn, *Christianity, Patriarchy, and Abuse*, 2.

51. Engel, "Evil," 160.

52. Brown and Bohn, *Christianity, Patriarchy, and Abuse*, 107.

53. Ibid., 105–115. Bohn critiques the kind of theology of ownership that is at the heart of much of Christian theology.

54. Ibid., 105.

55. Ibid., 113.

56. Ibid., 114.

57. Ibid., 114.

58. Ibid., 115.

59. Fortune, "Forgiveness," 216.

60. Suggested by the poem that opens this chapter.

4 / Grace Transforms Condemnation — HETEROSEXISM

1. Audre Lorde, "A Litany for Survival," in *The Black Unicorn* (New York: W. W. Norton & Co., 1978), 31–32.

2. Letha Dawson Scanzoni, "A Religious Perspective," in Janet Kalven and Mary I. Buckley, eds., *Women's Spirit Bonding* (New York: Pilgrim Press, 1984), 246–247. There is a brief discussion of condemnation, change, celibacy, and committed relationships as four attitudes exhibited by contemporary Christians.

3. Robert Nugent and Jeannine Gramick, "Homosexuality: Protestant, Catholic, and Jewish Issues; A Fishbone Tale," in Richard Hasbany, ed., *Homosexuality and Religion* (New York: Harrington Park Press, 1989), 31.

4. For a more thorough discussion of homosexuality and scriptural interpretation, Christian tradition, natural law, ecclesiastical structures, and denominational principles, see John J. McNeill, *The Church and the Homosexual* (Boston: Beacon Press, 1988); Jeannine Gramick and Pat Furey, eds., *The Vatican and Homosexuality: Reactions to the "Letter to the Bishops of the Catholic Church on the Pastoral Care of Homosexual Persons"* (New York: Crossroad, 1988); Letha Scanzoni and Virginia Ramey Mollenkott, eds., *Is the Homosexual My Neighbor? Another Christian View* (San Francisco: Harper & Row, 1978); and James B. Nelson, *Between Two Gardens: Reflections on Sexuality and Religious Experience* (New York: Pilgrim Press, 1983).

5. For a fuller and more detailed account of this event, see Rosemary Denman, *Let My People In : A Lesbian Minister Tells of Her Struggles to Live Openly and Maintain Her Ministry* (New York: William Morrow & Company, 1990), 209–215.

6. Gary David Comstock, "Aliens in the Promised Land?: Keynote Address

for the 1986 National Gathering of the United Church of Christ's Coalition for Lesbian/Gay Concerns," in Hasbany, *Homosexuality and Religion,* 140.

7. John Shelby Spong, *Living in Sin: A Bishop Rethinks Human Sexuality* (San Francisco: Harper & Row, 1988), 23.

8. Carter Heyward, *Touching Our Strength: The Erotic as Power and the Love of God* (San Francisco: Harper & Row, 1989), 50.

9. Gerre Goodman et al., *No Turning Back: Lesbian and Gay Liberation for the '80s* (Philadelphia: New Society Publishers, 1983), 29.

10. Janice G. Raymond, *A Passion for Friends: Toward a Philosophy of Female Affection* (Boston: Beacon Press, 1986), 7.

11. Suzanne Pharr, *Homophobia: A Weapon of Sexism* (Inverness, Calif.: Chardon Press, 1988), 16.

12. Mary E. Hunt, "A Political Perspective," in Kalven and Buckley, *Women's Spirit Bonding,* 250.

13. Pharr, *Homophobia,* 1–2.

14. Mab Segrest and Leonard Zeskind, *Quarantines and Death: The Far Right's Homophobic Agenda* (Atlanta: Center for Democratic Renewal, 1989), 14.

15. Heyward, *Touching Our Strength,* 50.

16. Sarah Lucia Hoagland, *Lesbian Ethics: Toward New Value* (Palo Alto, Calif.: Institute of Lesbian Studies, 1988), 28.

17. Heyward, *Touching Our Strength,* 58.

18. Pharr, *Homophobia,* 18, 19.

19. Adrienne Rich, *Compulsory Heterosexuality and Lesbian Existence* (Denver: Antelope Publications, 1980), 19.

20. Pharr, *Homophobia,* 22.

21. Ibid., 41.

22. Ann Thompson Cook, *And God Loves Each One: A Resource for Dialogue about the Church and Homosexuality* (Nashville: Reconciling Congregation Program, 1988), 13.

23. Pharr, *Homophobia,* 2.

24. John E. Fortunato, *Embracing the Exile: Healing Journeys of Gay Christians* (San Francisco: Harper & Row, 1982), 35.

25. John Fortunato in *Embracing the Exile* speaks about this experience throughout his book. Suzanne Pharr in *Homophobia* also uses this metaphor to describe much of the existential experience of lesbians. Chris Glaser in *Uncommon Calling: A Gay Man's Struggle to Serve the Church* (San Francisco: Harper & Row, 1988) implies a kind of "exiled" reality for gay men and lesbians as well.

26. Goodman et al., *No Turning Back,* 27.

27. Ibid., 17.

28. Heyward, *Touching Our Strength,* 52–60. Throughout these pages there is a particular emphasis on the concept of alienated power, and its violent impact on all our social relations.

29. Susan Brooks Thistlethwaite and Mary Potter Engel, eds., *Lift Every Voice: Constructing Christian Theologies from the Underside* (San Francisco: Harper & Row, 1990), 165; see also pp. 11 and 12 for further discussion of the role of grace.

30. Ibid., 165.

31. Fortunato, *Embracing the Exile,* 86.

32. M. Douglas Meeks, "Love and the Hope for a Just Society," in Frederic B. Burnham, Charles S. McCoy, and M. Douglas Meeks, eds., *Love: The Foundation*

of Hope in the Theology of Jürgen Moltmann and Elisabeth Moltmann-Wendel (San Francisco: Harper & Row, 1988), 44–45. The image of home or household is a central one for Meeks's understanding of justice and God's economy.

33. Marsie Silvestro, "Blessing Song," in Diann Neu, ed., *Women Church Celebrations: Feminist Liturgies for the Lenten Season* (Silver Spring, Md.: WATER/Resources, 1985), 52.

34. Chris Glaser, *Come Home! Reclaiming Spirituality and Community as Gay Men and Lesbians* (San Francisco: Harper & Row, 1990), 213.

35. Glaser, *Uncommon Calling*, 162.

36. Leonardo Boff, *Liberating Grace* (Maryknoll, N.Y.: Orbis Books, 1979), 167.

37. James B. Nelson, *Embodiment: An Approach to Sexuality and Christian Theology* (Minneapolis: Augsburg Publishing House, 1978), 78–79.

38. Heyward, *Touching Our Strength*, 123–124.

39. Fortunato, *Embracing the Exile*, 18.

5 / Conversion Uproots Supremacy — WHITE RACISM

1. Sakae S. Roberson, "Okasan/Mother," in Asian Women United of California, eds., *Making Waves: An Anthology of Writings by and about Asian American Women* (Boston: Beacon Press, 1989), 29–30.

2. Jim Wallis, "America's Original Sin: The Legacy of White Racism," in Editors of Sojourners Magazine, eds., *America's Original Sin: A Study Guide on White Racism* (Washington, D.C.: Sojourners, 1988), 8.

3. Morris H. Bratton, "What Can Christians Do?" in *Racism: A White Prison* (Washington, D.C.: Engage/Social Action, 1981), 37.

4. I am indebted to Beverly Harrison for helping me make this important differentiation between discussing and analyzing the concrete, material realities of white racism, and analyzing the ideology that flows from and supports white racism.

5. Joel Kovel, *White Racism: A Psychohistory* (New York: Columbia University Press, 1984), xi.

6. Ibid., xiv.

7. Chris Lutz, *They Don't All Wear Sheets: A Chronology of Racist and Far Right Violence — 1980–1986* (Atlanta: Division of Church and Society of the National Council of Churches of Christ in the U.S.A., 1987), 11–18. These particular pages describe the rise of the white supremacist movement in the United States, the status of the Ku Klux Klan, and the relationship of bigotry-motivated crimes and hate-group activity.

8. Cornel West, *Prophesy Deliverance! An Afro-American Revolutionary Christianity* (Philadelphia: Westminster Press, 1982), 49.

9. Ibid., 50–59. In this section of the book West expands the discussion of the genealogy of modern racism beyond economics and the psychological needs of white people.

10. Ibid., 65.

11. In 1985 a policy statement on racial justice was published by the National Council of the Churches of Christ in the U.S.A., which includes over twenty denominations and religious bodies. In my own denomination, the United

Methodist Church, there was a national convocation on racism in 1989 entitled "Racism: The Church's Unfinished Agenda." There are countless other examples of mainline denominations attempting to address racism through study, implementation of policy, and the transformation of ecclesiastical structures.

12. In November 1988, the Association of Theological Schools convened a symposium to look at multicultural theological education and related implications for curriculum development. Following that gathering, *Theological Education* focused its autumn 1989 journal on the same issue. The journal suggests practical and theoretical insights as to how multicultural perspectives, including women's studies, might become fully integrated into the core disciplines of theological education. The journal reflects an assumption that multicultural theological education is one essential step in the honoring of cultural and racial diversity.

13. Audre Lorde, *Sister Outsider* (Trumansburg, N.Y.: Crossing Press, 1984), 128.

14. Katie G. Cannon, "Racism and Economics: The Perspective of Oliver C. Cox," in Beverly W. Harrison, Robert L. Stivers, and Ronald H. Stone, eds., *The Public Vocation of Christian Ethics* (New York: Pilgrim Press, 1986), 138.

15. Steve Charleston, "Victims of an American Holocaust," in Editors of Sojourners Magazine, *America's Original Sin*, 39.

16. Cannon, "Racism and Economics," 136.

17. On February 13, 1990, PBS showed a special documentary, entitled *Throwaway People*, on the Shaw neighborhood of Washington, D.C. The documentary focused on the social causes of the black underclass that has evolved in this country, with particular attention to the plight of black young men. Racial and economic injustice has devastated black neighborhoods across the United States. One-half of all young black men are unemployed, and nine thousand black men in Washington, D.C., are locked up in prisons. Black women and men are trapped at the bottom of our economy, and the impact of that reality on the lives of black men and women is violence and genocide.

18. Diane Yen-Mei Wong, with Dennis Hayashi, "Behind Unmarked Doors: Developments in the Garment Industry," in Asian Women United of California, *Making Waves*, 159–171.

19. Vicki Kemper, "When Aliens Live in Your Land: U.S. Immigration Policy," in Editors of Sojourners Magazine, *America's Original Sin*, 29–31.

20. Katie G. Cannon, *Black Womanist Ethics* (Atlanta: Scholars Press, 1988), 4.

21. Ibid., 34.

22. Ibid., 17. Even though Cannon utilizes the categories of invisible dignity, quiet grace, and unshouted courage throughout her book, she gives Mary Burgher credit for the original naming of these dimensions of black women's lives.

23. Ibid., 39.

24. Deborah Woo, "The Gap between Striving and Achieving: The Case of Asian American Women," in Asian Women United of California, *Making Waves*, 185.

25. Ibid., 188.

26. Ibid., 190.

27. Ibid., 191.

28. Karen Lebacqz, *Justice in an Unjust World: Foundations for a Christian Approach to Justice* (Minneapolis: Augsburg Publishing House, 1987), 31.

29. Ibid., 30–31. See also William Minoru Hohri, *Repairing America: An Account of the Movement for Japanese-American Redress* (Pullman, Wash.: Washington State University Press, 1988), 1–28; and Kathryn J. Waller, "A Question of Survival: Black Farmers Struggle to Keep Land," in Editors of Sojourners Magazine, *America's Original Sin,* 27–28.

30. Judith H. Katz, *White Awareness: Handbook for Anti-Racism Training* (Norman, Okla.: University of Oklahoma Press, 1978), 140. This book is a helpful tool for white people to work through their own white racism. Some of the language and illustrations in the book are outdated, but the general movement and stages described are valuable.

31. Ibid., 115, 116, 123. I think these questions only begin to address the issue of cultural imperialism. They are rather simplistic, yet for many white people this issue remains illusive and difficult to comprehend at its deepest levels of violence.

32. Gloria Anzaldúa, *Borderlands/La Frontera: The New Mestiza* (San Francisco: Spinsters/Aunt Lute, 1987), 53–54. This book is an excellent resource for understanding the many layers of violence that accompany cultural imperialism and white supremacy.

33. Ada María Isasi-Díaz, "A Hispanic Garden in a Foreign Land," in Letty M. Russell et al., eds., *Inheriting Our Mothers' Gardens: Feminist Theology in Third World Perspective* (Philadelphia: Westminster Press, 1988), 93. This is one of several articles in this volume that deals explicitly with racism and cultural imperialism.

34. Samuel Wong, "Asians Didn't Suffer as Much," in *Racism: A White Prison,* 15.

35. Bell Hooks, *Talking Back: Thinking Feminist, Thinking Black* (Boston: South End Press, 1989), 113.

36. Morris H. Bratton, "What Can Christians Do?" in *Racism: A White Prison,* 38.

37. Douglas John Hall, *God and Human Suffering: An Exercise in the Theology of the Cross* (Minneapolis: Augsburg Publishing House, 1986), 89.

38. Calvin S. Morris, "We, the White People," in Editors of Sojourners Magazine, *America's Original Sin,* 12.

39. Hall, *God and Human Suffering,* 82.

40. Ibid., 86.

41. Ibid., 87.

42. Robert B. Moore, *Racism in the English Language* (New York: Racism and Sexism Resource Center for Educators, 1979), 5.

43. Ibid., 6–14.

44. *An Inclusive-Language Lectionary: Readings for Year C,* rev. ed. (Atlanta: John Knox Press; New York: Pilgrim Press; and Philadelphia: Westminster Press, 1988), 262.

45. Letters to the Editor, *West Ohio News,* March 30, 1990, 2.

46. Blu Greenberg, *How to Run a Traditional Jewish Household* (New York: Simon & Schuster, 1983), 443–448. Holocaust Remembrance Day is a holy day in the Jewish calendar, a day set aside to remember the victims as well as the survivors of this unforgettable human atrocity.

47. Hohri, *Repairing America,* is an account of the internment of Japanese Americans and the movement for redress.

48. Anzaldúa, *Borderlands/La Frontera,* 7.

49. Susan Thistlethwaite, *Sex, Race, and God: Christian Feminism in Black and White* (New York: Crossroad, 1989), 89–90.

6 / Crosses Reveal Privilege — CLASSISM

1. Alice Walker, "The Diamonds on Liz's Bosom," in *Horses Make a Landscape Look More Beautiful* (San Diego: Harcourt Brace Jovanovich, 1984), 11.

2. Jon Sobrino and Juan Hernández Pico, *Theology of Christian Solidarity* (Maryknoll, N.Y.: Orbis Books, 1985), 9–10.

3. J. Philip Wogaman, *Economics and Ethics: A Christian Inquiry* (Philadelphia: Fortress Press, 1986), xi.

4. I am very grateful to Professor David Scotchmer at the University of Dubuque Theological Seminary for this insight.

5. This was the final comment that one of the women workers made to our seminary group upon departing from Barrio Esperanza. Her name is withheld for her own protection and the protection of the Guatemalan people with whom she works.

6. Karen L. Bloomquist, *The Dream Betrayed: Religious Challenge of the Working Class* (Minneapolis: Fortress Press, 1990), 18.

7. Richard Sennett and Jonathan Cobb, *The Hidden Injuries of Class* (New York: Vintage Books, 1972), 147.

8. Barbara Ehrenreich, *Fear of Falling: The Inner Life of the Middle Class* (New York: HarperCollins, 1989), 255–256.

9. Bloomquist, *Dream Betrayed,* 21.

10. Ibid., 39.

11. U.S. Bureau of the Census, *Poverty in the United States: 1990,* Current Population Reports, ser. P-60, no. 175 (Washington, D.C.: U.S. Government Printing Office, 1991), 2.

12. The title of the book by Bloomquist is *The Dream Betrayed.*

13. Paul L. Wachtel, *The Poverty of Affluence: A Psychological Portrait of the American Way of Life* (Philadelphia: New Society, 1989), 5.

14. Ibid., 48–71; see Wachtel's discussion of pollution, technology, decline of community, and wealth.

15. Ehrenreich, *Fear of Falling,* 139.

16. Sennett and Cobb, *The Hidden Injuries of Class,* 128.

17. Lillian B. Rubin, *Worlds of Pain* (New York: Basic Books, 1976), 38.

18. Michael Harrington, *The New American Poverty* (New York: Penguin Books, 1984), 1.

19. Michael Harrington, *The Other America: Poverty in the United States* (New York: Penguin Books, 1962), 8.

20. U.S. Bureau of the Census, *Poverty in the United States: 1990,* 2–6.

21. William Julius Wilson, *The Truly Disadvantaged: The Inner City, the Underclass, and Public Policy* (Chicago: University of Chicago Press, 1987).

22. Sheldon H. Danziger and Daniel H. Weinberg, eds., *Fighting Poverty: What Works and What Doesn't* (Cambridge, Mass.: Harvard University Press, 1986), especially chap. 10.

23. Francisco Jiménez, *Poverty and Social Justice: Critical Perspectives* (Tempe, Ariz.: Bilingual Press, 1987), 63–77.

24. National Conference of Catholic Bishops, *Economic Justice for All: Pastoral Letter on Catholic Social Teaching and the U.S. Economy* (Washington, D.C.: National Conference of Catholic Bishops, 1986), 85–90. See also Michael B. Katz, *The Undeserving Poor: From the War on Poverty to the War on Welfare* (New York: Pantheon Books, 1989), 241–244.

25. National Conference of Catholic Bishops, *Economic Justice for All,* 93.

26. Katz, *Undeserving Poor,* 187.

27. Ibid., 186.

28. Ibid., 187.

29. Ibid., 188.

30. Isaac Shapiro et al., *The States and the Poor: How Budget Decisions in 1991 Affected Low Income People* (Washington, D.C.: Center on Budget and Policy Priorities; Albany, N.Y.: Center for the Study of the States, 1991), 45.

31. Harrington, *New American Poverty,* 68–69.

32. U.S. Department of Labor, Bureau of Labor Statistics, *Employment and Earnings* (January 1992).

33. Wogaman, *Economics and Ethics,* 92.

34. U.S. Department of Labor, Bureau of Labor Statistics, *Employment and Earnings* (January 1992).

35. National Conference of Catholic Bishops, *Economic Justice for All,* 77.

36. Physician Task Force on Hunger in America, *Hunger in America: The Growing Epidemic* (Middletown, Conn.: Wesleyan University Press, 1985), 6–9.

37. Ibid., 8–9.

38. Jiménez, *Poverty and Social Justice,* 79.

39. Physician Task Force on Hunger in America, *Hunger in America,* 9.

40. Ibid., 132–138.

41. Ibid., 180.

42. Jack Nelson-Pallmeyer, *War Against the Poor: Low-Intensity Conflict and Christian Faith* (Maryknoll, N.Y.: Orbis Books, 1989), 14. Nelson-Pallmeyer suggests that there is a war against the poor being waged by the United States throughout Central America. However, this "low-intensity conflict" strategy has also been played out in Angola, the Philippines, Afghanistan, and countless other places around the globe. This book is a shocking analysis of the ideologies, structures, and systems that produce low-intensity warfare worldwide.

43. Jean-Marie Simon, *Guatemala: Eternal Spring — Eternal Tyranny* (New York: W. W. Norton & Co., 1987), 19–20.

44. Nelson-Pallmeyer, *War Against the Poor,* 11.

45. Susanne Jonas, Ed McCaughan, and Elizabeth Sutherland Martínez, eds. and trans., *Guatemala: Tyranny on Trial* (San Francisco: Synthesis Publications, 1984), 7.

46. Simon, *Guatemala,* 21.

47. Beatriz Manz, *Refugees of a Hidden War: The Aftermath of Counterinsurgency in Guatemala* (Albany, N.Y.: State University of New York Press, 1988), 30.

48. Leonardo Boff, *When Theology Listens to the Poor* (San Francisco: Harper & Row, 1988), ix.

49. Sobrino and Hernández Pico, *Theology of Christian Solidarity,* 10–11.

50. Boff, *When Theology Listens to the Poor,* 109.

51. Ibid., 114.

52. Ibid., 105–123. In this entire chapter Boff attempts to take a serious look at how Christians might preach about death and the cross in a world where crucifixions abound. He articulates seven instructive approaches to death and the cross, but I have chosen to focus on only three.

53. Ibid., 117.

54. Ibid., 119.

55. Ibid., 121.

56. Ibid., 122.

57. Leonardo Boff, *Passion of Christ, Passion of the World: The Facts, Their Interpretation, and Their Meaning Yesterday and Today* (Maryknoll, N.Y.: Orbis Books, 1987), 110.

58. "Re-imaging Redemption" was the title of a conference that took place in Boston, Massachusetts, on November 3–4, 1989. It was sponsored by the Anna Howard Shaw Center and focused on the work of six womanist and feminist scholars and their construction of new images of redemption.

59. Jon Sobrino, *Spirituality of Liberation: Toward Political Holiness* (Maryknoll, N.Y.: Orbis Books, 1988), 161. Throughout this volume, Sobrino looks at the kind of Christian spirituality that is emerging from within the communities and peoples of Latin America and the kind of spirituality that might be adequate in their struggle for justice. The way he weaves together the political and spiritual dimensions of life and faith strongly confronts the usual dichotomy between spirituality and political resistance.

60. Ibid., 163.

61. Simon, *Guatemala,* 159.

62. Sobrino, *Spirituality of Liberation,* 168.

7 / Sermons as Weeping, Confession, and Resistance

1. Renita J. Weems, *Just a Sister Away: A Womanist Vision of Women's Relationships in the Bible* (San Diego: LuraMedia, 1988), 61.

2. Marilou Awiakta, "Women Die Like Trees," in *Abiding Appalachia: Where Mountain and Atom Meet* (Memphis: St. Luke's Press, 1978), 35.

Index